Perspectives in Law, Business and Innovation

Over the last three decades, interconnected processes of globalization and rapid technological change—particularly, the emergence of networked technologies—have profoundly disrupted traditional models of business organization. This economic transformation has created multiple new opportunities for the emergence of alternate business forms, and disruptive innovation has become one of the major driving forces in the contemporary economy. Moreover, in the context of globalization, the innovation space increasingly takes on a global character. The main stakeholders—innovators, entrepreneurs and investors—now have an unprecedented degree of mobility in pursuing economic opportunities wherever they arise. As such, frictionless movement of goods, workers, services, and capital is becoming the "new normal".

This new economic and social reality has created multiple regulatory challenges for policymakers as they struggle to come to terms with the rapid pace of these social and economic changes. Moreover, these challenges impact across multiple fields of both public and private law. Nevertheless, existing approaches within legal science often struggle to deal with innovation and its effects.

Paralleling this shift in the economy, we can, therefore, see a similar process of disruption occurring within contemporary academia, as traditional approaches and disciplinary boundaries—both within and between disciplines—are being re-configured. Conventional notions of legal science are becoming increasingly obsolete or, at least, there is a need to develop alternative perspectives on the various regulatory challenges that are currently being created by the new innovation-driven global economy.

The aim of this series is to provide a forum for the publication of cutting-edge research in the fields of innovation and the law from a Japanese and Asian perspective. The series will cut across the traditional sub-disciplines of legal studies but will be tied together by a focus on contemporary developments in an innovation-driven economy and will deepen our understanding of the various regulatory responses to these economic and social changes.

More information about this series at http://www.springer.com/series/15440

Toshiyuki Kono
Editor

Security Interests in Intellectual Property

KYUSHU
UNIVERSITY

Springer

Editor
Toshiyuki Kono
Faculty of Law
Kyushu University
Fukuoka City, Fukuoka
Japan

ISSN 2520-1875 ISSN 2520-1883 (electronic)
Perspectives in Law, Business and Innovation
ISBN 978-981-13-5392-5 ISBN 978-981-10-5415-0 (eBook)
DOI 10.1007/978-981-10-5415-0

Printed on acid-free paper

This Springer imprint is published by Springer Nature
The registered company is Springer Nature Singapore Pte Ltd.
The registered company address is: 152 Beach Road, #21-01/04 Gateway East, Singapore 189721, Singapore

Preface

The importance of intellectual property in business management has been widely recognized. It applies not only to big corporations, but also to small- and medium-sized enterprises. It seems, however, that there is much less discussion on the issue of intellectual property and finance. This book is edited with the aim to contribute to the development of debates on how intellectual property could contribute to the finance of its holder. For this purpose, it is crucial to integrate interdisciplinary perspectives. Scholars in the fields of law, economics, business administration, as well as an expert in international organizations, are invited to participate in this project. This is an outcome of a research project funded with JSPS Kakenhi Grant (Type S).

Fukuoka City, Japan — Toshiyuki Kono

Contents

Editor and Contributors

About the Editor

Toshiyuki Kono is a Distinguished Professor at Kyushu University. After he obtained his LL.B. and LL.M. at Kyoto University and passed Japanese Bar Exam, he joined as the faculty of law at Kyushu University. His main research field is private international law and international heritage law. His recent research interests are economic analysis of private international law. He gave special lectures on "Efficiency in Private International Law" at The Hague Academy of International Law in 2013, which will be published in its Pocket Book series. He is currently, among others, Vice President and Titular Member of the International Academy of Comparative Law, Director of the International Academy of Commercial and Consumer Law, Chairman of the Committee for Intellectual Property and Private International Law, the International Law Association, Member of the Committee for Heritage Law, the International Law Association, Vice President of the Executive Committee of the International Council of Monuments and Sites (ICOMOS) as well as Chairman of the Committee for Cultural Affairs of UNESCO National Commission, Japan.

Contributors

Spyridon V. Bazinas is the Secretary of the UNCITRAL Working Group VI (Security Interests), which is preparing a draft Model Law on Secured Transactions. As Secretary of the Working Group, Mr. Bazinas is responsible for preparing comparative law studies, drafting legislative texts and commentaries, and servicing the Working Group. Mr. Bazinas served as Secretary of Working Group VI, when it prepared the UNCITRAL Legislative Guide on Secured Transactions (2007), the Supplement on Security Interests in Intellectual Property Rights (2010), and the UNCITRAL Guide on the Implementation of a Security Rights Registry (2013). He also served as Secretary of the Working Group on International Contract Practices, when it prepared the draft Convention on the Assignment of Receivables in International Trade (2001). He has also been involved in the Commission's work on insolvency, bank guarantees, procurement, and electronic commerce. He has co-authored eight books and has published numerous articles on various international trade law topics and, in particular, on secured financing. He has also provided technical assistance, lectured all over the world on a variety of UNCITRAL work topics, and taught classes on secured financing in various academic institutions, including the Law School of the University of Vienna, Austria, the London School of Economics, the Bristol University Law School, Bocconi University, Milan, Italy, University of Paris V, Paris, France, the Moscow State Institute of International Relations (MGIMO), the Moscow State University (Lomonosov), Moscow, Russian Federation, and the International Hellenic University in Thessaloniki, Greece.

Claire Wan-Chiung Cheng is Assistant Professor of Law at Taipei Medical University (TMU) Graduate Institute of Health and Biotechnology Law. Her recent research interests focus on the interplay between innovation and finance in a borderless world, which leads to her recently completed dissertation "Financing Innovation in the Global Arena: The Law Applicable to Security Interests in Intellectual Property Rights" (2013). Claire has published numerous articles in peer-reviewed academic journals and has made presentations at, inter alia, Stanford Law School, University of Chicago Law School, and University of British Columbia (UBC) Faculty of Law. Before joining TMU, Claire worked for law firm and technology-related think tanks in Taipei for years. She was also appointed as Academic Research Fellow at Kyushu University (Japan) in 2013. Claire obtained her law degrees at National Taiwan University (B.A. & LL.B.), National Central University (MBA), Erasmus University Rotterdam (LL.M.), Stanford University School of Law (JSM), and Kyushu University Graduate School of Law (LL.D.).

Janice Denoncourt B.A. (McGill), LL.B. (W. Australia), LL.M. (Murdoch), LL. M. (Bournemouth), Ph.D. candidate (Nottingham) Senior Lecturer in Law, Nottingham Law School. Janice is a graduate of McGill University (1988) and completed her law degree at the University of Western Australia (1995). She was a British Council Chevening Scholar and holds LL.M. degrees in Intellectual Property Law at Murdoch University (2002) in Western Australia and Intellectual Property Law and Management at Bournemouth University (2003). She is currently a Ph.D. candidate at the University of Nottingham. Before turning to academe, Janice worked in corporate legal practice in Perth, Western Australia, where she was a senior associate with Minter Ellison, an Australian Trade Mark Attorney as well as in-house corporate and IP counsel for a publicly listed mining technology company. She qualified as a solicitor of England and Wales (non-practicing) and is now Senior Lecturer at Nottingham Law School, Nottingham Trent University, where she teaches on the LL.M. in Intellectual Property Law and the LL.B. (Hons) Law. She also teaches business and entrepreneurship law within the Business School. Janice is strongly committed to IP law education and has presented on the subject at conference worldwide. Janice is presently researching the barriers to the use of intellectual property as collateral (security) for raising debt finance and potential solutions. She holds the position of Associate Editor of the Nottingham Law Journal and is an External Examiner in Law at Queen Mary, University of London and Middlesex University.

Kazuaki Kagami is a Professor of Economics at Toyo University. He received his Ph.D. and M.A. from the University of Tokyo, and BA from Waseda University. He has been a visiting scholar at Strasbourg University (2010–2011). He has attempted to apply microeconomic theory to various institutions, such as marketing channels, transaction and production systems in the machine industry, legal procedure and public intervention, and private international law. His recent research interests focus on economic analysis of private international law.

Takashi Shimizu is an Associate Professor of the Department of Advanced Social and International Studies, Graduate School of Arts and Sciences, The University of Tokyo. Dr. Shimizu received his Ph.D., M.A., and B.A. in economics from The University of Tokyo. He has written a book and has published several articles in journals including International Journal of Production Economics, Benchmarking: An International Journal, International Journal of Services and Operation Management, International Journal of Business Innovation and Research, and Organizational Science. Dr. Shimizu has been a visiting scholar at Yale University and a visiting professor at Seoul National University. His research interests are in organization theory, corporate systems, and the interactions between legal systems and corporate behaviors.

IP Debt Finance and SMEs: Revealing the Evolving Conceptual Framework Drawing on Initiatives from Around the World

Janice Denoncourt

Just as physical assets were used to finance the creation of more physical assets during the industrial age, intangible assets should be used to finance the creation of more intangible assets in the information age.

—Intangible Asset Monetization, Athena Alliance, 2008

Abstract This chapter surveys and analyses how the increased integration of the intellectual property (IP) rights system within the globalized economy could accelerate business outcomes for young IP-rich small and medium size enterprises (SMEs) if lenders adopt a new mind-set to IP-backed debt finance. The phenomenon of globalization, namely, the increased interconnectedness of the world's countries, has a profound influence on the business, legal and finance framework. In this post-financial crisis environment, the banking and finance sector has largely retreated from traditional lending practice. Although access to finance is a universal issue, how can IP-backed debt finance grow in a globalized world? What IP finance trends and initiatives are currently afoot to support national competitive advantage and economic growth? The range of international initiatives to enhance IP-backed debt finance has never been fully explored in any of the innovation or IP finance literature. This chapter reviews a variety of international initiatives being undertaken to facilitate the expansion of IP-backed debt finance to improve liquidity and to support young IP-rich SMEs in the UK, the E.U., the US and Asia. It attempts to set a high level agenda for informing IP debt financing for SMEs policy. It also analyses the contributions of certain regional Intellectual Property offices, international inter-governmental organizations, the World Intellectual Property Office (WIPO), the United Nations Commission on International Trade Law (UNCITRAL) and leading commercial banks in this regard. By combining the body of knowledge emanating from over two decades of developments from a global perspective, this chapter

J. Denoncourt (✉)
Nottingham Law School, Nottingham, UK
e-mail: janice.denoncourt@ntu.ac.uk

T. Kono (ed.), *Security Interests in Intellectual Property*, Perspectives in Law, Business and Innovation, DOI 10.1007/978-981-10-5415-0_1

provides a synthesized understanding to inform future IP finance policy directions. It introduces the systemic changes needed to support the agile development of globally enhanced SME access to IP finance in the post-recession economy.

1 Introduction

Governments in a number of countries are evaluating their intellectual property (IP) frameworks to further their understanding of how IP can help shape sustainable economic growth, whether they are mature economies who wish to maintain their competitive edge in the global market, or emerging economies seeking to build up their economic base. This chapter focuses on intellectual property (IP) assets within the context of the wider term 'intangible assets'[1] which includes such things as goodwill or intellectual capital. The internationalization of the debate over the viability of IP-backed debt finance is due in part to the increasing economic importance of IP. IP is a bundle of legally created rights that arise through law.[2] The term IP itself refers to: creations of the mind, such as scientific inventions; literary and artistic works; designs; and commercially employed symbols, names and images. In the IP law framework, they entail complex intangible legally recognized exclusive rights.[3] In order to come into existence, some IP rights must be registered with the relevant national statutory registry (e.g., patent, trademark and design registries) though certain IP rights subsist even as unregistered rights (e.g., copyright and confidential information). IP rights are personal property rights protected in law, which enable people to earn recognition or financial benefit from what they invent or create. IP is like any other property, allowing the creators, inventors or owners of IP rights to benefit from their own work or investment in a creation by licensing or selling their IP rights.[4] As such, in commercial terms they are assets which can be used to generate additional value or provide liquidity and in accounting terms, assets are credits to the balance sheet.

---

[1]In accounting, banking and finance and company law terms, intangible assets are those whose value equals the aggregate market share value less the portion that can be explained by tangible assets.

[2]IP rights are intangible assets are assets that do not have a physical or financial embodiment. They have also been referred to as knowledge assets or intellectual capital in other non-legal disciplines.

[3]See WIPO (2011), http://www.wipo.int/publications/en/details.jsp?id=99&plang=EN. Accessed 13 May 2017.

[4]See WIPO (2011), http://www.wipo.int/publications/en/details.jsp?id=99&plang=EN. Accessed 13 May 2017. IP rights are confirmed in Article 27 of the Universal Declaration of Human Rights and their importance was first recognized in the Paris Convention for the Protection of Industrial Property (1883) and the Berne Convention for the Protection of Literary and Artistic Works (1886). Both treaties are administered by WIPO.

From a legal perspective however, most jurisdictions do not offer adequate legal means for IP financing, a concept which refers using IP rights to obtain or secure finance. We should first specify what is meant by 'security'. The basic questions of the theoretical literature concern why debtors grant security for their loans and how security is used by debtors to mitigate market imperfections and whether this is socially beneficial.[5] In Anglo-American law secured finance provides asset-based priority credit. A secured debt has full priority over any unsecured claim on insolvency. Certain academic fields such as law, economics, accounting and finance are increasingly aware of these deficiencies, and the issue of IP financing is the subject of policy development at the international level. Although IP policy is now firmly established in the political arena, there is still a need to help governments understand the different components needed to create a platform to encourage IP financing of transactions and to stimulate the growth of innovative and creative industries.

Further, across the world the mainstream financial press is now more aware of the value of IP assets as a core component of business strategy. High profile IP corporate finance stories with global impact have been widely reported in recent years. These involve multi-national companies operating in a variety of industrial sectors, including Apple, Disney, Facebook, GSK, Lucasfilm, IBM, Microsoft, Samsung, Sony, Toshiba, Panasonic and Pfizer, to name a few. Although the increased awareness of the value of IP assets has mainly focused on high profile global corporations, in most OECD[6] countries it is small-to-medium sized enterprises (SMEs) that generate between 60 and 70% of employment and make the most significant contribution to economic growth in the globalized world. Many of these SMEs are constrained in their access to traditional banking or debt financing due to a lack of traditional security. The IP system is a precondition for the markets for technologies, innovations and creative activities that are often developed by SMEs. Young SMEs are also often linked to universities and research institutions, which are themselves also using IP assets to leverage their research and work with commercial partners.[7]

Why are IP rights valuable as commercial assets? The fundamental value of IP arises from its exclusivity. The law confers the right or ability of the IP owner to exclude others, assuring its uniqueness. This enables the owner the time to monetize

[5]Siebrasse (1997), https://www.researchgate.net/publication/237830835_A_Review_of_Secured_Lending_Theory, pp. 2–3.

[6]The Organization for Economic Cooperation and Development.

[7]An overview of business and government action is published by the International Chamber of Commerce (ICC) in its biennial publication. See https://iccwbo.org/media-wall/news-speeches/icc-releases-2014-intellectual-property-roadmap. Accessed 17 May 2017. This link provided contains the 2014 press release and has now been updated with the full text of the ICC IP Roadmap 2017. See ICC (2017), https://cdn.iccwbo.org/content/uploads/sites/3/2014/11/icc-IProadmap-intellectual-property-roadmap-current-emerging-issues-business-policymakers.pdf. Accessed 18 May 2017.

personal innovations and creations by the route that creates greatest corporate value without undue concern that third parties will copy them. IP rights also confer pricing power. The value of an IP right (or portfolio of IP rights) is basically the value of supra-normal profits earned from exploiting the innovation or creation, compared with what might be earned without the IP right. The commercialization of innovations and creations and the IP rights that protect them are therefore two different issues. For example, if a patent is declared invalid, the IP owner may still beat other competitors to market and thus earn revenue from the invention. Conversely, if that owner fails to develop the invention, a revenue stream can still be earned from the patent by licensing out to others the right of its use.[8] In theory, young IP-rich SMEs are less likely to suffer margin erosion, and this should be central to a lender's valuation as a form of security.

For our purposes, the company law term SME refers to young enterprises involved in IP creation, whether with respect to innovation or the creative sector. We assume here that the young SME with IP assets adopts a private limited company legal structure in the relevant international jurisdiction. SMEs do not issue publicly tradable securities, making such enterprises reliant on credit from banks to grow their businesses. With quoted share offerings listed on a stock exchange and available to the public as well as to large private companies the value of intangible IP assets is recognized in their market value. However, for unquoted SMEs there is no comparable mechanism to measure and demonstrate how IP assets will create value for their business for use as security for bank loans.[9]

There are four reasons for the interest in enhancing young SME access to IP-backed debt finance.

First, there is the scale of commercial value dependency on intangibles and IP assets, which has often been recognized.[10] A growing body of research shows rapid expansion of investment in intangible assets by companies in the United States (US), Japan and Europe, with significant impact on productivity. Data shows investment in IP assets is growing and continues to outstrip investment in tangible assets. In many countries, the proportion of 'off balance-sheet' assets to 'on-balance-sheet' assets (the price-to-book ratios of companies) has risen for decades. These figures signal the growing value business attaches to knowledge, innovation and creativity. Young SMEs in the technology and creative industry sectors are likely to be IP-rich. In terms of fundamental policy relating to secured debt finance, high-growth, young IP-rich companies typically do not possess suitable security on their corporate balance sheets for financing from a capital

---

[8]See Walmsley (2001).

[9]See Garrett (1995), p. 99.

[10]New figures published today (21 March 2014) show that UK business is building success through knowledge and creative assets. See UK Department for Business, Innovation and Skills and Viscount Younger of Leckie (2014), https://www.gov.uk/government/news/uk-knowledge-investment-continues-to-grow. Accessed 13 May 2017.

adequacy perspective (IP is a 100% risk-weighted asset).[11] Thus the corporate finance options for young IP-rich SMEs are limited and they remain largely dependent on bank lending to raise capital due to limited means of self-finance (e.g., savings, government grants etc.) and the high cost of equity finance. Debt finance is advantageous for SMEs as it is typically less expensive than other funding methods and does not involve diluting equity in the business. Operationally, it is relatively easy to implement. Yet, most lenders only rarely identify and consider IP assets in SME credit appraisal decisions, instead focusing their attention on the familiar: traditional tangible assets such as land and equipment.

Second, as early as 1979 it has been known that the smaller the borrower, the more likely security will be required. In other words, smaller risker borrowers are more often required to provide security.[12] This is because security is traditionally regarded by lenders as a signaling device to indicate poor quality borrowers rather than good quality borrowers who are able to rely on their cash flow and income streams to repay loans. In terms of secured lending theory, this directly affects IP-rich SMEs in the innovation and creative sectors.

Third, following the global financial crisis which began in 2007,[13] SME access to finance was formally recognized as an issue of pressing importance at the G20 summit held in 2009.[14] Since that period, the ability and willingness of commercial banks to fund SMEs globally has generally declined despite government initiatives to increase lending. At the same time, a bank loan or commercial mortgage is the preferred method of finance.[15]

Fourth, young IP-rich SMEs are largely dependent on bank lending to raise capital as it does not involve diluting equity and control of decision-making within the business is retained by the directors.

---

[11]Capital regulation requires that a sufficient fraction of a bank's investments or assets be funded with un-borrowed money. Because un-borrowed funds are obtained without any promise to make specific payments at particular times, having more equity enhances the bank's ability to absorb losses on its assets.

[12]Hester (1979), pp. 349–57. The pilot survey gathered information on 1072 business loans of $10,000 or more made by sixty-two banks in 1972.

[13]See The run on the Rock Fifth Report of Session 2007–2008 House of Commons Treasury Committee (2008) Vol. 1, House of Commons London: The Stationer Office Ltd p. 4–20. Also known as a credit crunch, it is a decline in the general availability of loans (or credit) coupled with a tightening of the conditions required to obtain bank loans. A credit crunch is accompanied by a "flight to quality" by lenders, as they search for less risky investments, often at the expense of SMEs.

[14]See G20 (2009), https://www.oecd.org/g20/summits/pittsburgh/publicationsdocuments/. Accessed 13 May 2017.

[15]See Lomax and Davies (2013), http://www.bmgresearch.co.uk/sme-journey-towards-accessing-external-finance/. Accessed 13 May 2017. A Report by BMG Research commissioned by UK Department of Business and Innovation in p. 68 which found that for banks loans were preferred by 36% of SMEs, followed by a bank overdraft (23%) and loans/equity from friends and family (10%).

Against the dramatic rise of IP value as a percentage of corporate value is the setback from the contraction of the banking sector and the availability of financing for growth across the globe generally. Therefore, even though IP rights are corporate assets that drive technological 21st century innovation and the creative industry, IP-backed debt finance is underdeveloped in virtually every country in the world due to the understandable risk-aversion of many banks in dealing with intangible IP assets which they find difficult to identify, value and register their security interest. Secured creditors enjoy a priority status in insolvency (bankruptcy) situations and are repaid ahead of unsecured creditors and company shareholders. Nevertheless, the use of intangible IP assets as security for loans has existed for over a century and needs to grow and eventually become commonplace if young SMEs are to thrive in the post-recession economy.

The advantage of IP rights as corporate assets is that in addition to creating a new asset which can be used as a source of security for loans, IP assets have the potential to create a royalty revenue stream, to bolster financial statements and to provide a shield against aggressive competitors. However, this requires a largely upfront financial investment by the owner. IP-savvy young SMEs accumulate as many IP rights as possible with a view to maintaining their discretion in choosing the most suitable commercialization strategy. When funding is limited, young SMEs focus on acquiring those IP rights that are most likely to generate a financial return. Imperfect access to debt finance funding has a comparatively greater negative impact on young SMEs at the beginning of the business life cycle. This is because entrepreneurs and young SMEs frequently lack the internal financial resources to engage in the IP rights registration process that supports commercialization, compared with larger firms who have more finance and security options.[16] Lenders prefer to deal with registered granted IP rights because they are legally enforceable against infringers, more liquid and therefore seen as more valuable. There are also gaps in the level of finance and IP law knowledge among many young SMEs and lenders.[17] There is a pressing need to facilitate the use of IP as the underlying asset in a loan transaction to support young SMEs worldwide. Poor—or non-existent—access to financing is the main barrier to achieving growth aspiration plans that underpin nation states' economic goals.[18] This chapter proceeds as follows: the debt versus equity debate is examined in Sect. 1 and provides a theoretical framework for the discussion of the international initiatives to facilitate IP-backed debt finance in Sects. 2, 4 and 5. Following the critical analysis of the global initiatives, Sect. 6 introduces the concept of 'systemic change' and a new conceptual framework for IP finance, with a view to informing policy to support the agile development of globally enhanced SME access to IP finance.

---

[16]See European Commission (2012), p. 18, https://www.iprhelpdesk.eu/node/867. Accessed 13 May 2017.

[17]See Gower (2006), p. 3, https://www.gov.uk/government/publications/gowers-review-of-intellectual-property. Accessed 13 May 2017.

[18]Federation of Small Business (2012), http://www.fsb.org.uk/docs/default-source/Publications/reports/fsb_2012_access_to_finance.pdf?sfvrsn=1. Accessed 17 May 2017.

1.1 IP Finance and SMEs: Debt Versus Equity

IP-backed debt finance simply involves using a portfolio of IP rights as security (collateral)[19] for a loan.[20] However, most lenders rarely consider IP assets in SME credit appraisal decisions, instead focusing their attention on the familiar: namely, traditional tangible assets. However, the duration of the IP rights, some of which have the potential to exist indefinitely (registered trademarks and confidential information) allowing lenders to forecast revenue and possibly enabling the young SME to generate high-value income through licensing, thus reducing cost/income ratios. Debt finance needs to become a viable alternative to venture capital (VC) and private equity finance, the availability of which has also decreased over the past decade.

1.2 Equity Finance

In terms of access to finance, economies with robust IP regimes are more likely to attract venture capital and private equity funding.[21] IP assets are a resource with great appeal for venture capitalists; however, a variety of finance options is needed by young IP-rich SMEs, given the decline in VC investment since the onset of the global financial crisis in 2008. Presently there are fewer markets for initial public offerings (IPOs) as companies stay private for longer periods of time. Further, in many jurisdictions, especially in Asia, South America, Africa and the Middle East, the IPO market is small and/or immature. For example, even in a highly developed nation such as Japan, the amount of investment by Japanese VC is very small compared with that of North America and Europe.

Unsurprisingly, companies increasingly seek financing from outside the VC arena. VC finance is limited by the fact that it primarily serves the capitalist interests of VCs over the public's interest in supporting innovation and creative activity. In other words, what VCs choose to invest in may not take into account the public interest and ultimately may limit choice in the innovation ecosystem. It is suggested that if governments would take a more active role in shaping the activities of lenders to enhance SME access to IP-backed debt finance, this would reduce the need for VC finance and increase the likelihood of young SME business activities

---

[19]Collateral is the American term for "security".

[20]In many OECD countries, investment in intangible assets is growing rapidly. In some cases, this investment matches or exceeds investment in traditional capital. Intensified global competition, ICTs, new business models, and the growing importance of the services sector have all amplified the importance of intangible assets to firms, industries and national economies.

[21]Global Intellectual Property Center of US Chamber of Commerce (2016), http://www.theglobalipcenter.com/wp-content/themes/gipc/map-index/assets/pdf/2016/GIPC_Index_2016_Final.pdf. Accessed 13 May 2017.

aligning with national and international innovation policy. Improving access to additional public and private capital is where the government, IP debt finance, secured transactions, bankruptcy and insolvency law all have roles to play. In addition, sharing valuable VC experience as to how to deal with IP assets and strategy with lenders and other e-finance platforms will be a key skill in the modern innovation ecosystem.

1.3 IP-Backed Debt Finance and Information Asymmetry

There are various types of IP debt-financing practice depending on the type of IP asset involved. For example, lending practices may differ between the use of patents to secure pharmaceutical borrowing, a copyright for a movie or software financing or trademark inventory financing. Regardless of the type of IP asset offered as security, at its core, the key objectives of IP financing are: (1) to allow IP owners to use their IP rights as security for credit to the extent permitted under IP law; and (2) to allow secured creditors to obtain a security interest in an IP right, determine its priority and enforce it within the limits of IP law.

In credit decisions involving young SMEs, lenders use a variety of information sources in order to arrive at a decision on whether to lend. This may include corporate regulator records as well as credit history, automated tools and scoring systems. However, according to Richard Holden, Head of Manufacturing at Lloyds Banking Group in London, the current position within the SME debt finance market is that lenders initially only require the SME to provide a breakdown of its assets and liabilities via its traditional financial statements, the balance sheet and a profit and loss statement. He advises that:

> At present, these seldom if ever include intangibles or IP; they don't get offered or asked for —they are just not on the agenda. As a result, it is unlikely in most cases, that the credit decision process considers IP to any degree. Paying much attention to IP at the moment would be a big leap in any event, but at least when it comes to understanding a company's overall position, it may provide comfort between doing something or not. It doesn't necessarily follow even at that point that lending will be increased or be directly assigned to IP, but it might make the difference between lending and not lending.[22]

In other words, in the UK, lenders are not 'IP information demanders'. The fact that traditional lending practice does not include non-financial performance adversely impacts knowledge-based young IP-rich SMEs. Those that wish to raise capital in the debt market are particularly affected (Footnot 204 in chapter "IP and Debt Finance: Cross-Border Considerations"). Holden opines that improving the quality of IP information available to lenders would probably involve a nonstandard form or process with custom-made documentation, at least initially. This would have a

[22]See Brassell and King (2013), https://www.gov.uk/government/uploads/system/uploads/attachment_data/file/312008/ipresearch-bankingip.pdf. Accessed 13 May 2017.

cost attached to it, which the bank would have to pass on in some way, unless standardized approaches were available.[23] Lowering the lender's costs to obtaining IP asset information (transaction costs) decreases the cost of credit. In contrast, older companies with a corporate reporting history are less likely to secure loans[24] and larger and longer term loans generally indicate that borrowers are safer or that there are economies of scale.

There are a number of actors with different roles in the IP-debt finance transaction involving a young SME. Some of these are represented in Table 1 below. An IP-debt finance transaction encompasses the young IP-rich SME or its professional advisors dealing with a lender to leverage its IP assets to raise money for business purposes (Column 1). However, many finance solutions for young SMEs end up being hybrids, combining equity and debt finance, from traditional providers such as venture capitalists, business angels and banks, as well as alternative providers such as crowd funding, with grant aid (Column 2). Exploitation relates to the generation of income through the sale of products and services in which IP assets are embedded or via the licensing of IP (Column 3).

In summary, according to Edwards, a confluence of factors has combined to set the stage for the need to develop access to IP-backed debt finance:

- the increase in technological innovation and creative activity and the ensuing growth in corporate IP assets;
- an environment of restricted capital markets, especially in the venture capital and private equity arenas; and
- the growing realization that IP represents a strategic advantage that, when viewed as financial assets, can greatly impact market value.[25]

Fortunately, in a variety of countries around the world, a number of interesting developments have emerged, lifting the awareness of IP-backed debt finance, and perhaps even more importantly, its provocative potential.

The remainder of this chapter draws together the fragmented contributions at the international, national and private levels in an effort to tackle how to increase young SME access to IP-debt finance. A comparative functionality approach is relevant here because functionalism is an orientation towards the practical application of aspects of the finance practice.[26] The aim is to consolidate the body of knowledge and explore the gradual advances being made with respect to this exceptional method of financing.

---

[23]See Brassell and King (2013), https://www.gov.uk/government/uploads/system/uploads/attachment_data/file/312008/ipresearch-bankingip.pdf. Accessed 13 May 2017.

[24]Leeth and David (1983), pp. 371–387.

[25]See Edwards (2001).

[26]See Brand (2006), p. 409.

Table 1 Actors in IP debt finance

1. Innovation	2. IP-debt finance transaction	3. Exploitation
The SME (corporate person) SME creators/inventors, entrepreneurs, R&D (natural persons) Company directors Professional advisors (accounting, legal and IP) Statutory IP rights registers (e.g., state intellectual property office)	Grant funders (public government or third sector money) Equity funders (private money) Debt finance (lenders) Crowd-funding and e-platforms Statutory registers to record the security (corporate and IP) Proceedings and court judgments within the formal legal system (due diligence)	SME Sales and distribution channels, licensees, retailers and publishers etc. Business partners Competitors Customers/clients/the public Statutory IP registers to record licence transactions

2 International Economic Research to Underpin IP Finance Policy Developments

At the international level, the global economic crisis has shone a light on how policies may assist in the accumulation of these types of IP assets as a source of growth. In addition, many emerging economies are pursuing new policies to develop the IP assets necessary to succeed in high value-added economic activities.

2.1 Office for Economic Cooperation and Development (OECD) Research

OECD research demonstrates that young SMEs play a central role in creating jobs and enhancing growth and innovation[27] and that a successful finance ecosystem needs to develop SME access to IP-debt financing to increase the supply of available credit. A further OECD study concluded that targeting resources to IP-rich young SMEs is important as those resources are critical to implementing new ideas and bringing innovation to market.[28]

The empirical economic studies discussed above are designed to support evidence-based policy making. The key issue however for IP finance is to increase a lender's risk tolerance for using IP assets as security. Two international organizations in particular, the World Intellectual Property Organization (WIPO) and the UN Commission on International Trade (UNCITRAL) have taken the lead in

[27]See Criscuolo et al. (2014), http://cep.lse.ac.uk/pubs/download/dp1274.pdf. Accessed 13 May 2017.

[28]See Andres et al. (2014), http://www.oecd-ilibrary.org/economics/do-resources-flow-to-patenting-firms_5jz2lpmk0gs6-en. Accessed 13 May 2017.

driving the agenda for analyzing the barriers that need to be overcome if IP-backed debt finance is to thrive in the future, rather than be left on the margin.

2.2 *World Intellectual Property Organization (WIPO) and United Nations Commission on International Trade (UNCITRAL) Initiatives*

WIPO's involvement in IP-backed financing is to raise awareness among its member states' IP offices, and the wider IP community of the current international policy development. WIPO's Director-General, Francis Gurry, has identified what he believes to be the principal reasons for the considerable difficulty in developing IP-backed debt financing. These are:

1. the lack of a clear connection between the security and the underlying asset; and
2. the complexity and lack of transparency in the IP system that results in distrust of the intangible economy.[29]

Since 2004 WIPO has cooperated with UNCITRAL to ensure that the views of the IP community are taken into consideration in policy development on the issue,[30] participating in deliberations to develop the *Legislative Guide on Secured Transactions* (LGST) to assist states in modernising their secured transactions laws and enabling effective access to finance. If implemented, a general credit registration system (such as that envisaged by the LGST) will provide legal certainty for lenders, by giving transparency as regards the debtor's credit structure, and giving visibility to secured transactions.

Next, in 2005 WIPO recognized that current international accounting standards (IAS) are ill-equipped to address the IP dimension of business, and it issued the following statement:

> Clearly, the various challenges associated with determining the value of internally held IP, paired with the inherent volatility associated with the value of some forms of IP, can be cited as major reasons why accounting has been reluctant to report on internally generated IP, which is seen as too subjective and risky. Furthermore, accounting has always been reluctant to anticipate future gains, overstate the value of assets or include assets on the balance sheet whose value is more volatile.[31]

WIPO held its inaugural 'IP Financing' meeting shortly afterwards in 2008, with the WIPO-Argentina Conference entitled "Intellectual Readiness: The Role of

---

[29]See Tuncak (2009), http://www.ip.finance/2009/03/wipo-information-meeting-on-ip.html. Accessed 13 May 2017.

[30]See WIPO (2009), http://www.wipo.int/pressroom/en/articles/2009/article_0003.html. Accessed 13 May 2017.

[31]See WIPO (2015), http://www.wipo.int/sme. Accessed 13 May 2017.

Intangibles as a Tool for Raising Finance".[32] This was followed by a WIPO Information Meeting on 'IP Financing' in 2009 in Geneva, Switzerland. Theme 5 focused on 'Financial Institutions' Perspective of IP Financing'. Ms. Megan Deane, Deputy Managing Director of the national Export-Import Bank (E-IB)[33] of Jamaica gave a presentation entitled, 'Taking IP to the Bank'.[34] She stated that the 2010 Vision for E-IB was to increase the bank's tolerance for credit risk. In addition, Ms. Helena Tenoria Veiga de Almeida, Head of Policy Design Department, Intangible Assets Evaluation Program of the Brazilian Development Bank (BNDES) discussed IP asset valuation for finance purposes. BNDES uses an internally developed methodology for intangibles to evaluate 56 quantitative and qualitative and patent information indicators to derive an intangible capital (IC) rating.[35]

Theme 6 dealt with international policy development for IP financing.[36] Mr. Spiros Bazina, Senior Legal Secretary of UNCITRAL, and Working Group VI[37] explained the relationship between IP, secured transactions law and the interaction between the LGST and the IP Annex. Briefly, the LGST is not a restatement of current law, but rather a guide to reform of secured transactions law with the economic goal of facilitating the use of both movable and intangible property as security to facilitate increased access to credit at lower cost.

On 6 December 2010, UNCITRAL adopted the *Supplement on Security Rights in Intellectual Property* (*hereafter the IP Supplement*) in order to include IP in the general security right system under the LGST. The *IP Supplement* aims to address the problem of insufficient coordination between secured transactions and IP law by facilitating the extension of credit at a lower cost while deferring to IP law to the extent there is a conflict between the two bodies of law—in particular, without interfering with fundamental policies of IP law.[38]

In the analysis, the *IP Supplement* largely concentrates on providing guidelines for the development of law at a national level. There is no guarantee that all states will make the same conflict-of-laws rules. What is still needed to facilitate IP-backed debt finance is a focus on designing a substantive secured transactions

---

[32]See details of WIPO's IP Finance related meetings at http://www.wipo.int/meetings/en/details.jsp?meeting_id=16342. Accessed 13 May 2017.

[33]A bank wholly-owned by the government of Jamaica.

[34]See Deane (2009), http://www.wipo.int/meetings/en/doc_details.jsp?doc_id=118034. Accessed 13 May 2017.

[35]The author has been unable to locate any further information in English on the success or otherwise of BNDES IP-backed debt financing and it certainly would be of interest to follow up this Brazilian banking IP finance initiative.

[36]See WIPO (2008b), http://www.wipo.int/wipo_magazine/en/2008/05/article_0001.html. Accessed 13 May 2017.

[37]See Bazinas (2009), http://www.wipo.int/meetings/en/doc_details.jsp?doc_id=118036. Accessed 13 May 2017.

[38]UNCITRAL (2010), http://www.uncitral.org/uncitral/en/uncitral_texts/security/ip-supplement.html. Accessed 13 May 2017.

law at the private international level.[39] The publication of the *IP Supplement* has led to vigorous debates on the legal policy of promoting IP finance on both levels, which is a positive development. If countries determine to promote IP finance, it will be important for policy makers to study the current situation whereby IP financing methods are in fact infrequently used at the national level, and to create a substantive secured transactions law that is suitable to the characteristics of the IP law framework in that state. In this process, the LGST and the *IP Supplement* will be helpful references for reform. Reform to secured transactions law is a key pillar in the effort to support the development of IP finance.

Since 2010, both UNICITRAL and WIPO have continued to play vital roles as facilitators for the international debate on IP finance, signaling the credibility and need for additional research. In terms of specific state-sponsored research into IP finance policy, the contribution of the UK and Europe is gaining momentum.

3 IP Finance Developments in the UK and Europe

Important and meaningful recent developments in IP finance have taken place in the UK and Europe, in particular with the *Banking on IP? Report in* 2013[40] and the *Final Report from the Expert Group on Intellectual Property Valuation* (*IP Valuation* Report) in 2014. These research initiatives are providing the impetus to consolidate knowledge with respect to this under-exploited yet promising financing method.

3.1 The United Kingdom (UK)

The UK has a highly advanced and sophisticated IP environment.[41] The first notable UK initiative for IP finance took place in 2006 when the UKIPO jointly organized a conference on "Patents: realising and securing value" together with the European Patent Office (EPO) and the Organization for Economic Cooperation and Development (OECD). This high-level event was aimed at raising awareness of the crucial role of intellectual capital (IC) in the knowledge economy.[42]

---

[39]Sato (2013), https://www.iip.or.jp/e/e_summary/pdf/detail2012/e24_18.pdf. Accessed 13 May 2017.

[40]Brassell and King (2013), https://www.gov.uk/government/uploads/system/uploads/attachment_data/file/312008/ipresearch-bankingip.pdf. Accessed 13 May 2017.

[41]Global Intellectual Property Center of US Chamber of Commerce (2016), p. 73, http://www.theglobalipcenter.com/wp-content/uploads/2017/04/GIPC_Index_Report_2016.pdf. Accessed 13 May 2017.

[42]EPO, the OECD, and the UK Patent Office (2006), http://www.prnewswire.co.uk/news-releases/patents-realising-and-securing-value—an-international-conference-in-london-154779345.html. Accessed 13 May 2017.

In 2008, the UKIPO partnered with the Austrian and Hungarian Patent Offices and the National Board of Patents and Registration of Finland to hold four international symposiums on "IP Valuation in Business", the primary aim of which was to raise awareness of IP valuation issues and increase dialogue among stakeholders. Further interest in UK IP finance issues has been led by Professor Jeremy Phillips,[43] founder of the weblog *IP finance* in January 2008 whose webpage banner declares:

> …Where money issues meet IP rights. This weblog looks at financial issues for intellectual property rights: securitization and collateral, IP valuation for acquisition and balance sheet purposes, tax and R&D breaks, film and product finance, calculating quantum of damages —anything that happens where IP meets money.[44]

The *IP finance* blog is an offshoot of Professor Phillips' earlier blog the *IPKat*,[45] which began in June 2003 and covers IP issues generally, from a UK and European perspective. The *IPKat* team organized the first UK IP finance conference in London on 15 October 2009. A second conference, *IP and Finance 2010: exploring and explaining the financial dimensions of IPRs*, soon followed which shared the knowledge of speakers from a range of disciplines to identify the complex issues arising when IP and finance interact.

The UKIPO commissioned the comprehensive *Banking on IP?* Report[46] published in late 2013 which catalogued the challenges facing IP-backed debt financing, making recommendations as to how these obstacles might be surmounted. Speaking at the Alliance for IP Conference in London on 17 October 2013, the then UK Business Secretary Vince Cable said:

> SMEs are the lifeblood of the economy. Most of our successful creative businesses are SMEs and we know that IP represents a big part of their assets and growth potential. But too often, through risk aversion or banks' conservative lending practices linked to property as security, IP is not catered to by traditional bank lending. Intellectual property is too important an asset to be undervalued by banks who are the main source of finance. That is why I commissioned a report to explore how we can improve SMEs' access to capital. We will look carefully at its recommendations in order to better support this country's creators and IP-rich businesses.[47]

[43]Professor Phillips is an IP consultant for commercial law firm, Olswang and editor of the *European Trade Mark Reports* and the *Journal of Intellectual Property Law and Practice* and formerly Research Director of the UK's Intellectual Property Institute.

[44]See http://ipfinance.blogspot.co.uk/. Accessed 13 May 2017.

[45]See http://www.ipkat.com/. Accessed 13 May 2017.

[46]European Commission (2014), https://ec.europa.eu/research/innovation-union/pdf/Expert_Group_Report_on_Intellectual_Property_Valuation_IP_web_2.pdf. Accessed 14 May 2017.

[47]Department for Business, Innovation & Skills, Intellectual Property Office and Cable V (2013), https://www.gov.uk/government/news/plans-unveiled-to-support-ip-rich-businesses-get-funding. Accessed 14 May 2017.

The *Banking on IP?* report broadly discusses SMEs, IP awareness, IP value and accounting rules, UK debt and equity finance and policy initiatives, Clydesdale Bank's Growth Fund, liquidity and recording security interests. The key findings for the purpose of this chapter are: (1) IP and intangibles must be identified during the financing process; (2) IP value needs to be taken into account; and (3) lenders need additional guidance by way of legal templates and a resource toolkit.[48] The authors state:

> …If IP and intangibles are to be given any consideration within credit decision-making, tools to identify and describe the actual assets (not merely evidence of expenditure) need to be embedded within the lending process. Businesses must use them, and lenders must understand and take note of them. This step will have the wider benefit of boosting IP awareness amongst the business community as a whole and will establish base data for the possible future use of IP as "full" security. The first steps are to provide a means for companies to identify the assets they own and to build information on IP and intangibles into the templates companies use when presenting information to prospective funders.[49]

Following publication of *Banking on IP?*, the UKIPO convened a series of roundtable discussions with a multi-disciplinary group comprising of representatives from the financial services sector, including banks, equity investors and insurers, from the business advisory community, including the IP profession, lawyers, accountants and general commercial advisers, and from a number of SMEs. On 31 March 2014, the UK government formally responded to the *Banking on IP* report promising to promote a greater understanding of IP within businesses seeking finance and the financial sector, and to create systems to give lenders confidence in assessing the value of IP and the risks involved in lending using IP as security.[50] The UKIPO stated:

> …In 2014/15 the IPO will therefore focus attention on improving the ability of IP-rich businesses to secure access to growth finance: by building understanding of IP in the business and the financial services communities, by enabling a more productive dialogue between businesses and lenders, and by building greater confidence in the value of IP assets as collateral.[51]

---

[48]Brassell and King (2013), p. 216, https://www.gov.uk/government/uploads/system/uploads/attachment_data/file/312008/ipresearch-bankingip.pdf. Accessed 13 May 2017.

[49]See Brassell and King (2013), https://www.gov.uk/government/uploads/system/uploads/attachment_data/file/312008/ipresearch-bankingip.pdf. Accessed 13 May 2017.

[50]UK Intellectual Property Office (2014), https://www.gov.uk/government/publications/banking-on-ip-an-active-response. Accessed 14 May 2017.

[51]UK Intellectual Property Office (2014), p. 20, https://www.gov.uk/government/publications/banking-on-ip-an-active-response. Accessed 14 May 2017.

The UKIPO published *Banking on IP: An Active Response* confirming that, 'early action must focus on raising awareness and stimulating an appetite for change within both business and the financial services community'.[52] The UKIPO intends to develop a series of real life case studies showing how these businesses have, through their IP management, secured finance and are working with the British Bankers' Association (BBA) and its Business Finance Roundtable to create an awareness campaign.[53] The UK is pressing ahead with its IP finance agenda.

3.2 The European Union (EU)

In 2014, the *Final Report from the Expert Group on Intellectual Property Valuation* (*IP Valuation* Report) was published.[54] The European Commission appointed a multi-disciplinary panel of experts to consider how IP valuation plays a part in innovation policy and where bottlenecks occur. This report investigated European best practices in IP valuation as performed by financial institutions that provide capital to SMEs, including examples relating to debt-financing. The panel noted a significant difference in the approach to lending to SMEs compared with large companies with strong trading histories and further, financial institutions interviewed expressed the view that IP is usually too risky to be used as security for traditional commercial loans.[55] The Final Report explored the inadequacy of IAS38 intangibles and recommended the filing of a "management report" together with a company's annual report, giving detailed information about IP value in order to improve publicly available information on intangibles generally.[56]

The crux of the problem is that if internally generated 'off balance sheet' corporate IP assets are inadequately financially recorded for modern purposes, the result is a lack of financial transparency. From the lender's point of view, this 'invisibility' creates a key problem in that nothing exists on the financial statements (documents that they are familiar with) to quickly tell them how to value the firm's internally developed IP assets and their potential for use as security (collateral).

---

[52]UK Intellectual Property Office (2014), p. 4, https://www.gov.uk/government/publications/banking-on-ip-an-active-response. Accessed 14 May 2017.

[53]UK Intellectual Property Office (2014), https://www.gov.uk/government/publications/banking-on-ip-an-active-response. Accessed 14 May 2017.

[54]European Commission (2014), https://ec.europa.eu/research/innovation-union/pdf/Expert_Group_Report_on_Intellectual_Property_Valuation_IP_web_2.pdf. Accessed 14 May 2017.

[55]European Commission (2014), p. 6, https://ec.europa.eu/research/innovation-union/pdf/Expert_Group_Report_on_Intellectual_Property_Valuation_IP_web_2.pdf. Accessed 14 May 2017.

[56]European Commission (2014), https://ec.europa.eu/research/innovation-union/pdf/Expert_Group_Report_on_Intellectual_Property_Valuation_IP_web_2.pdf. Accessed 14 May 2017.

The undesirable level of uncertainty from the lender's perspective is a formidable barrier which prevents appropriately informed credit appraisal decisions from being made. In other words, financing the young SME is adversely affected. The weaknesses inherent in the financial reporting of IP asset value was also confirmed in the *IP Valuation Report* (2014) which states:

> …There are limitations on when and how it is possible to place the value of IP assets on the balance sheet of the company. The complexity of IP from an accounting perspective leads to problems in its reporting, which may result in the vulnerability of firms which base most of their performance on IP.[57]

IP assets are often worth much more than their historic financial value, for any number of commercially strategic reasons. If their value is limited in traditional financial statements, then the young SMEs themselves, as well as the lenders, may not be aware of their role and what they can offer in terms of business strategy and performance.

Demand for relevant, accurate and timely information regarding young SMEs' intangible IP assets is needed. Limited access to VC finance, IP-backed debt finance, public government grants and self-finance have resulted in a funding gap that hits young SMEs particularly hard. Lenders are unable to value and use as security IP assets that are not made known (disclosed) either quantitatively in traditional financial reports or qualitatively in narrative corporate reports.

The author hypothesizes that increased voluntary corporate disclosure relating to IP assets by young SMEs should assist to facilitate credit appraisal and potentially favorable lending decisions, reduce transaction costs and support annual IP asset monitoring by banks. The importance of IP finance and using IP assets as security should in theory lead to young SMEs being offered better credit terms than unsecured credit, opening up an existing but underused path to liquidity. Lowering legal risk, through a higher level of borrower disclosure of relevant, accurate and timely IP asset information and the business strategy for creating value from those corporate assets should enable lenders to better assess and quantify risk, thereby lowering the cost of credit.

The IP finance research and literature taking place in the UK and the EU show a high level of momentum in the region to tackle this important commercial problem. The UKIPO-sponsored *Banking on IP?* (2013)[58] report and the EU-sponsored *Final Report from the Expert Group on IP Valuation* (2014)[59] indicate that the EU seeks to achieve a better understanding of the interplay between IP rights and how their value as financial assets is understood.

---

[57]European Commission (2014), p. 6, https://ec.europa.eu/research/innovation-union/pdf/Expert_Group_Report_on_Intellectual_Property_Valuation_IP_web_2.pdf. Accessed 14 May 2017.

[58]Brassell and King (2013), https://www.gov.uk/government/uploads/system/uploads/attachment_data/file/312008/ipresearch-bankingip.pdf. Accessed 13 May 2017.

[59]European Commission (2014), https://ec.europa.eu/research/innovation-union/pdf/Expert_Group_Report_on_Intellectual_Property_Valuation_IP_web_2.pdf. Accessed 14 May 2017.

4 The United States Patent Quality Initiative (PQI)[60]

The US is a key global player, has one of the largest economies in the world and is also steadily advancing the IP finance agenda. In October 2014 the Clearing House,[61] a US banking industry group representing more than 20 US and international financial institutions, formed the PQI, a project aimed at eliminating inferior patents through better prior art searching, research and filing thereby enhancing patent quality as a form of intangible property capable of being used as security.[62] According to Lloyd, the initiative reflects the increased sophistication of financial institutions with respect to IP assets. The new term 'fin-tech' covers the software programs and other technology used to enable banking and financial services that are disrupting sectors such as mobile payments and money transfers. As financial institutions begin to realize the value of their own e-commerce patent portfolios, they are creating internal IP teams to more effectively manage their patent strategies.[63] The premise is that low quality patents are subject to more litigation resulting in legal uncertainty which reduces patent value. Although this initiative is limited to one type of IP right—patents—higher quality patents will enhance legal certainty as to the validity and thus the value of patents and their potential to secure loan transactions.

5 Government IP-Backed Debt Finance Initiatives in Asia to Stimulate Economic Growth and Address the Young SME Funding Gap

5.1 Singapore's 'IP Financing Scheme'

Asia is currently setting the pace in IP-backed lending and governments have adjusted their mind-sets to profit from the changing environment. At the forefront of

[60]See www.patentqualityinitiative.com.

[61]The Clearing House is the oldest banking association in the US and is owned by the world's biggest commercial banks, who hold more than half of all US deposits. It is self-described nonpartisan advocacy body representing the interests of its owners on significant banking issues. The Clearing House Payments Company L.L.C. provides payment, clearing and settlement services to its member banks and other financial institutions, clearing just under $2 trillion USD daily. See https://www.theclearinghouse.org/. Accessed 14 May 2017.

[62]See Oblack (2014), http://www.patentqualityinitiative.com/news/press%20releases/2014_oct%2015_pqi%20launch. Accessed 14 May 2017.

[63]See Lloyd (2014), http://www.iam-magazine.com/blog/detail.aspx?g=972D0D5D-D116-42FD-945D-82AC28C33B3A. Accessed 14 May 2017.

such initiatives is Singapore. In April 2014 the IP Office of Singapore (IPOS)[64] launched a substantial S$100 million 'IP Financing Scheme' designed to support local SMEs to use their IP as security for banks loans.[65] To be eligible, applicants must be incorporated and have IP or granted registered rights such as trademarks, design or patents to use as security. The scheme has three steps. First, with its granted IP right(s), an applicant can approach a participating financial institution for a preliminary assessment. The participating banks are: DBS Bank Ltd[66]; Overseas-Chinese Banking Corp Ltd[67]; and the United Overseas Bank Ltd.[68] Next, a panel of IPOS-appointed valuers assess the applicant's IP portfolio using standard guidelines to provide lenders with a basis on which to determine the amount of funds to be advanced. The development of a national valuation model is a noteworthy aspect of the scheme which could lead to an accepted valuation methodology for the future. Finally, the applicant submits a formal application to the participating lender.[69] Under the terms of the loan agreement, the interest rate for repaying the loan is not fixed and depends on the granted patent portfolio valuation.[70] The Singapore government will subsidize the valuation but this is capped at 50% of the IP valuation cost, or 2% of the value of the IP, whichever is lower.[71] If the borrower defaults, the loan will be partially underwritten by the Singapore government, thus the liquidity of the patent assets on default is minimized.[72]

The IPOS IP Financing Scheme is contributing to the evolution of IP-backed debt finance with the Singaporean government investing a substantial sum in creating an environment in which IP-backed debt finance has the potential to thrive. If the scheme proves to be a credible model, it could become the preferred template within the international IP community. Singapore ranks first in Asia, and second globally, for IP protection according to the World Economic Forum's Global Competitiveness Report 2014–2015.[73] The country's strong IP regime together

---

[64]IPOS is a statutory board under the Ministry of Law that advises and administers the IP regime, promotes its usage and builds expertise to facilitate the development of Singapore's IP eco-system. See www.ipos.gov.sg. Accessed 14 May 2017.

[65]See IPOS (2014b), https://www.ipos.gov.sg/MediaEvents/Readnews/tabid/873/articleid/272/category/Press%20Releases/parentId/80/year/2014/Default.aspx. Accessed 14 May 2017.

[66]See www.dbs.com.sg.

[67]See www.ocbc.com.sg.

[68]See www.uob.com.sg.

[69]See IPOS (2014a), http://www.ipos.gov.sg/IPforYou/IPforBusinesses/IPFinancingScheme.aspx. Accessed 14 May 2017.

[70]See Collopy and Chun (2014), http://www.managingip.com/Article/3362420/Singapore-IP-financing-scheme-launched.html. Accessed 14 May 2017.

[71]See Collopy and Chun (2014), http://www.managingip.com/Article/3362420/Singapore-IP-financing-scheme-launched.html. Accessed 14 May 2017.

[72]See Leung (2014), http://www.managingip.com/Article/3382687/From-idea-to-asset-Singapores-IP-financing-scheme.html. Accessed 14 May 2017.

[73]See IPOS (2014c), https://www.ipos.gov.sg/MediaEvents/Readnews/tabid/873/articleid/249/category/Press%20Releases/parentId/80/year/2013/Default.aspx. Accessed 14 May 2017.

with its well-established and diverse finance sector and support from major financial institutions adds to its credibility.

5.2 *The People's Republic of China (PRC) IP Pledge Financing Program*

Also of interest, but less influential, is the People's Republic of China's (PRC) State IP Office (SIPO) patent-backed debt finance initiatives.[74] In terms of a functional comparative analysis of IP finance related issues, a foreign system should always be seen from the inside and within a socio-cultural context.[75] The PRC's IP regime is just over 30 years old, yet its government has been extremely proactive in raising awareness to ensure that domestic enterprises understand the future value-creating potential of IP.[76] In 2004, SIPO began to design the nation's IP strategy which evolved from its membership in the World Trade Organization. In 2006, the landmark policy, *The Guidelines on National Medium and Long-Term Program for Science and Technology Development* (2006–2020) was issued.[77] A pilot "IP pledge financing" program followed in 2008. According to *China IP News*, only 6 years later in 2014, SIPO reported that Chinese companies had secured over £6 billion GPB in IP-backed loans since the program launched. For example, in 2013, Chinese companies had apparently secured over £2.4 billion GPB (25.4 billion yuan) of credit against patent assets.[78] Unfortunately, SIPO does not appear to have published information about how the scheme works. From the standpoint of Western lenders and borrowers, it is difficult to determine how Chinese financial institutions carry out credit appraisals leading to positive decisions to grant patent-backed loans. However, the fact that the Chinese government has more direct control and input into commercial bank lending policy and capital adequacy requirements enables it to vigorously and potently implement its strategic goal of increasing IP-backed lending. In 2012, China's Ministry of Finance issued the new "Measures for the Administration of Special Funds for Subsidizing Foreign Patent Applications". The regulation outlines policies for PRC citizens and entities that file patent applications abroad.[79]

---

[74]See IP China News (2014), http://www.chinaipr.gov.cn/article/nocategory/201403/1801673.html. Accessed 14 May 2017.

[75]See Palmer (2004), pp. 2–5.

[76]See Shao and Feng (2014).

[77]See Shao and Feng (2014), pp. 30–31.

[78]See Cohen (2012), http://chinaipr.com/2012/06/. Accessed 14 May 2017.

[79]Wild (2014), http://www.iam-media.com/blog/Detail.aspx?g=481b76b6-637f-427f-b8d6-78d06cece504. Accessed 14 May 2017.

Further, in 2014 the largest-ever IP-backed debt finance loan emerged in the PRC. A trade publication, *China Paper*, reported[80] that Quanlin Paper, a Shandong province-based company, secured a loan of approximately £78 million GPB (RMB 7.9 billion) against a small portfolio of 110 patent and 34 trademark rights from a lending consortium led by the China Development Bank (CDB).[81] Although the quality of Quanlin's patent and trademark portfolio is indeterminate, the scale of the loan speaks for itself, and for that reason alone, is worthy of attention. The loan was reportedly recorded on 21 February on SIPO's IP asset register. The CDB is a PRC government-owned financial institution created in 1994 by the Policy Banks Law of 1994.[82] At its head is a cabinet minister level Governor, under the direction of the State Council. It is one of three policy-making banks in the PRC primarily responsible for raising finance for large infrastructure projects. The CDB was involved in financing the Three Gorges Dam and the Shanghai Pudong International Airport and is described as 'the engine that powers the national government's economic development policies'.[83] Most of Quanlin Paper's small portfolio of IP rights is limited to China.[84] The portfolio was valued at £600 million GPB (RMB 6 billion)[85] but details as to the valuation process for credit purposes has not been officially reported to date. This would assist to confirm if the sale of Quanlin's portfolio would enable the CDB to recoup its loan in the event it defaults. Whether the PRC credit appraisal methodology is capable of being adopted by Western economies, and thus is a compelling and credible case for change, is certainly debatable and an area for future research. In a public statement, Jiang Lurong, general manager of the Shandong branch of Bank of Communications (part of the consortium that syndicated the loan) said:

> …IP seems intangible, but it reflects the ability of value creation and sustainable operation of enterprises. Banking risk is not increased, but may be able to get a hold of high-quality customers early and improve the structure/makeup of the client base.[86]

Debts issued by the CDB owned by local banks are treated as "risk-free assets". Under the proposed PRC's capital adequacy rules for intangibles, they receive the same treatment as government bonds and the CDB is effectively insured by the

[80]The original report was in Mandarin and was translated into English.

[81]See IPOS (2014c), https://www.ipos.gov.sg/MediaEvents/Readnews/tabid/873/articleid/249/category/Press%20Releases/parentId/80/year/2013/Default.aspx. Accessed 14 May 2017.

[82]See http://www.cdb.com.cn/web/ (no English translation).

[83]See Forsythe and Sanderson (2011), https://www.bloomberg.com/markets/markets-magazine. Accessed 14 May 2017.

[84]See IAM Magazine (2014), pp. 5–6, www.iam-media.com/ctredir.ashx?g=cc6edf40-3f31-4157-b1aa-0cb886775091. Accessed 14 May 2017.

[85]See IPOS (2014c), https://www.ipos.gov.sg/MediaEvents/Readnews/tabid/873/articleid/249/category/Press%20Releases/parentId/80/year/2013/Default.aspx. Accessed 14 May 2017.

[86]See IPOS (2014c), https://www.ipos.gov.sg/MediaEvents/Readnews/tabid/873/articleid/249/category/Press%20Releases/parentId/80/year/2013/Default.aspx. Accessed 14 May 2017.

government. In contrast, under Basel III,[87] applicable to the UK and the EU, intangibles are rated as more risky types of assets requiring banks to hold more capital under the capital adequacy regulations which is a deterrent to IP-backed lending.[88] Intangibles are treated as lower-quality security, and intangible assets are not usually counted toward the loan's security because they are considered too difficult to value. The amount of funding Quanlin secured against its IP portfolio signals the substantial support for IP-backed debt finance initiatives in the PRC. Empirical research has shown that the increase in government subsidies, equity capital and bank loans have all helped to improve the capacity for self-driven innovation in Chinese enterprises.

5.3 Malaysia Debt Ventures Bhd (MDV) IP Financing Scheme (IPFS)

This RM200 million[89] IPFS was introduced by the Malaysian government on 13 December 2013 by the country's Minister of Finance II to assist the technology sector. According to Malaysia Debt Ventures Bhd (MDV), an innovative technology financier, the IPFS aims to further inculcate innovation and increase productivity. The initiative of RM200 million in financing is offered solely by MDV and enables companies to use their IP assets as an additional source of security to obtain funding and spur more investments for companies with technology capabilities, in turn encouraging innovation. The scheme also helps alleviate the difficulties faced by companies in the tech sector when they seek funding from financial institutions. The key features of the scheme are as follows:

- Financing of up to RM10 million or 80% of valued IP, whichever is lower;
- 5 years financing tenure (inclusive of a grace period of up to 12 months);
- 2% p.a. interest/ profit equalization payment;
- 50% guarantee provided by the Government of Malaysia and administered by Credit Guarantee Corporation Malaysia Berhad;
- Applicable for all MDV financing products (except post-shipment); and
- Discounted guarantee fee of 0.5% per annum.[90]

---

[87]See Basel Committee for Banking Supervision, Bank for International Settlements (2011), pp. 6–23, http://www.bis.org/publ/bcbs189.pdf. Accessed 14 May 2017.

[88]See Basel Committee for Banking Supervision, Bank for International Settlements (2011), pp. 6–23, http://www.bis.org/publ/bcbs189.pdf. Accessed 14 May 2017.

[89]Malaysian Ringgit currency.

[90]See Malaysia Debt Ventures Berhad, http://www.mdv.com.my/en/product-services/government-schemes/intellectual-property-financing/. Accessed 14 May 2017.

The scheme will lend against registered IP (patent and trademarks are preferred). However, MDV generally requires a corporate guarantee and takes a debenture[91] over the company's other assets.

The scheme has since disbursed RM40 million in loans to 11 companies and there are reportedly 19 new applications worth RM70.8 million, 6 of which are in the final evaluation stage. The applicants, most of whom emanate from the ICT[92] sector, are qualified to enjoy the 2% government rebate and 50% government guarantee administered by Credit Guarantee Corp Malaysia BhD. The loan term is 5 years (including a grace period of up to 12 months) carrying an interest rate of between 7.5% and 9.5%. MDV allocates a margin of 80% of the value of the IP (if the IP is valued at RM10 million then the amount advanced can be up to RM8 million).[93]

The Malaysian government has recognized IP as an alternative source of security in finance transactions and the funds allocated by the IPFS should support the growth of business operations of eligible IP-rich companies.

IP valuation is increasingly relevant. Valuation is a key tool in the process of financing based on IP assets. Technical valuations are required of intangible assets to give a point in time value of the IP for the purpose of assets to secure loans. Numerous valuation techniques have been developed, but since the value of IP is context-based and may have various value dimensions at the same time, the development of international standardized techniques will be a challenge. Moreover, international accounting standard (IAS) 38 Intangibles may require amendment to provide an effective method for valuing IP to allow the impact of internally-generated corporate IP to be visualized.[94]

The available methodologies for IP valuation work best with individual major patents and brands, which are the focus of the IPFS scheme.[95] Presently, there is no global standard for patent valuation. In 2007, the German Institute for Standardization (DIN) published PAS 1070 *General Principles of Proper Patent Valuation* (SAB) to assess the quality of valuation reports and expert appraisals. DIN initiated an international standardization project on patent valuation at the International Organization for Standardization (ISO). In 2010 ISO issued a standard on trademarks ISO 10668:2010.[96] This standard is a good starting point for brand valuation.

---

[91]A form of loan contract.

[92]Information and communication technology.

[93]See Wong (2015), https://www.pwc.com/my/en/assets/press/150209-theedge-banking-on-intellectual-property.pdf. Accessed 14 May 2017.

[94]See ICC (2017), https://cdn.iccwbo.org/content/uploads/sites/3/2014/11/icc-IProadmap-intellectual-property-roadmap-current-emerging-issues-business-policymakers.pdf. Accessed 19 May 2017.

[95]See, for example, Haigh (2004), http://brandfinance.com/images/upload/2004_05_brand_valuation_iam.pdf. Accessed 14 May 2017.

[96]See ISO (2010) at http://www.iso.org/iso/catalogue_detail?csnumber=46032. Accessed 14 May 2017.

The move to train a specialized team of IP valuation professionals is an inspiring initiative and will help Malaysian banks and financial institutions, which were previously unlikely to engage in IP-backed finance, to accept registered and valued IP assets as security. The Intellectual Property Corporation of Malaysia (MyIPO) is responsible for coordinating the training of the IP valuation team.[97]

Note however that in secured lending practice, it is increasingly common for the debtor to agree to grant a security interest in all its present and future IP assets, in which case the security is not based on a specific IP asset. The legal documentation is asset-based only in a formal sense. There is a problem then, in terms of secured lending theory, as to why the extent of priority is often linked to the value of specific assets.[98]

5.4 *Hong Kong*

The ground-breaking intellectual capital statement (ICS) initiative was introduced in 2010 by five Hong Kong Banks which offer young SMEs more favorable financial and/or service privileges if they prepare their own ICS. In relation to IP-backed lending, since 2010 five Hong Kong banks[99] have offered more favorable financial and/or service privileges to successful business loan applicants who have voluntarily prepared their own ICS. The Hong Kong Intellectual Property Department (HKIPD) worked closely with the Hong-Kong based banks to facilitate this. HKIPD have also produced a helpful *Guide to Intellectual Capital Management* to assist credit applicants on how to produce a narrative disclosure of their IC/IP assets.[100]

The effect of this initiative is to turn lenders into 'information demanders' who use the information to inform their credit appraisal and lending decisions. Whereas, we have seen in Sect. 1 above that most European lenders only rarely identify and consider IP assets in SME credit appraisal decisions, instead focusing their attention on the familiar: traditional tangible assets such as land and equipment. Lenders in other countries, with the exception of Japan (the next jurisdiction to be discussed), are not yet 'IP information demanders'.

In essence, this initiative passed on the cost of preparing the ICS to the young IP-rich SME. By providing their *Guide to Intellectual Capital Management*, the HKIPD have attempted to support SMEs to manage, capture and disclose their IC/IP information.

---

[97]See http://www.myipo.gov.my/.

[98]See Siebrasse (1997), p. 3.

[99]Bank of China (Hong Kong) Limited, Chon Hing Bank Limited, Citi Commercial Bank, Hang Seng Bank Limited and the Bank of East Asia. See Hong Kong Intellectual Property Department, http://www.ipd.gov.hk/eng/home.htm.

[100]See Hong Kong Intellectual Property Department, http://www.ipd.gov.hk/eng/ICM/guide_icm_e.pdf. Accessed 14 May 2017.

However, it appears that what is also needed, but which is currently lacking, is a standardized approach for young SMEs to provide a useful, timely and relevant IC/IP management report tailored specifically to set out non-financial qualitative IC/IP information to assist lenders make IP-backed finance lending decisions. In relation to the corporate disclosure of IP assets by SMEs, the author has created in a simple triage-style model that is extensively discussed in her Ph.D. thesis "Patent-backed Debt Finance: Should Company Law Take the Lead to Provide a True and Fair View of SME's Patent Assets?.[101] Japan, the subject of the next section, is unique in that it has developed its own official guidelines specifically for corporate IP asset and strategy disclosure in its efforts to enhance IP awareness in the business community as well as access to IP finance by young Japanese SMEs.

5.5 Japan

Japan is an interesting country renowned for its innovativeness in bringing to market new technologies and is largely a nation built on IP offsetting the low level of natural resources. The country has a robust and sophisticated national IP framework in place. Over the past decade, the Japanese government has introduced initiatives regarding the disclosure of intellectual capital (IC) which comprises IP among other things. Following business research in the field of knowledge management that began in earnest in the 1980s, in 2004 Japan's Ministry of Economy, Trade and Industry (METI) introduced the *Guideline for Intellectual Property Information Disclosure* (GIPID)[102] to increase the acknowledgement of IP assets through the voluntary extension of corporate reporting.[103] The Guideline states that the rationale for implementing an IP disclosure regime is that:

> Becoming a nation that quests for sustained growth of its economy and society through vigorous promotion of creation, protection and exploitation of intellectual property, in short a "nation built on intellectual property," is an urgent goal for Japan to strengthen its industrial competitiveness… the METI also established a "Pilot Model for Disclosing Patent and Technical Information" with the hope that those companies that practice "intellectual property-backed management" will disclose information concerning their intellectual property and gain fair market valuation.[104]

As a result, Japanese lenders and other stakeholders presently have a greater awareness of the nature of IP assets and a more detailed understanding of firms' IP

[101] See Denoncourt (2015).

[102] See Ministry of Economy, Trade and Industry, Japan (2004), http://www.meti.go.jp/english/information/downloadfiles/cIPP0403e.pdf. Accessed 14 May 2017.

[103] Johansen et al. (2006), pp. 474–491.

[104] IAM Magazine (2014), p. 3, www.iam-media.com/ctredir.ashx?g=cc6edf40-3f31-4157-b1aa-0cb886775091. Accessed 14 May 2017.

strategies for value creation than those in other countries. This makes it easier for Japanese lenders to link the corporate IP asset and strategy information to the cost of debt.

The Japanese Government also shifted its IC and IP disclosure target from publicly listed-company investor communications to non-listed SME-financial institution communications with a view to adjusting the perceptions of lenders to IC and IP assets when contemplating loans to SMEs.[105] This shift occurred precisely for the reasons outlined earlier in Sect. 1 of this chapter, namely that young Japanese SMEs (in common with young SMEs around the world) still rely heavily on loans from financial institutions. During the shift, Japanese lenders were under the 'Action Program Concerning the Enhancement of Relationship Banking Functions'.[106]

As a result of these government-led initiatives, Japanese lenders have also become 'information demanders'. More timely, relevant and useful IP asset information serves to better inform credit appraisal and lending decisions to young IP-rich Japanese SMEs. In addition, there is presently a higher degree of communication between SMEs and Japanese lenders, given the adoption of a closer 'relationship-banking' approach to SME lending. 'Relationship-banking is a form of retail banking that involves direct advice to the client/borrower by a bank officer, who remains a point of contact on a range of value-added services. This is a strategy used by banks to enhance their profitability, by strengthening their relationships with clients and thereby increasing their loyalty. Shinji Hino, founder and CEO of Patent Finance Consulting, Inc.,[107] has had direct experience of successful IP-backed debt financing transactions with Mitsubishi Bank, the Development Bank of Japan and Fukuoka Bank. According to Hino, as the Japanese economy moves out of recession and begins to expand, IP finance is returning to pre-2008 levels, although lenders are insisting on lower loan to value (LTV) rates of circa 30% coupled with tighter annual monitoring of the secured IP assets.

In Japan, there already appears to be a different mind-set towards the viability of IP finance. The difference in the general governance structure of companies, however, is an important and unique factor, given the direct role banks have in the corporate governance structure. This is a unique approach which warrants discussion. According to Learmount,[108] the main bank system is widely perceived to be an important component of Japanese corporate governance arrangements, playing a significant role in the monitoring of company managers in lieu of shareholders. Japanese banks may hold company shares (up to a maximum of 5% of the company's

[105]Ordonez de Pablos and Edvinsson (2015), pp. 187–191.

[106]Introduced by the Financial Services Agency (FSA) in March 2003. See FSA (2003), http://www.fsa.go.jp/news/newse/e20030328-1a.pdf. Accessed 14 May 2017.

[107]See http://www.ptfc.co.jp/english/.

[108]A Lecturer at the Judge Institute of Management, University of Cambridge.

total company equities), which is considered to give banks some incentive to monitor their clients.[109] More importantly, economists argue that the high gearing of Japanese companies has meant that bank lending takes on many of the characteristics of equity finance, which obliges banks to monitor client companies.[110] A high percentage of the loans are secured (60–70%) against general rather than specific assets and banks generally ask companies for extensive ongoing access to company financial information when making a loan. This in turn leads to the lender playing an active role in supporting client companies during financial distress. According to Suzuki, who carried out a detailed analysis of 52 companies facing financial distress, the main determinant of recovery was the strength of the relationship with the main bank, defined in terms of the amount of outstanding loan, the extent of bank shareholding and the existence of employee transfers between the firm and the bank.[111] The main bank tends to provide only 20–30% of the total loan to an individual company. Learmount concludes:

> … there is a broad consensus that banks have played a more prominent role in the Japanese financial system than is the case in other developed countries, particularly the US. Moreover, it is widely believed that the main bank has been important for corporate governance in Japan, as it is in a position to monitor company management in lieu of shareholders and is able to intervene quickly and effectively in the case of financial distress. For economists the main bank-company relationship is often summarized as being a system of 'contingent corporate governance'. When performance is good, corporate affairs are left to the incumbent management. When it deteriorates, the main bank, using its power as a lender and shareholder, intervenes in the management of companies to supervise down-sizing and reorganization where necessary.[112]

Research into the role the main bank plays in Japanese corporate governance and lending practice is a relatively embryonic new area with little empirical data, especially in relation to young IP-rich SMEs.

In summary, various types of IP-backed debt finance initiatives have taken root in Asia. Asian government policy makers are the catalysts and together with private commercial lenders they have developed various initiatives and innovations in IP finance to attempt to stimulate young IP-rich SMEs' access to credit. Although beyond the scope of this chapter due to the language barrier and lack of publicly available English translation of key documents, there is an opportunity for further work here. The progress of Singapore, the PRC, Malaysia, Hong Kong and Japan with IP-backed debt finance should be carefully studied by international and nation-state government policymakers to learn lessons as to which IP finance methods prove to be effective and which are not. The notion of the lender as an IP

[109]See Learmount (2002), p. 27.

[110]See Sheard (1987).

[111]See Suzuki (1980), pp. 18–39.

[112]See Learmount (2002), pp. 28–29.

asset 'information demander' appears to be the first step in the process towards systematizing IP finance practice as it opens the door to facilitate a valuable dialogue between the directors of young IP-rich SMEs and lenders. The initiatives in Singapore, Malaysia, Hong Kong and Japan appear to create this new behavior in their relationship with the potential borrower. Company directors appear to tolerate demands for timely, relevant and useful information about their IP assets when they are expected to provide such information as the opportunity to acquire debt finance is a powerful incentive.[113]

6 Analysis of the Global Initiatives

Across the globe, lenders currently place trust in tangible assets, intangible equity assets (shares) and all kinds of other tricky, risky and complex financial products (e.g., derivatives and hedge funds etc.). What lenders are really saying to young IP-rich SMEs is "we trust borrowers who own other classes of assets more". But is this trust in other asset classes misplaced? Are IP assets really more risky? Banks perceive less risk in lending against land, shares and other financial products, but the global financial crisis tells a different story. Traditional forms of security have turned out to be riskier than many lenders originally perceived.

We have seen that intergovernmental organizations such as WIPO and the OECD arrange seminars and compile resources specifically on this issue. UNCITRAL has included IP assets in the scope of its Legislative Guide on Secured Transactions (LGST). The LGST recommended that domestic secured transaction laws be harmonized internationally to reduced legal restrictions that impact on the availability of low-cost finance and credit. More recently, a number of governments have provided financial support for and established initiatives to encourage their young SMEs to exploit their IPR. The valuation of IPR and a formal IP asset and strategy report are critically important for young SMEs in this context.

The IP finance developments above indicate that IP assets will, in the future, play a greater part in the financial calculations of lenders than they have in the past. However, the high level of public funds to support IP finance in Asia stands in marked contrast to the position in the UK, Europe, the United States and other IP-intensive developed nations. In Asia, there is clear evidence of government-led collaborations between public and private sector organizations. These fledgling approaches should be encouraged and supported to link together, develop and support the direct participation and involvement of lenders in IP finance by lifting their awareness of IP and their use of IP in secured transactions. Such initiatives could have enormous impact.

[113]See Learmount (2002), p. 64.

6.1 Systemic Change and a Conceptual Framework for IP Finance

Evidence from a variety of different countries, all seems to be pointing in the same direction (subject to the caveat that cautions not to draw conclusions from one legal system and apply them to another) which is that lenders need to become IP asset and strategy 'information demanders' as the first step in systematizing IP finance.

The most broadly valid definition of systemic change is 'change that pervades all parts of a system, taking into account the interrelationships and interdependencies among those parts'. The international community will need to collectively rethink the underemployed IP finance method and make it more viable as a finance alternative by integrating systemic thinking with the goal of reformatting it. In this vein, it is beneficial to distinguish 'systemic change' from 'piecemeal change'. Piecemeal change entails changing one or several parts of a system. Systemic change recognizes interdependencies and makes the necessary changes in those other parts and their interrelationships. If the changes are compatible with the rest of the system, they will often be more successful.[114] When a system's 'systemic environment' undergoes few and small changes, piecemeal change to that system is most appropriate. When the systemic environment undergoes big changes, systemic change is needed.[115] In the area of IP finance, 'extreme' systemic change (which is referred to as paradigm change) is necessary as IP assets have largely replaced traditional forms of security especially in the context of young IP-rich SMEs. There are still large gaps in our understanding of the impact and consequence of IP rights as commercial assets on other disciplines such as finance, and vice versa. Now that economies have evolved from the industrial age to the information age, there is a need for a paradigm change in finance. The term most commonly used for this kind of change is 'transform', to actually create a new form or structure for the system. 'Systemic Design' begins with broad and tangential information gathering in order to examine the array of issues surrounding any given problem, precisely what has been undertaken in this chapter which has surveyed the range of initiatives in a variety of jurisdictions. As the exploration develops, related information begins to cluster into what Berger terms 'Systemic Bundles'.[116] These bundles connect one discipline (e.g., secured transaction law) with a framework that is unrelated (e.g., IP law), within the new framework. An example of another bundle is IP law with International Accounting Standards, IP assets valuation standards and practice, and corporate regulation with respect to disclosure of intangibles.[117] These connections represent clusters of issues that are imperative to examine in theory and in practice.

---

[114]See Systemic Change at https://systemicchange.wordpress.com/systemicchange/. Accessed 14 May 2017.

[115]See Berger (2009).

[116]See Berger (2009).

[117]Denoncourt (2015).

Consider the following systemic changes in the field of transportation, (an example involving tangibles). An initial system of human transport was the horse. The first mode of such transport was to ride the horse bareback, but eventually change occurred by way of fitting the horse with a saddle and bridle, making riding easier and less dangerous. The next critical change was the innovative horse-drawn wagon or coach, facilitating the transport of more passengers and cargo. The third change was a revolutionary one: replacing the horse with a gasoline engine vehicle, a new invention. A similarly revolutionary change eventually exceeded ground transport with another ground-breaking innovation, the airplane, facilitating the shift to air transport over longer distances in a faster way that ever before, even intercontinentally. Space travel and travel between planets is currently in the embryonic stage. These all represent vastly different points on the continuum from piecemeal to systemic change.[118]

Another example of successful systemic change that has direct import for IP finance is the Nobel prize-winning microfinance initiative by Grameen Bank. The Grameen Bank pioneered and popularized a methodology for extending small security-free loans for self-employment to some of the worlds' poorest people. Microfinance has had enormous impact, and is a prime example of systemic change to solve a problem. Academic Muhammed Yunus challenged banking theory by showing how to systematically extend security-free loans on a cost-effective basis to poor villagers on a large scale. The Grameen Bank now has over 7 million borrowers among approximately 77,000 villages in India. Microfinance is now a global movement and has been taken up by banking giants like Citigroup.[119] IP finance is a complex issue, but the starting point for a global IP finance movement to produce systemic change is international public policy to coordinate the bundles of changes that are needed to accelerate the secured lending model to accommodate intangible IP assets.

6.2 *Lenders and IP-Backed Finance Policy*

Engaging with commercial lenders is a key component of systemic change in IP finance. Government policy-makers can encourage and guide commercial lending banks to develop contemporary written 'IP-Backed Lending' policies to provide a blueprint for lending decisions. According to Howard Crosse, formerly Vice-President of the Federal Reserve Bank of New York, "the very act of formulating a policy and expressing it in words that all agree, will sharpen the issues and make the end product more effective".[120] IP-backed debt lending strategies of

[118]See Systemic Change at https://systemicchange.wordpress.com/systemicchange/. Accessed 14 May 2017.

[119]See www.grameen.com. Accessed 14 May 2017.

[120]See Crosse (1962).

commercial lending institutions should be drafted, if they do not already exist, or upgraded to attain the following broad objectives with respect to IP-backed lending:

1. profit maximization in the short and long term (taking into account the nature of the IP asset commercialization cycle) based on the lender's strategic plan;
2. conducting the IP-backed lending function within a managed risk framework; and
3. complying with existing capital adequacy requirements.

Such policies need to align with the lending codes of practice to ensure that the standards expected of banks in connection with the assessment of lending applications are met.

Profit maximization remains the chief concern of bankers around the world. In modern commercial lending, as in any other enterprise, the planning exercise must begin with a profit objective in view. The profit maximization elements of an IP-backed lending policy will primarily be drawn from a banks' strategic plan. In order for the commercial lender to strategically plan its approach to IP-debt finance and its central focus, namely profit, consideration of several issues will be needed. It is profit planning from which other policy sub-goals like targeted deposit growth, credit-deposit ratio, portfolio-mix, 'access to liquidity', transaction cost, loan repayment norms etc. will follow.[121]

The commercial lender's strategic plan for IP-backed lending will then give rise to the formulation of a loan policy document to enhance and upgrade IP-backed debt finance as a priority sector of development. The bank will need to analyse how the decision to make IP-backed loans will impact on its profitability. This is important for the purpose of the bank implementing an appropriate appraisal system of the potential borrower's IP assets. This requires a clear understanding of different operating and financial variables relating to IP rights as secured assets. Central to the development of a healthy IP-backed lending environment is the creditworthiness of both the IP-owning borrower and the lender.

In terms of the commercial lender's strategic plan, the aim should be for the IP-backed lending policy to encompass a five-year operational plan, keeping the profit objective in full view. The lender's short-term objectives to upgrade IP-backed lending will necessarily emanate from a medium-term goal, once it is translated into actionable strategies, and could be influenced by exposure to the existing IP finance initiatives taking place in various parts of the world (especially in Singapore, Malaysia, Hong Kong and Japan). The strategic plan should be straightforward and well-communicated to all levels of bank management, especially those dealing with young IP-rich SMEs who will know to ask for an IP asset and strategy report (or a more comprehensive IC report). Professional development for loan officers in terms of IP education as well as an engaged group of accredited IP valuers will be necessary.

[121] Bhattacharya (2010), p. 15.

The IP ecosystem is perceived as being complex, although its fundamental principles are simple. In time, lenders' trust in IP assets will develop and the IP asset class will mature and foster a reputation (a past credit history). Gaining a lenders' trust does not mean young IP-rich SMEs will successfully commercialize their IP assets; rather it provides the funding to move forward. Lenders will have an opportunity to dynamically monitor their loans by comparing the SME's financial information with its real time current account activity. Clearing banks across the world already have both a unique understanding of SMEs and the infrastructure to monitor small debt-financing.[122]

In conclusion, at an international level, a 'Summit on the Global IP Finance' agenda is needed to further the work already begun by WIPO, UNCITRAL and the national state IP offices to nurture the necessary paradigm shift. An international IP finance brainstorming event, assembling those experienced in the IP finance initiatives outlined, as well as professional IP valuers and representatives from the accounting profession, would jointly explore and advance knowledge to foster the systemic change need to critically shape the fledgling piecemeal developments in IP finance.

7 Conclusions and Outlook: Supporting the Agile Development of Globally Enhanced Access to IP Finance

This chapter has consolidated global perspectives, knowledge, recent trends and developments in IP-backed debt finance around the globe to inform future policy directions to encourage lending to young IP-rich SMEs in the post-recession economy. Government research and initiatives have begun to play an expanding role in encouraging initiatives to support the extreme systemic change needed to support the development of IP-backed debt finance. IP assets comprise a rich and diverse set of intangible assets, behaviors and networks that influence both short-term and long-term economic growth. There are now real advances in various jurisdictions which were examined in a critical manner adopting a "What is the current practice?" approach. Studies of the UK, EU, Asian and American initiatives have import for systemic change in IP finance across the globe in first tier, second tier and third countries. The success or otherwise of such initiatives can provide a unique view of the future, a world where IP finance will become increasingly significant, as IP assets are a relatively untapped source of value and security, while tangible personal and business assets, such as buildings and land, continue to decline within the young SME community. In consequence, IP assets should be made available as sources of security in loan transactions.

[122]In the UK for example, large clearing banks (institutions which clear bankers' cheques) in England and Wales include Barclays, HSBC, Lloyds Banking Group and Natwest.

The examples of positive momentum in economies that have recognized the infinite possibilities provided by robust IP finance systems aimed at enhancing young IP-rich SME access to IP finance through practical initiatives are:

- The UK government commissioned the *Banking on IP?* Report in 2013 and has followed this up with its *Banking on IP? an active response*,[123] published in March 2014, setting out the actions the UKIPO will take to improve access to finance for IP-rich SMEs.
- The EU published the *Final Report from the Expert Group on Intellectual Property Valuation* (*IP Valuation* Report) in 2014.
- In the US in October 2014, the Clearing House banking industry group formed the Patent Quality Initiative, a project aimed at eliminating inferior patents through better prior art searching, research and filing, thereby enhancing patent quality as a form of intangible property capable of being used as security.[124]
- In April 2014 the IP Office of Singapore launched the S$100 million 'IP Financing Scheme' to support local SMEs' access to IP-backed debt finance with the involvement of DBS Bank, Ltd; Overseas-Chinese Banking Corp, Ltd; and the United Overseas Bank, Ltd.[125]
- In 2008 the PRC implemented an 'IP pledge financing' program which has secured over £6 billion GPB in IP-backed loans and involves the China Development Bank, a PRC government-owned financial institution.
- In December 2013 the Malaysian government introduced the RM200 million Intellectual Property Finance System to assist the technology sector which is administered by Malaysia Debt Ventures Bhd (MDV), an innovative technology financier and Credit Guarantee Corporation Malaysia Berhad[126];
- In 2010 the Hong Kong Intellectual Property Department introduced the intellectual capital statement (ICS) initiative whereby five Hong Kong Banks (Bank of China [Hong Kong]) Limited, Chon Hing Bank Limited, Citi Commercial Bank, Hang Seng Bank Limited and the Bank of East Asia offer young SMEs more favorable financial and/or service privileges if they prepare their own ICS.[127]
- In 2004 Japan's Ministry of Economy, Trade and Industry (METI) introduced the *Guideline for Intellectual Property Information Disclosure* (GIPID) to increase the acknowledgement of IP assets through a voluntary extension of

[123]See https://www.gov.uk/government/publications/banking-on-ip-an-active-response. Accessed 14 May 2017.

[124]Oblack (2014), http://www.patentqualityinitiative.com/news/press%20releases/2014_oct%2015_pqi%20launch. Accessed 14 May 2017.

[125]See www.ocbc.com.sg.

[126]See Malaysia Debt Ventures Berhad, http://www.mdv.com.my/en/product-services/government-schemes/intellectual-property-financing/. Accessed 14 May 2017.

[127]See http://www.ipd.gov.hk/eng/ICM.

corporate reporting,[128] shifted its IC and IP disclosure target to non-listed SME-financial institution communications and implemented an 'Action Program Concerning the Enhancement of Relationship Banking Functions'.[129]

The majority of the initiatives involved a government agency acting in a supportive capacity and as a facilitator connecting lenders with SMEs. This research could form the basis for a larger more in-depth project to follow up the success or otherwise of the various initiatives and to share information regarding policy development and practical advice in the IP finance field. This could see a greater coherence of government involvement in stimulating IP finance beyond the present situation and work to systematize a tailored form of IP asset and strategy report tailored for lenders and financiers.

This chapter also considered how government policy-makers can work together with commercial lenders to take forward their IP-backed commercial lending policy with a view to creating systemic change by supporting them to become IP 'information demanders'. Lenders who recognize and act to benefit from the enormous security potential in IP assets will have "first mover" advantage in the market.

In essence, the government initiatives examined are aimed at fostering a culture that encourages young SME success by adapting the 'one-size-fits-all' of corporate debt finance to a more tailored approach to benefit young IP-rich SMEs. By encouraging entrepreneurs, start-ups and young IP-rich SMEs to succeed, government policy will also boost competition which breeds innovation. There is ample room for countries to improve their IP finance environment in order to unleash the benefits of IP for young SMEs and the wider economy.

Policy makers have to constantly strive to maintain the delicate balance necessary to satisfy the rights of the IP assets owner and the interests of lenders, so that the IP finance system benefits society as a whole. Research that builds on this theme to better coordinate the piecemeal IP finance initiatives that are taking place may have import with respect to potential reforms to legal frameworks. While there will be clear efficiency capital advantages for IP-rich SMEs if IP finance becomes more commonplace, there are also efficiency losses for creditors (transaction, registration of security and enforcement costs) that need to be addressed. Setting the agenda of IP debt financing theory and a framework will require the careful coordination of several areas of law: corporate governance and corporate reporting of corporate IP assets; secured debt finance theory as it applies to IP portfolios and secured transactions; the registration of security interests in IP rights and IP licences; financial institution regulation; and bankruptcy and insolvency laws. These are the pillars of IP finance that require coordination in order to provide more certainty for lenders who become IP owners on default of the borrower.

---

[128]See Ministry of Economy, Trade and Industry, Japan (2004), http://www.meti.go.jp/english/information/downloadfiles/cIPP0403e.pdf. Accessed 14 May 2017.

[129]See Ordonez de Pablos and Edvinsson (2015), pp. 187–191. See also FSA (2003), http://www.fsa.go.jp/news/newse/e20030328-1a.pdf. Accessed 14 May 2017.

Creating a successful future for IP financing where lenders are IP 'information demanders' should result in better understanding of the value and potential of young IP-rich SMEs' IP assets, making lenders more willing to secure loans against those assets which would have previously been deemed 'too risky'. This would be a significant step in the further development of the IP-based economy for enterprises that do business domestically and internationally, enabling governments to achieve their economic goals for innovation and the creative industries.

The range of international governments and public bodies addressing IP finance policy, including the state Intellectual Property Offices, should encourage and support systemic change in this area, leading to capacity building and the synergistic development of IP finance frameworks, lowering the cost of accessing credit and garnering more trust in IP assets as a form of security for lending.

References

Andres D, Criscuolo C, Menon C (2014) Do resources flow to patenting firms: cross-country evidence from firm-level data. http://www.oecd-ilibrary.org/economics/do-resources-flow-to-patenting-firms_5jz2lpmk0gs6-en. Accessed 13 May 2017

Brand O (2006) Conceptual comparison: towards a coherent methodology of comparative legal studies brook. J. Int'l L 32:405–466

Bazinas S (2009) International policy development on IP financing: United Nations commission on international trade law (UNCITRAL) legislative guide on secured transactions and current work on security interests in IP rights. http://www.wipo.int/meetings/en/doc_details.jsp?doc_id=118036. Accessed 13 May 2017

Berger A (2009) Systemic design can change the world. SUN Architecture, Amsterdam

Bhattachary H (2010) Banking strategy, credit appraisal and lending decisions: a risk-return framework. Oxford University, Oxford, p 15

Basel Committee for Banking Supervision, Bank for International Settlements (2011) Basel III: a global regulatory framework for more resilient banks and banking. http://www.bis.org/publ/bcbs189.pdf. Accessed 14 May 2017

Brassell M, King K (2013) Banking on IP? The role of intellectual property and intangible assets in facilitating business finance final report. https://www.gov.uk/government/uploads/system/uploads/attachment_data/file/312008/ipresearch-bankingip.pdf. Accessed 13 May 2017

Crosse HD (1962) Management policies for commercial banks. Prentice-Hall Inc., Englewood, New Jersey

Cohen M (2012) China to provide financial incentives for filing patent applications abroad China. http://chinaipr.com/2012/06/. Accessed 14 May 2017

Collopy D, Chun KH (2014) Singapore: IP financing scheme launched. http://www.managingip.com/Article/3362420/Singapore-IP-financing-scheme-launched.html. Accessed 14 May 2017

Criscuolo C, Gal PN, Menon C (2014) The dynamics of employment growth: new evidence from 18 countries. http://cep.lse.ac.uk/pubs/download/dp1274.pdf. Accessed 13 May 2017

Deane M (2009) Financial institutions' perspective of IP financing. http://www.wipo.int/meetings/en/doc_details.jsp?doc_id=118034. Accessed 13 May 2017

Department for Business, Innovation & Skills, Intellectual Property Office and Cable V (2013) Plans unveiled to support IP-rich businesses get funding. https://www.gov.uk/government/news/plans-unveiled-to-support-ip-rich-businesses-get-funding. Accessed 14 May 2017

Department for Business, Innovation and Skills and Viscount Younger of Leckie (2014) UK knowledge investment continues to grow. https://www.gov.uk/government/news/uk-knowledge-investment-continues-to-grow. Accessed 13 May 2017

Denoncourt J (2015) Patent-backed debt finance: should company law take the lead to provide a 'true and fair' view of SME patent assets. Dissertation, University of Nottingham

Edwards D (2001) Patent backed securitization: blueprint for a new asset class. https://www.researchgate.net/publication/241479825_Patent_Backed_Securitization_Blueprint_For_a_New_Asset_Class. Accessed 13 May 2017

EPO, OECD, and the UK Patent Office (2006) Patents: realising and securing value—an international conference in London. http://www.prnewswire.co.uk/news-releases/patents-realising-and-securing-value—an-international-conference-in-london-154779345.html. Accessed 13 May 2017

European Commission (2012) Options for an EU instrument for patent valorisation. https://www.iprhelpdesk.eu/node/867. Accessed 13 May 2017

European Commission (2014) Final report from the expert group on intellectual property valuation EU. https://ec.europa.eu/research/innovation-union/pdf/Expert_Group_Report_on_Intellectual_Property_Valuation_IP_web_2.pdf. Accessed 14 May 2017

FSA (2003) Action program concerning enhancement of relationship banking functions (background and basic policy concept). http://www.fsa.go.jp/news/newse/e20030328-1a.pdf. Accessed 14 May 2017

Forsythe M, Sanderson H (2011) Financing China costs poised to rise with CDB losing sovereign-debt status. http://www.cn-c114.net/583/a599201.html. Accessed 14 May 2017

Federation of Small Business (2012) ALT + finance: small firms and access to finance. http://www.fsb.org.uk/docs/default-source/Publications/reports/fsb_2012_access_to_finance.pdf?sfvrsn=1. Accessed 18 May 2017

Garrett JF (1995) Banks and their customers. Oceana Publications, Dobbs Ferry NY, p 99

Gower A (2006) Growers review of intellectual property. https://www.gov.uk/government/publications/gowers-review-of-intellectual-property. HM Treasury on behalf of the Controller of Her Majesty's Stationery Office, p. 3

G20 (2009) G20 leaders statement: the Pittsburgh summit. https://www.oecd.org/g20/summits/pittsburgh/publicationsdocuments/. Accessed 13 May 2017

Global Intellectual Property Center of US Chamber of Commerce (2016) Infinite possibilities US chamber international IP index forth edition February 2016. http://www.theglobalipcenter.com/wp-content/themes/gipc/map-index/assets/pdf/2016/GIPC_Index_2016_Final.pdf. Accessed 13 May 2017

Haigh D (2004) Brand valuation: what it means and why it matters. http://brandfinance.com/images/upload/2004_05_brand_valuation_iam.pdf. Accessed 14 May 2017

Hong Kong Intellectual Property Department (2009) Put your enterprise knowledge to work: a guide to intellectual capital management. http://www.ipd.gov.hk/eng/ICM/guide_icm_e.pdf. Accessed 14 May 2017

ISO (2010) 10668:2010: Brand valuation—Requirements for monetary brand valuation. http://www.iso.org/iso/catalogue_detail?csnumber=46032. Accessed 14 May 2017

IAM Magazine (2014) A revolution postponed (May/June 2014). www.iam-media.com/ctredir.ashx?g=cc6edf40-3f31-4157-b1aa-0cb886775091. Accessed 14 May 2017

IP China News (2014) Patent right pledge financing amounted to 25 billion Yuan as reported in English at http://www.chinaipr.gov.cn/article/nocategory/201403/1801673.html. Accessed 14 May 2017

IPOS (2014a) IP financing scheme. http://www.ipos.gov.sg/IPforYou/IPforBusinesses/IPFinancingScheme.aspx. Accessed 14 May 2017

IPOS (2014b) Singapore launches s$100 m IP financing scheme & first one-stop IP service centre. https://www.ipos.gov.sg/MediaEvents/Readnews/tabid/873/articleid/272/category/Press%20Releases/parentId/80/year/2014/Default.aspx. Accessed 14 May 2017

IPOS (2014c) Singapore ranks tops in Asia for IP Protection at https://www.ipos.gov.sg/MediaEvents/Readnews/tabid/873/articleid/249/category/Press%20Releases/parentId/80/year/2013/Default.aspx. Accessed 14 May 2017

ICC (2017) The ICC intellectual property roadmap. https://cdn.iccwbo.org/content/uploads/sites/3/2014/11/icc-IProadmap-intellectual-property-roadmap-current-emerging-issues-business-policymakers.pdf. Accessed 13 May 2017

Johansen U et al (2006) The Japanese government's intellectual capital reporting guideline: what are the challenges for firms and capital market agents? J Intellect Capital 7(4):474–491

Learmount S (2002) Corporate Governance: what can be learned from Japan?. Oxford University, Oxford, p 27

Lomax S, Davies E (2013) SME journey towards raising external finance. http://www.bmgresearch.co.uk/sme-journey-towards-accessing-external-finance/. Accessed 13 May 2017

Leung P (2014) From ideas to assets: Singapore's IP financing scheme. http://www.managingip.com/Article/3382687/From-idea-to-asset-Singapores-IP-financing-scheme.html. Accessed 14 May 2017

Lloyd R (2014) New banking group launches with focus on improving patent quality at http://www.iam-magazine.com/blog/detail.aspx?g=972D0D5D-D116-42FD-945D-82AC28C33B3A. Accessed 14 May 2017

Ministry of Economy, Trade and Industry, Japan (2004) Reference guideline for intellectual property information disclosure in the pursuit of mutual understanding between companies and capital markets through voluntary disclosures of information on patent and technology. http://www.meti.go.jp/english/information/downloadfiles/cIPP0403e.pdf. Accessed 14 May 2017

Oblack S (2014) Patent quality initiative launched to facilitate better patents and fewer disputes. http://www.patentqualityinitiative.com/news/press%20releases/2014_oct%2015_pqi%20launch. Accessed 14 May 2017

Ordonez de Pablos P, Edvinsson L (2015) Intellectual capital in organizations: Non-financial reports and accounts. Routledge, Abingdon, pp 187–191

Palmer VV (2004) From Lerotholi to Lando: some examples of comparative law methodology. Global Jurist Frontiers 4(2):1–31

Suzuki S (1980) Kyuusai yuushi ni okery "meinu banku" chikara (The strength of relief capital from main banks) Keiou Keiei Ronshuu, 18–39

Sheard P (1987) Intercorporate shareholdings and structural adjustments in Japan. Research School of Pacific Studies, Australia-Japan Research Centre Australian National University, Canberra

Sato I (2013) Study on governing law on security rights in intellectual property. https://www.iip.or.jp/e/e_summary/pdf/detail2012/e24_18.pdf. Accessed 13 May 2017

Shao F, Feng X (eds) (2014) Innovation and intellectual property in china: strategies, contexts and challenges. Edward Elgar, Cheltenham

Tuncak B (2009) The WIPO information meeting on ip financing: some notes. http://www.ip.finance/2009/03/wipo-information-meeting-on-ip.html. Accessed 13 May 2017

UNCITRAL (2010) Uncitral legislative guide on secured transactions supplement on security rights in intellectual property available. http://www.uncitral.org/uncitral/en/uncitral_texts/security/ip-supplement.html. Accessed 13 May 2017

UK Intellectual Property Office (2014) Banking on IP?-an active response https://www.gov.uk/government/publications/banking-on-ip-an-active-response. Accessed 14 May 2017

www.patentqualityinitiative.com

Walmsley J (2001) Patenting finance: financing patents. http://www.icmagroup.org/assets/documents/Patenting%20Finance%20Financing%20Patents.pdf. Accessed 13 May 2017

WIPO (2008a) Conferencia subregional de la OMPI-AGENCIA-MinCyT sobre la disponibilidad del capital intelectual: el rol de los activos intangibles como herramienta para obtener financiamiento. http://www.wipo.int/meetings/en/details.jsp?meeting_id=16342. Accessed 14 May 2017

WIPO (2008b) IP financing—an introduction. http://www.wipo.int/wipo_magazine/en/2008/05/article_0001.html. Accessed 13 May 2017

WIPO (2009) WIPO meeting to explore ip as a financing tool. http://www.wipo.int/pressroom/en/articles/2009/article_0003.html. Accessed 13 May 2017

WIPO (2011) What is intellectual property? http://www.wipo.int/publications/en/details.jsp?id=99&plang=EN. Accessed 13 May 2017

Wild J (2014) Chinese company's $1.3 billion patent and trade mark loan enters the IP deal Pantheon at http://www.iam-media.com/blog/Detail.aspx?g=481b76b6-637f-427f-b8d6-78d06cece504. Accessed 14 May 2017

WIPO (2015) WIPO SME e newsletter. http://www.wipo.int/sme. Accessed 13 May 2017

Wong A (2015) Banking on IP. https://www.pwc.com/my/en/assets/press/150209-theedge-banking-on-intellectual-property.pdf. Accessed 13 May 2017

Intellectual Properties and Debt Finance for Startups

Takashi Shimizu

Abstract This paper is an attempt to answer whether we can utilize intellectual properties for the financing of startups and why that is so. In order to tackle these questions, we conducted a questionnaire survey for startups and fund providers in Japan. Based on the results of this survey, we will examine how intellectual properties are actually used for their financing and why they are used in such a way.

1 Introduction

In general, securing funding is crucial for a business. This is especially true in the case of a startup, whose business has not yet developed and thus cannot produce enough money to sustain itself. At the same time, however, it is not an easy task to obtain financing from fund providers for the same reason—the business of a startup is still in its infancy and thus the risk of providing money is extremely high.

In such a situation, fund providers need more return on their money than in the situation where they provide funds for big enterprises or stable businesses. They cannot obtain high returns when they use debt financing—i.e., lending money to a startup which must repay the money with interest—since the interest rate is usually fixed at the time of the contract. Moreover, startups usually do not own enough tangible assets for use as collateral.[1] For these reasons, debt financing for startups usually does not function well. Thus, startups as well as fund providers are often

[1]See Berger and Udell (1998), pp. 613–673.

T. Shimizu (✉)
Department of Advanced Social and International Studies,
Graduate School of Arts and Sciences, The University of Tokyo, Tokyo, Japan
e-mail: tshimizu@waka.c.u-tokyo.ac.jp

T. Kono (ed.), *Security Interests in Intellectual Property*, Perspectives in Law, Business and Innovation, DOI 10.1007/978-981-10-5415-0_2

dependent on equity financing, i.e., investing money in a startup, obtaining shares in it, and therefore obtaining high returns when the business succeeds (by selling the shares and/or by receiving dividends).

Does this mean debt financing for startups is totally unnecessary? The answer is no for several reasons. One reason is that not all countries have a well-established IPO market. If a mature IPO market exists in a country, then it is relatively easy for a startup in that country to obtain funding because an investor—such as a venture capital or an investment fund—can easily sell the acquired stocks when the startup's business turns out to be successful, and thus will be more willing to invest his/her money in startups. Conversely, an investor will be less willing to invest in startups if there is no IPO market, and thus it will not be easy for startups to secure sufficient funds from investors. Another reason is that even though an IPO market may exist, there may be various difficulties regarding IPO: the market conditions may not be so good, the stock market may be controlled by the government, and so forth.

Thus, startups may prefer debt financing. Moreover, there is another reason for startups to prefer debt financing, namely maintaining secure control of their businesses. If a startup is heavily dependent on equity financing, the control right of the business may fall into the hands of investors and thus the founder of the company may lose his/her power. Startups may prefer debt funding in order to avoid such a situation. For fund providers, there are other reasons to let startups use debt financing. A debt provider could secure a certain amount of money as the repayment on the principal and interest even when the business is not so successful. For an investor (the provider of equity financing), a much higher return could be expected by letting startups use debt financing when the startup's business is very successful, since the interest rate is usually fixed and thus the rest of the profit goes to investors and founders (the leverage effect).

We can understand from the above that debt financing for startups is especially important in countries where financial industries are in their infancy. For example, Japan until the 1980s (or even in the 1990s) was in such a situation. The IPO market for startups did not exist until 1999 (two new markets for startups were established in 1999, one being the Tokyo Stock Exchange and the other, the Osaka Stock Exchange), and the financial system had been heavily dependent on banks or other types of banking institutions (such as credit associations, credit cooperatives, and agricultural cooperatives). Though several venture capitals were established even in the 1960s and the 1970s, their activity was somewhat limited. A survey on newly established Japanese manufacturing companies shows many still dependent on banking institutions, and about half of the funds for starting businesses came from banking institutions.[2]

Of course, Japan is not the only such case. In China, for example, the IPO market is still in its infancy, and the number of venture capitals is limited.

[2]See Sakakibara et al. (2000), http://data.nistep.go.jp/dspace/bitstream/11035/817/1/NISTEP-RM073-FullJ.pdf. Accessed 15 May 2017.

Thus China is now trying to find a way to provide money for startups by using debt financing. Even in the U.S., it was pointed out that debt financing has been important for small businesses.[3]

Then, several questions arise. As we have already pointed out, startups in Japan often prefer equity financing because of the risks, insufficient collateral, and so forth. How can we meet their needs? One idea for this was the use of intellectual properties as collateral–so-called "IP-backed lending" or "IP-based lending." This is often the case when a startup does not have enough tangible properties but has intellectual properties such as patents or copyrights (especially those for software). Banking institutions can provide money in various ways by using IPs as collateral. Thus, it would be beneficial for startups in Japan as well as Japanese banking institutions if they could utilize IPs as collateral.

In the U.S., for example, this idea has already been put into practice. Moreover, many other countries that did not have such means of financing welcomed this idea. As we will show in the next section, the Japanese government tried to introduce IP-backed lending in the late 1990s and early 2000s, while the Chinese government has also been pursuing this course. Recently, the U.K. government issued a report about the introduction of IP-backed lending (IPO 2013).[4]

In Japan, however, IP-backed lending is not popular even after the government struggled for its introduction for several years. The situation in Japan will be explained in detail here, but this means careful consideration should be given on whether or not IPs can be utilized for debt financing as well as the reason why. Moreover, we should also think how IPs could be utilized for debt financing, if it is possible at all.

This paper is multi-pronged. First, it contributes to the discussion of how financing can be secured for startups, by investigating the attempts of the Japanese government to introduce IP-backed lending and the results. Secondly, this paper can provide some ideas for policymakers on how to utilize IPs to secure financing for startups. Thirdly, it contributes to the discussion on how to legally deal with IPs as collateral. There was a long discussion about this issue in UNCITRAL and related organizations.[5]

The structure of the paper is as follows. In the next section, we will explain the Japanese government's attempts to introduce IP-backed lending. In the third section, we will introduce the method and results of our questionnaire survey, while in the fourth one we will discuss the results and consider how we can utilize IPs for debt financing. We will consider the implications of our study in our final section.

---

[3]See Berger and Udell (1998), pp. 613–673.

[4]UK IPO (2013), https://www.gov.uk/government/uploads/system/uploads/attachment_data/file/312008/ipresearch-bankingip.pdf. Accessed 15 May 2017.

[5]UNCITRAL (2011), https://www.uncitral.org/pdf/english/texts/security-lg/e/10-57126_Ebook_Suppl_SR_IP.pdf. Accessed 15 May 2017.

2 Japan's Attempts to Introduce IP-Backed Lending and the Aftermath

In 1995, IP-backed lending was introduced to Japan by the Development Bank of Japan (DBJ), and the Ministry of Trade and Industry (MITI), the current Ministry of Economy, Trade and Industry (METI). For several years after this development, however, IP-backed lending failed to attract much attention from fund providers as well as startups.

In 2002, the Japanese government organized the Strategic Council on Intellectual Property to strengthen its intellectual property policy. In the same year, the Strategic Council issued the "Intellectual Property Policy Outline" and laid out Japan's strategy to make the country more innovative. The Outline indicated that IP-backed lending should be introduced widely, and the main target of the IP-backed lending was startups.

The document stated that, "financial institutions in Japan should introduce financing based on Intellectual Properties proactively,"[6] and this is particularly for "startups, which do not own enough fixed assets such as lands,"[7] since "if the potential value of a company is not evaluated properly by financial institutions, then enough funds would not be provided to companies with the high potential for growth."[8]

Based on this Outline, the Japanese government established the Intellectual Property Strategy Headquarters in 2003 for its intellectual properties policies and it continuously issued the Intellectual Property Strategic Program from the year of its establishment in 2003. From 2004 to 2009, the Intellectual Property Strategic Plan continuously stressed that IP-backed financing should be introduced, especially for the sake of financing startups. The following[9] was taken from the 2004 version of the Strategic Program:

> In order for businesses including SMEs and venture companies that regard intellectual property as an important element in their management strategies to raise funds smoothly with the use of their intellectual property, in FY 2004, the GOJ [Government of Japan] will continue to promote efforts by the Development Bank of Japan to extend loans secured by intellectual property and also actively encourage similar efforts in the private sector.

Moreover, the Financial Service Agency of Japan also considered IP-backed lending as a way to promote financing to small and medium-sized enterprises. In 2003, a subcommittee of the Financial Systems Council, an advisory board for the

---

[6]Japan Strategic Council on Intellectual Property (2002), http://japan.kantei.go.jp/policy/titeki/kettei/020703taikou_e.html. Accessed 15 May 2017.

[7]Japan Strategic Council on Intellectual Property (2002), http://japan.kantei.go.jp/policy/titeki/kettei/020703taikou_e.html. Accessed 15 May 2017.

[8]Japan Strategic Council on Intellectual Property (2002), http://japan.kantei.go.jp/policy/titeki/kettei/020703taikou_e.html. Accessed 15 May 2017.

[9]Japan Intellectual Property Policy Headquarters (2004), http://japan.kantei.go.jp/policy/titeki/kettei/040527_e.html. Accessed 15 May 2017.

government regarding financial systems, issued a report regarding the enhancement of so-called "relationship banking", i.e., a method of lending based on the relationships with customers.[10] FSA also issued its Action Program Concerning Enhancement of Relationship Banking Functions on the next day.[11] Those documents recommended evaluation of IPs in small and medium-sized enterprises in order to utilize them as a way to obtain financing. In 2005, the FSA renewed its Action Program,[12] and it was also promoting the idea of "loans secured by intellectual property rights."

Based on these efforts by the government, from around 2004 to 2007, the Development Bank of Japan and some other regional financial institutions tried to expand their lendings to startups by using IPs as collateral. For example, DBJ had dealt with about 310 IP-backed lendings by March of 2008.[13] But the number of IP-backed lendings started to decrease around 2007. In the period from 2004 to 2006, the number of IP-backed financings by DBJ per year was around 30, but in 2007, the number decreased to around 10.[14] This indicates that the IP-backed lending boom has passed.

According to the questionnaire survey to financial institutions in Japan conducted in 2012 and 2013 by Teikoku Databank, of the 366 financial institutions that were surveyed, only 8 had experience with IP-backed lending.[15] Moreover, METI, which had advocated the idea of IP-backed financing, started to change its focus to financing by evaluating the business as a whole, and IPs are regarded as a part of business.[16]

Those are indications that even though the government made efforts to promote it, IP-backed lending, especially for startups, could not take root in Japan.[17] The question is why IP-backed lending for startups has not been widely employed in Japan. In the next section, we will investigate this matter by using our own questionnaire survey.

---

[10]Japan Financial Systems Council, Second Subcommittee (2003), http://www.fsa.go.jp/news/newsj/14/singi/f-20030327-1.pdf (in Japanese). Accessed 16 May 2017.

[11]See Japan FSA (2003), http://www.fsa.go.jp/news/newse/e20030328-1a.pdf. Accessed 15 May 2017.

[12]Japan FSA (2005), http://www.fsa.go.jp/news/newsj/16/ginkou/f-20050329-4/01.pdf (in Japanese). Accessed 16 May 2017.

[13]See Japan Intellectual Property Strategy Headquarters (2009), http://warp.da.ndl.go.jp/info:ndljp/pid/998223/www.kantei.go.jp/jp/singi/titeki2/keikaku2009_e.pdf. Accessed 15 May 2017.

[14]See Japan METI Intellectual Property Policy Office (2007), http://www.meti.go.jp/policy/intellectual_assets/guideline/list8.html. Accessed 15 May 2017. See also, Japan Intellectual Property Strategy Headquarters (2009), http://warp.da.ndl.go.jp/info:ndljp/pid/998223/www.kantei.go.jp/jp/singi/titeki2/keikaku2009_e.pdf. Accessed 15 May 2017.

[15]See Teikoku Databank (2013), https://www.jpo.go.jp/shiryou/toushin/chousa/pdf/zaisanken/2012_10.pdf. Accessed 15 May 2017.

[16]See Japan METI Intellectual Property Policy Office (2009), http://www.meti.go.jp/policy/intellectual_assets/english.html. Accessed 15 May 2017.

[17]In 2011, Howa bank, a regional bank in Japan, started to provide IP-backed financing based on its cooperation with Patent Finance Consulting, a consulting firm specialized in IP and finance.

3 The Questionnaire Survey

3.1 Method

In order to investigate how IP-backed lendings were used in Japan and why it could not take root, our research project entitled "Private International Law & Securities in Intellectual Property, Applying a Law and Economics Approach with the Aim of Developing and Disseminating the Methodology of PIL," conducted a questionnaire survey. This questionnaire survey had two parts: one for startups and the other for fund providers, such as people from consulting firms, venture capital, or law firms. By investigating Japan's case, in which the government tried to introduce IP-backed financing but failed, understanding was sought as to how people might better utilize IP-backed financing. The project and the survey were supported by the Grant-in-Aid for Scientific Research (S) by the Ministry of Education, Culture, Sports, Science and Technology.

The main survey was conducted from January to February of 2013, after two preliminary surveys. The questionnaire for startups was sent to 631 startups, which were randomly selected from various sources (i.e., reports issued by the government and related institutions, websites of financial institutions, news articles, etc.). The questionnaires for fund providers were sent to financial institutions, investment funds, venture capital, law firms, patent attorney offices, auditing firms, and so forth, which were randomly selected again from above-mentioned sources. The questionnaire was sent by mail.

Unfortunately, since the questionnaire was so complex and respondents were not familiar with the details of the legal issues related to financing, we received only 25 valid responses from startups and 12 from fund providers. The response rate was 4% for both surveys. As far as we know, this is the first questionnaire survey regarding the legal issues involved in financing for ventures. Thus, we believe this result is unavoidable. At the same time, we consider this result to be worth investigating.

Regarding possible biases to the answers, we have examined this possibility but could discover no biases related to types, industry, size, and so forth. Thus we regard our sample as properly representative of the respondents involved. Moreover, because of the small sample size, we analyzed the result by simply counting the numbers and also used cross tabulation.

3.2 Result of the Survey for Startups

First, from among the 25 respondent companies, 3 companies have not received any funding from fund providers in the past or at the present. We asked the remaining 22 companies about the method of financing they used, allowing multiple answers. In reply, 15 companies stated they obtained funds for investment from VCs, 14 companies indicated investment funds from individuals, and 13 companies said they were using loans from financial institutions. Furthermore, we asked about the primary source of funding, and from the answers we realized that 9 companies depended on loans from financial institutions as their primary funding source. We can thus conclude that loans were still used by many companies.

Next, we asked about the IPs they had and how they were used. Among 22 companies which received or had received funding from the outside, 7 companies did not have any IPs. These 7 were mainly sales and service companies. The remaining 15 companies could use their IPs to secure funding. As for those 15 companies, most of the intellectual property rights (IPRs) they owned were patents and trademarks, but some companies also owned copyrights for software.

One interesting result is that, among 7 companies not owning any IPRs, 6 companies indicated that their primary method of funding was debt financing (i.e., loans from financial institutions). On the other hand, among 15 companies that owned IPRs, 11 companies answered that their primary funding method was equity (investment from VCs/individuals/investment funds). Below is the cross tabulation of the relationship. The Chi-squared statistic is 6.812 and the hypothesis that there is no relationship between the primary method of financing and ownership of IPRs is rejected at 0.1% level.

		Own IPRs?		Total
		Yes	No	
Primary source of financing	Equity	11	1	12
	Debt	4	6	10
Total		15	7	22

Moreover, among those 4 companies owning IPRs and also dependent on debt financing, only 1 company owned patents. The other 3 companies indicated their IPRs consisted of trademarks, copyrights, and know-hows. This means that technology-based startups (tech startups) are mainly using equity financing, while those startups that are not based on technology (non-tech startups) are using debt financing.

We also asked several questions regarding how they deal with their IPRs when they obtain funding. All 4 companies that owned IPRs and were dependent on debt financing had conducted the valuation of their IPRs, and 1 company actually used its IPRs as collateral. On the other hand, among the 11 companies that owned IPRs and were mainly using equity financing, only one company conducted valuation. The other 4 companies made the confirmation of ownership of IPRs, and the remaining 6 companies did not report anything about IPR ownership. However, fund providers can confirm ownership by using the database of patents, for example, so it does not mean that fund providers actually are unaware of the IPRs of startup companies.[18]

[18]Japan has a database for patents, trademarks, utility model rights and design rights. See Japan Platform for Patent Information, available at https://www.j-platpat.inpit.go.jp/. Moreover, copyrights for software can be registered at the Software Information Center, and the information about them can be obtained from this Center.

In summary, tech startups were mainly dependent on equity financing, while non-tech startups were often using debt financing. When startups use debt finance, fund providers conduct the valuation of IPRs. On the other hand, when startups use equity financing, fund providers usually do not conduct the valuation.

3.3 Results of the Survey for Fund Providers

Next, we will introduce the results of the survey for fund providers. Though we have received 24 answers, many respondents said that they had not dealt with matters related to startups (11 out of 24). Especially, many patent attorney offices answered thus. Those responses were not regarded as valid. Moreover, another response was excluded because of its inconsistency. So the number of valid response was 12: 1 in-house fund of a manufacturing company, 2 law firms, 1 patent attorney office, 3 consulting firms, 1 securities company, 1 banking institution, and 3 VCs.

We asked them the method of financing they usually use, though methods vary based on the type of fund provider (VCs usually use investment, while banking institutions use loans). Law firms usually deal with equity financing, while some consulting firms deal with both equity and debt financing.

As for the use of IPs for financing, among 12 respondent companies (including law firms, patent attorney offices, etc.), 3 were not dealing with any IPs, thus 9 companies were dealing with financing with IPs. Among them, 4 companies were dealing with debt financing, and the other 5 companies were not dealing with debt financing (only with equity financing). All of the former 4 companies answered they were using IPRs as collateral, and also conducted the valuation of those IPRs. On the other hand, among the remaining 5 companies which only used equity financing, only 1 conducted the valuation while 3 other companies said they only confirmed the ownership of IPRs.

Moreover, among 4 companies that were using IPRs as collateral, 3 companies had the experience of exercising security rights (or, at least, attempted to do so). But only 1 company finally exercised the right. According to their answers, they considered the security rights difficult to exercise or that collateral could not be sold to others. One company answered that it abandoned the security rights. These answers indicated the difficulty of exercising the security rights of IPRs.

In summary, fund providers dealing with debt financing used IPRs as collateral, and they usually conducted the valuation. Fund providers that used equity financing only confirmed the ownership of IPRs and did not conduct the valuation. Moreover, fund providers considered that in reality the exercise of security rights was difficult when they used IPRs as collateral.

4 Discussion

The results of our questionnaire survey can be summarized by the following four points:

1. While fund providers can provide IP-based lending, startups usually do not use this method of funding.
2. Tech startups are especially dependent on equity financing. On the other hand, non-tech startups often use debt financing, but they frequently do not have IPRs and thus do not use IPRs as collateral.
3. When startups use debt financing by using IPRs, fund providers usually conduct the valuation of them. When startups use equity financing, however, fund providers usually do not conduct the valuation and only confirm the ownership of IPRs.
4. Fund providers consider the exercise of security rights to be difficult when they use IPRs as collateral.

The results initially show that while IP-backed lending had been promoted by the government, in fact startups do not use this type of financing method. But why is that so? There are two clues to the answer. The first is that non-tech startups are using debt financing while tech startups are using equity financing, and the second is that fund providers conduct valuation of IPRs when they use the IPRs as collateral, but they only confirm the ownership when they provide funding by equity financing.

Actually, it is often pointed out by the government and some other organizations in Japan that the valuation of IPRs is difficult and thus costly [see Organization for Small & Medium Enterprises and Regional Innovation (OSMERI) (2000)].[19] This is basically because the valuation requires an estimation of future cash inflow produced by the business as well as the contributions of the IPRs to the business (and cash inflow). It implies that valuations are difficult to carry out and not so reliable in their conclusions.

However, in order to provide funding using IPRs as collateral, banking institutions insist that they must accurately evaluate IPRs as collateral. This has been a traditional bank practice in Japan. If the evaluation of the IPRs proved to be unreliable, banking institutions would not want to lend large sums of money, since there is the risk of overestimation of the value of IPRs and so the debt could not be secured by those IPRs.

If fund providers are using equity finance, on the other hand, they do not have to do such valuations. If the fund provider regards a business as being profitable (and if they can estimate how profitable it is), then they can provide the money. If the evaluation of IPs is difficult, costly, and unreliable but required for debt financing,

[19]See OSMERI (2000), https://web.archive.org/web/20130212041813/http://www.smrj.go.jp/keiei/dbps_data/_material_/common/chushou/b_keiei/keieisaimu/pdf/titeki_manual.pdf. Accessed 16 May 2017.

and startups cannot borrow sufficient money because of the unreliability of the evaluation, then it is natural for both fund providers and startups to avoid debt financing by using IPRs. When fund providers use equity financing for a startup, there is no need to evaluate the IPRs it owns. What fund providers do have to do is to evaluate the profitability of the business as a whole and whether IPs that are used for the business are actually owned by the startup. IPRs are only needed, first, to show the technical capability of the startup and, secondly, to prevent intervention in the business by others.

If startups have no IPRs, then there is no need to consider evaluation of IPRs. But it is difficult for them to persuade VCs or other kinds of fund providers using equity finance to invest in them since they do not have any IPs to prove their technical competitiveness. In such a situation, a non-tech startup must somehow try to borrow money from banking institutions rather than by attracting investment. Moreover, non-tech startups usually use money more often to purchase tangible assets (buildings, facilities, etc.) than intangible assets (i.e., advanced technology) and thus they can use debt financing more easily than tech startups can.[20]

Another matter we should consider is the difficulty related to the exercise of security rights. In Japan, the exercise of security rights was considered difficult because IPRs are not so useful when the owner changes and thus it is usually almost impossible to find a buyer for IPRs.[21]

In summary, there are two reasons why IP-backed financing is difficult. One is that fund providers must conduct the valuation of IPRs, which is difficult and costly but unreliable. The other is that the exercise of the security rights is in fact almost impossible.

If this is correct concerning Japan, then why is debt financing using IPRs as collateral popular in some other countries (especially the U.S.)?

Pertinent is that the above explanation is basically relevant only to how Japanese companies create and use IPs, and how they set up IPRs. In Japan, IPs are "embedded" in business. Basically, owners create IPs specifically for their own businesses, where they are used. They usually do not consider the possibility of selling or licensing those IPs. Because of this way of thinking, they do not consider how to make money by using IPs themselves. Instead, they consider how to make money by using IPs as a part of their business. They usually only consider the IPRs that are directly related to business, and do not try to "enlock" all of the related IPRs.

Since IPRs are embedded in the business of Japan, it is difficult to determine the value of IPRs per se. It is also difficult to exercise security rights, since IPRs are developed under the specific context of the particular business, and companies do not consider the possibility of using IPRs in a different setting. This means they are not useful if those IPRs are separated from the original businesses.

---

[20]See Bezant (1997), pp. 237–263.

[21]See OSMERI (2000), https://web.archive.org/web/20130212041813/http://www.smrj.go.jp/keiei/dbps_data/_material_/common/chushou/b_keiei/keieisaimu/pdf/titeki_manual.pdf. Accessed 16 May 2017.

However, there are types of IPRs which are independent from businesses and thus their valuation is rather easy. For example, if an IPR (or a group of IPRs) is licensed to other companies, we can estimate the cash flow that the IPR(s) produces. For this kind of IPR, the valuation and the exercise of security rights are rather easy. It seems to us that, in the U.S., the majority of IPRs are independent from particular businesses and an IPR or a group of IPRs can produce its own cash flow. If this understanding is correct, then we can say that debt financing using IPs as collateral is easy in the U.S. but difficult in Japan.

This conclusion is related to the discussions in UNCITRAL and other organizations. If IPs are embedded in businesses in some countries but not in some other countries, then probably the legal framework suitable for the former countries is different from that of the latter countries.

5 Conclusion

In this paper, we have examined whether or not we can utilize IPs to secure funding for startups and the reasons why. We also considered how we could use IPs for finance of startups.

We have first reviewed the Japanese government's efforts to introduce IP-backed financing in Japan and the results. After 2004, the Japanese government tried to stimulate innovation in Japan and, as a part of this effort, it promulgated the idea of IP-backed lending for startups. In fact, IP-backed lending attracted attention, and the DBJ actively pursued it. However, after 2007, the boom was over and, in the end, IP-backed financing could not take root in Japan.

We have also introduced the results of our questionnaire survey. What we found was that IP-backed financing was not popular among startups, and that tech startups are mostly dependent on equity financing. Non-tech startups are more dependent on debt financing, but they usually do not have IPRs and thus IP-backed lending is not useful for them. We also found that investors (i.e., fund providers using equity financing) usually do not conduct the valuation of IPRs, while lenders (fund providers using debt financing) often conduct valuations. Finally, lenders recognize that the exercise of security rights is difficult even when they try to use such rights.

Based on the results, we consider that though startups in Japan often try to develop and use IPs as a part of their businesses, it is usually difficult to determine the value of IPs, and they are often useless when they are transferred to someone else. In this sense, IPs are "embedded" in business and thus debt finance using IPs as collateral does not work. On the other hand, it is working in the U.S., probably because in that country people are developing IPs as independent assets and often use them for profits (i.e., licensing them to obtain fees). In that case, the valuation of IPs is rather easy and they can also serve as collateral. In such a country, IP-backed financing works well, but in Japan it does not. The situation in Japan may change in the future, but at present there is a substantial difference between countries. The legal framework must be constructed based on this difference.

References

Berger AN, Udell GF (1998) The economics of small business finance: the roles of private equity and debt markets in the financial growth cycle. J Bank Financ 22(6):613–673

Bezant M (1997) The use of intellectual property as security for debt finance. J Knowl Manag 1 (3):237–263

Japan FSA (Financial Services Agency) (2003) Action program concerning enhancement of relationship banking functions (Background and Basic Policy Concept). http://www.fsa.go.jp/news/newse/e20030328-1a.pdf. Accessed 15 May 2017

Japan Intellectual Property Policy Headquarters (2004) Intellectual property strategic program 2004 http://japan.kantei.go.jp/policy/titeki/kettei/040527_e.html. Accessed 15 May 2017

Japan Intellectual Property Strategy Headquarters (2009) Intellectual property strategic program 2009. http://warp.da.ndl.go.jp/info:ndljp/pid/998223/www.kantei.go.jp/jp/singi/titeki2/keikaku2009_e.pdf. Accessed 15 May 2017

Japan METI (Ministry of Economy, Trade and Industry) Intellectual property policy office (2007) Chiteki Zaisan-no Ryutsu Shikin Chotatsu Jirei Chosa Hokoku (A report on cases of the trade of and financing using intellectual properties). http://www.meti.go.jp/policy/intellectual_assets/guideline/list8.html Accessed 15 May 2017

Japan METI (Ministry of Economy, Trade and Industry) Intellectual property policy office (2009) keys to intellectual asset-based management evaluation finance, Ministry of Economy, Trade and Industry. http://www.meti.go.jp/policy/intellectual_assets/english.html. Accessed 15 May 2017

Japan Strategic Council on Intellectual Property (2002) Intellectual property policy outline http://japan.kantei.go.jp/policy/titeki/kettei/020703taikou_e.html. Accessed 15 May 2017

OSMERI (Organization for Small & Medium Enterprises and Regional Innovation) (2000) Chiteki Zaisan-ken Tanpo Yushi Manyuaru (Manual on lending secured by intellectual property right). https://web.archive.org/web/20130212041813/http://www.smrj.go.jp/keiei/dbps_data/_material_/common/chushou/b_keiei/keieisaimu/pdf/titeki_manual.pdf. Accessed 16 May 2017

Sakakibara K, Koga T, Honjo Y, Kondo K (2000) Nihon-ni Okeru Gijutukei Bencha no Keiei Jittai to Sogyosha ni Kansuru Chosa Kenkyu (Survey research on technology-based startups and their entrepreneurs in Japan). http://data.nistep.go.jp/dspace/bitstream/11035/817/1/NISTEP-RM073-FullJ.pdf. Accessed 15 May 2017

Teikoku Databank, Ltd. (2013) Kin-yu Kikan-to kara Mita Kigyo no Chiteki Zaisan wo Katsuyo shita Shikin Chotatsu ni Kansuru Chosa Kenkyu Hokoku-sho (A report on the financing of companies utilizing intellectual properties from the perspective of financial institutions). https://www.jpo.go.jp/shiryou/toushin/chousa/pdf/zaisanken/2012_10.pdf. Accessed 15 May 2017

UK Intellectual Property Office (IPO) (2013) Banking on IP? The role of intellectual property and intangible assets in facilitating business finance, final report. https://www.gov.uk/government/uploads/system/uploads/attachment_data/file/312008/ipresearch-bankingip.pdf. Accessed 15 May 2017

UNCITRAL (2011) UNCITRAL legislative guide on secured transactions: supplement on security rights in intellectual property. https://www.uncitral.org/pdf/english/texts/security-lg/e/10-57126_Ebook_Suppl_SR_IP.pdf. Accessed 15 May 2017

IP and Debt Finance: Cross-Border Considerations

Toshiyuki Kono and Claire Wan-Chiung Cheng

Abstract Innovation in both technology and finance has greatly changed the definition of national borders in the past decades. This brings vibrant commercial possibilities as well as legal challenges to the age-old loan industry. One relevant question may be: how to stimulate innovative endeavor by providing a globally well-functioning financial infrastructure. As of today, however, not only is it true that national laws rarely address security rights in intellectual property rights ("IPRs"), but also almost no provisions are provided on the international level to determine the law applicable to these kinds of security interests. On the other hand, the tension between the protecting state (i.e. the underpinning *lex loci protectionis* principal of traditional IPRs jurisprudence) and the efficiency goal of secured transaction law, has become stalemated. This paper digs into this complexity by exploring more than twenty variants of proposals after five major international meetings at UNCITRAL. The introduction session is divided into two parts: historical analysis and policy-debate review. The first part of the introduction section concentrates on the summarization of each proposal, while the second part provides detailed analysis of the rationales raised to support them. A comparative private international law analysis consisting of four jurisdictions follows in the next section to assist the understanding of the current legal *status quo* in different countries. Finally, the conclusion reflects what is missing in previous discussions, and proposes harmonization of reforms to solve the "self-duplicating" problem embedded in the current *lex loci protectionis* intellectual property system.

T. Kono
Kyushu University, Fukuoka, Japan
e-mail: glyndebourne@gmail.com

C.W. Cheng (✉)
National Chengchi University, Taipei, Taiwan
e-mail: clairexl@nccu.edu.tw

T. Kono (ed.), *Security Interests in Intellectual Property*, Perspectives in Law, Business and Innovation, DOI 10.1007/978-981-10-5415-0_3

1 Introduction

1.1 Background

Even in China, one of the most booming and influential markets in the world, using intellectual property rights as collateral in secured transactions was still an almost unheard business practice until the year 2006.[1] To accommodate such a cutting edge financing tool, it is imaginable that a society's entire legal system must strenuously devote itself to responding to the accompanying regulatory demands and/or civil disputes that are arising.

Hence it becomes understandable that when in many countries, the domestic and substantive security right in intellectual property (hereafter "SR-in-IP") law issues are still under-addressed and require enormous legislative attention from the general public, a next-stage conflict-of-laws concern would most likely find difficulty being placed on pre-occupied law-makers' priority lists.

However, innovation in both technology and finance has greatly changed the definition of national borders in the past decades. This brings vibrant commercial possibilities as well as legal challenges to the age-old loan industry. One relevant question may be: how to stimulate innovative endeavor by providing a globally well-functioning financial infrastructure. Imagine, for instance, the following scenario: instead of relying on the local businesses, how much can the cross-border financing practices contribute to the above-mentioned goal? For instance, wouldn't both the capital-scarce country A and the technology-stagnant society B benefit from each other—if a potential future inventor in A no longer has to sacrifice or postpone the realization of his or her creative ideas, but simply to obtain timely funding from B's financial institutions, who are also searching for new investment targets?

One of the obstacles lies in the reality that in today's world, States (sovereignties) still intensively regulate both money (e.g. "banks") and proprietary aspects of technologies (i.e. intellectual property rights; hereafter "IPRs") . Hence, there exist considerable legal barriers or uncertainties that impede the achievement of cross-border intellectual property ("IP") financing practice as such. Finding or proposing a set of transparent, efficient and predictable conflict-of-laws rules may help clarify the concerns of stakeholders (including the States), and reduce the transaction cost by eliminating the ambiguities in/from laws. This paper investigates the institutional reasoning of the fuzzy *status quo*, as well as addressing the real conflicts which shape the determination of applicable law (準拠法) for multiple-state IPRs' secured transactions.

The United Nations Commission on International Trade Law ("UNCITRAL") recognizes and addresses both the commercial possibilities alongside of the legal challenges attached to this issue. Besides, even though UNCITRAL's legislative

[1]According to State Intellectual Property Office ("SIPO") of the PRC (People's Republic of China), there are more than 1.73 million patents granted in China accumulatively by the end of 2006. Among such a huge amount of granted patents, however, only 323 patent pledge contracts were registered with SIPO. See SIPO (2007), p. 499; see also Lu (2007), p. 46.

discussion started with a focus on tangible encumbrances, intangible assets were quickly addressed in the secured transaction law-drafting processes. Intellectual property rights, in particular, were intensively discussed as a separate category of encumbrance, and eventually an independent "IP Supplement" ("IP Supplement" is the abbreviation for "UNCITRAL Legislative Guide on Secured Transactions: Supplement on Security Rights in Intellectual Property") was produced with harmonization or legal reform recommendations.

Paying equal attention to diversified categories of collateral assets is not the only factor that makes UNCITRAL's contribution unique and irreplaceable for this subject. Follow-up researchers may also be interested in UNCITRAL's unprecedented action to include not only domestic dealings but also cross-border secured transaction laws in its legislative initiative. When it comes to secured transactions embedded with foreign elements, however, conflicts among multiple national laws inevitably arise. Searching and determining which law applies in such cases was an extremely complicated task, but fortunately one not rejected by UNCITRAL. For both tangible and intangible encumbrances, the conflict-of-laws topic constitutes an independent chapter in the presented "Legislative Guideline" ("Legislative Guideline" is the abbreviation for "UNCITRAL Legislative Guide on Secured Transactions") and IP Supplement, respectively. For intellectual property collateral, this is particularly valuable as the conflict-of-laws issue has never been this comprehensively debated in other policy or academic forums before.

In this connection, this paper will commence by conducting a thorough examination of UNCITRAL's past discussions on this issue: choosing the law applicable for security interest in intellectual property with a narrowed-down focus on public notice, perfection, and third party effectiveness issues.

This paper is arranged as follows: firstly, since there are still more than twenty variants of proposals after five major international meetings at UNCITRAL, the introduction session will be divided into two parts (historical analysis and policy-debate review) to facilitate readers' understanding. The first part of the introduction section concentrates on the summarization of each proposal, while the second part provides detailed analysis of the rationales raised to support them. A comparative private international law analysis consisting of four jurisdictions follows in the next section to assist the understanding of the current legal *status quo* in different countries. Finally, the conclusion reflects what is missing in previous discussions, and proposes harmonization of reforms to solve the "self-duplicating" problem embedded in the current *lex loci protectionis* intellectual property system.

1.2 Proposals and Debates at Milestone UNCITRAL Meetings

As will be elaborated later, readers can find twenty-two different legislative proposals being raised, accumulatively, at UNCITRAL meetings. In addition,

UNCITRAL appoints different applicable laws based on different connecting factors. Therefore, since there are four major connecting factors (creation, third-party effectiveness, priority and enforcement of a security right) on laws applicable to property matters,[2] there could potentially be more than eighty conflict-of-laws rules. Thus, to avoid confusion, the following discussion focuses on only one of the four abovementioned aspects: third-party effectiveness.

1.2.1 13th Session (19–23 May 2008, New York)

Compared to the early UNCITRAL study on non-IP encumbrances, i.e. the general legislative guide on secured transactions prepared at UNCITRAL since 2002,[3] security interest in IPRs has a relatively short history. According to the official recording of UNCITRAL, it wasn't until the Working Group VI 13th session (held in the year 2008)[4] that intellectual property rights began to be formally introduced as a separate type of encumbrance for exploration.

Even though before 2008, intellectual property has never appeared as an independent collateralization asset for UNCITRAL's Working Group VI (but merely mentioned in scattered discussions), the conflict-of-laws issue was immediately brought up after this topic emerged. The reason is perhaps understandable: the discussion context still follows the previous setting for non-IP assets, and the conflict-of-laws issue is always included there.[5]

Accordingly, since the conflict-of-laws issue has always been apparent ever since the very first meeting discussing non-IP assets,[6] in which the topic moved on

---

[2]UNCITRAL divides conflict-of-laws rules for IPRs collateral into two classifications: (1) Law Applicable to Property Matters and, (2) Law Applicable to Contractual Matters. See UNCITRAL (2011b), http://www.uncitral.org/pdf/english/texts/security-lg/e/10-57126_Ebook_Suppl_SR_IP.pdf, pp. 127–147. Accessed 16 May 2017.

[3]UNCITRAL keeps very comprehensive documentary of its Working Group meetings and discussion tracks. For this specific issue of security interest and to view from the 1st session to the current 25th session, please see http://www.uncitral.org/uncitral/en/commission/working_groups/6Security_Interests.html. Accessed 16 May 2017.

[4]See the 13th session on 19–23 May 2008 in New York, http://www.uncitral.org/uncitral/en/commission/working_groups/6Security_Interests.html and See also UNCITRAL (2008c), https://documents-dds-ny.un.org/doc/UNDOC/GEN/V08/539/36/PDF/V0853936.pdf?OpenElement . Accessed 16 May 2017.

[5]See, e.g., UNCITRAL (2007), https://documents-dds-ny.un.org/doc/UNDOC/GEN/V07/810/60/PDF/V0781060.pdf? OpenElement. Accessed 16 May 2017. Conflict-of-laws issue constitutes the Chapter XIII of the twelfth session Working Group VI Report. See UNCITRAL (2007), https://documents-dds-ny.un.org/doc/UNDOC/GEN/V07/810/60/PDF/V0781060.pdf?OpenElement.

[6]Even though only briefly, conflict-of-laws has been mentioned since the first traceable record of UNCITRAL meetings, "the conflict-of-laws rules applicable outside insolvency should also be applicable in an insolvency proceeding." See UNCITRAL (2002), https://documents-dds-ny.un.org/doc/UNDOC/GEN/V02/549/74/PDF/V0254974.pdf?OpenElement, p. 22. Accessed 16 May 2017.

to IP,[7] it logically has appeared as one of the main debating issues on the discussion table. The conflict-of-laws issue is therefore listed as one of the main focuses of discussion ever since the early IP-related meeting at UNCITRAL.[8]

Five conflict-of-laws suggestions are considered at the first UNCITRAL security rights in intellectual property meeting. In the final report, proposals contain general rules for SR-in-IP but sometimes with certain exceptions for more specific issues like perfection (third-party effectiveness). The five proposals are as following:

Lex protectionis[9]: i.e. the applicable law would be the law of the state in which protection of the (intellectual property) was sought.

Grantor's location[10]: One is the absolute grantor's location approach (without any exceptions), and the other is the grantor's location approach with an exception for the priority issue. For the latter, it is suggested that the rule could be formulated as "apply the law of the grantor's location generally, with the exception of priority conflicts in which a competing claimant had obtained a security right under the *lex protectionis*."[11]

Lex protectionis for register-able IP, and grantor's location for non-register-able IP: the original text is "to limit the application of the *lex protectionis* to security rights that could be created by registration in an intellectual property rights registry."[12]

The last proposal divides rules into two categories, with the criteria being the number of encumbered assets. For security right in the case of a single intellectual property, *lex protectionis* applies; for security interest attached to multiple encumbrances (e.g. the case when more than one IP is pledged as collateral, or when IP is

[7]To be more precise, at the beginning stage, UNCITRAL's discussion only makes distinction between "tangible" and "intangible" assets (but not "IP" and "non-IP" assets). As a matter of fact, IP was not even originally intended to be part of the legislative guide discussion, "it was also agreed that securities and intellectual property should not be dealt with." See UNCITRAL (2002), https://documents-dds-ny.un.org/doc/UNDOC/GEN/V02/549/74/PDF/V0254974.pdf?OpenElement, p. 3.

[8]See, generally, UNCITRAL (2008c), https://documents-dds-ny.un.org/doc/UNDOC/GEN/V08/539/36/PDF/V0853936.pdf?OpenElement. Accessed 16 May 2017. See also UNCITRAL (2008d), https://documents-dds-ny.un.org/doc/UNDOC/LTD/V08/521/28/PDF/V0852128.pdf?OpenElement. Accessed 16 May 2017.

[9]See UNCITRAL (2008d), https://documents-dds-ny.un.org/doc/UNDOC/LTD/V08/521/28/PDF/V0852128.pdf?OpenElement, para. 77. Accessed 16 May 2017.

[10]See UNCITRAL (2008d), https://documents-dds-ny.un.org/doc/UNDOC/LTD/V08/521/28/PDF/V0852128.pdf?OpenElement, para. 77. Accessed 16 May 2017.

[11]See UNCITRAL (2008d), https://documents-dds-ny.un.org/doc/UNDOC/LTD/V08/521/28/PDF/V0852128.pdf?OpenElement, para. 77. Accessed 16 May 2017.

[12]See UNCITRAL (2008d), https://documents-dds-ny.un.org/doc/UNDOC/LTD/V08/521/28/PDF/V0852128.pdf?OpenElement, para. 77. Accessed 16 May 2017. See also UNCITRAL (2008d), https://documents-dds-ny.un.org/doc/UNDOC/LTD/V08/521/28/PDF/V0852128.pdf?OpenElement, para. 56. Accessed 16 May 2017.

pledged along with other tangible encumbrances) located in several different countries and owned by a single grantor, the law of the grantor's location applies.[13]

1.2.2 14th Session (20–24 October 2008, Vienna)

Three proposals were brought up at the 14th session of UNCITRAL Working Group VI meeting. They are summarized as the three following alternatives[14]:

Alternative A:
"The law should provide that the law applicable to the creation, effectiveness against third parties, priority and enforcement of a security in intellectual property is the law of the State in which the intellectual property is protected."[15]
Alternative B:
"The law should provide that the law applicable to the creation, third-party effectiveness, priority and enforcement of a security right in intellectual property is the law of the State in which the grantor is located."[16,17]
Alternative C:
"The law applicable to the creation, effectiveness against third parties, priority and enforcement of a security right in intellectual property subject to registration in an intellectual property registry is the law of the State under whose authority the registry is maintained."[18]

---

[13]See UNCITRAL (2008d), https://documents-dds-ny.un.org/doc/UNDOC/LTD/V08/521/28/PDF/V0852128.pdf?OpenElement, para. 78. Accessed 16 May 2017.

[14]Since the written conflict-of-laws rules can sometimes be very lengthy and complicated, and it does not seem necessary to replace the original language of UNCITRAL with descriptions, this paper chose to quote the crucial UNCITRAL texts instead of re-phasing them in the following analysis.

[15]See UNCITRAL (2008a) https://documents-dds-ny.un.org/doc/UNDOC/LTD/V08/562/95/PDF/V0856295.pdf?OpenElement, para. 97. Accessed 16 May 2017.

[16]See UNCITRAL (2008a) https://documents-dds-ny.un.org/doc/UNDOC/LTD/V08/562/95/PDF/V0856295.pdf?OpenElement, p. 33. Accessed 16 May 2017.

[17]There do exist exceptions (and conditions attached to certain exceptions) for Alternative B. However, that situation is applicable only to the priority issue and is quoted as follows:

"However, the law applicable to a priority conflict involving the right of a [competing claimant] [transferee or licensee] is the law of the State in which the intellectual property is protected [if under that law the intellectual property may be registered in an intellectual property registry] [if under that law a security right may be registered in an intellectual property registry.]" See UNCITRAL (2008a), see UNCITRAL (2008a) https://documents-dds-ny.un.org/doc/UNDOC/LTD/V08/562/95/PDF/V0856295.pdf?OpenElement, p. 33. Accessed 16 May 2017.

However, due to the concerns for uncertainty and searching cost, the bracketed text in the above text was recommended to be deleted. See UNCITRAL (2008b), https://documents-dds-ny.un.org/doc/UNDOC/GEN/V08/577/88/PDF/V0857788.pdf?OpenElementat, para. 126. Accessed 16 May 2017.

[18]See UNCITRAL (2008a), https://documents-dds-ny.un.org/doc/UNDOC/LTD/V08/562/95/PDF/V0856295.pdf?OpenElement, para. 97. Accessed 16 May 2017.

According to the above-proposed rules, when examining perfection and/or third-party effectiveness, there should be three different sets of applicable laws, applying three different proposed approaches. They are:

Under Alternative A: the law of the State in which the intellectual property is protected (*lex protectionis*);
Under Alternative B: the law of the State in which the grantor is located;
Under Alternative C: if the encumbered intellectual property is register-able in an intellectual property registry, the applicable law shall be the law of the State where the registry authority is located; if the collateralized intellectual property is not subject to any intellectual property registry's recording requirement, the law of the State in which the grantor is located[19] seems to prevail.[20]

1.2.3 15th Session (27 April–01 May 2009, New York)

With remarkable modifications, three variant conflict-of-laws rules are proposed with preliminary analysis at UNCITRAL 15th session meeting with a plea for consideration at Working Group VI. To truly reflect their constituents, Alternatives are literally cited below without annotation or explanatory comment.

Alternative A:
"The law should provide that the law applicable to the creation, effectiveness against third parties, priority and enforcement of a security in intellectual property is the law of the State [or region] in which the intellectual property is protected."[21]
Alternative B:

---

[19]To be more precise, in the official text of UNCITRAL, the law applicable for SR-in-IP that is not subject to registration in an intellectual property registry is not clearly provided, but deferred to the contract law principle.

Grantor's location, however, seems to be a convincing candidate for cases involving connector factors of this kind, "[…] or, under contract law principles, defers to the law of the State in which the secured creditor, the grantor or a third party is located, in particular where a security right in a specific type of intellectual property may not be registered in an intellectual property registry (e.g. copyright or trade secret)." See UNCITRAL (2008a), https://documents-dds-ny.un.org/doc/UNDOC/LTD/V08/562/95/PDF/V0856295.pdf?OpenElement, para. 97. Accessed 16 May 2017.

[20]It has to be noted that in the final report of 14th session, Alternative C was not supported and was suggested to be deleted. The stated reason is because of uncertainty and searching cost, "by referring to the law of the State under whose authority the registry was maintained, alternative C would introduce uncertainty as to the law applicable or, at least, increase the time and cost of a transaction, since a secured creditor would need to undertake a search to identify the relevant registry in which the intellectual property to be encumbered was registered." See UNCITRAL (2008b), https://documents-dds-ny.un.org/doc/UNDOC/GEN/V08/577/88/PDF/V0857788.pdf?OpenElement, para. 124. Accessed 16 May 2017.

[21]See UNCITRAL (2009a), https://documents-dds-ny.un.org/doc/UNDOC/LTD/V09/808/23/PDF/V0980823.pdf?OpenElement, para. 20. Accessed 16 May 2017.

"The law should provide that the law applicable to the creation and enforcement of a security right in intellectual property is the law of the State in which the grantor is located. However, the law applicable to the third-party effectiveness and priority of a security right in intellectual property is the law of the State [or region] in which the intellectual property is protected."[22]
Alternative C:
"The law should provide that the law applicable to the creation, third-party effectiveness, priority and enforcement of a security right in intellectual property is the law of the State in which the grantor is located. However, the law applicable to a priority conflict involving the right of a transferee or licensee is the law of the State [or region] in which the intellectual property is protected.]"[23]

According to the three proposed conflict-of-laws rules described above, the law applicable for perfection or third-party effectiveness shall be:

Under Alternative A: the law of the State [or region] in which the intellectual property is protected (i.e. *lex protectionis*);
Under Alternative B: the law of the State [or region] in which the intellectual property is protected, i.e. also *lex protectionis* (on the other hand, the law of the State in which the grantor is located applies to the creation and enforcement of a security right in intellectual property exclusively);
Under Alternative C: the law of the State in which the grantor is located (the conditional *proviso* of this Alternative only plays a role when a priority conflict arises between the secured creditor and the right of a transferee or licensee. In that case, *lex protectionis* principle applies).

1.2.4 16th Session (2–6 November 2009, Vienna)

Even when judged merely by the volume of output alone, the 16th session of UNCITRAL Working Group VI presented considerably advanced work. For instance, there are three main reference documents[24] and in terms of quantity, all three of them are also more information-abundant than the previously accumulated ones.

[22]See UNCITRAL (2009a), https://documents-dds-ny.un.org/doc/UNDOC/LTD/V09/808/23/PDF/V0980823.pdf?OpenElement, para. 20. Accessed 16 May 2017.

[23]See UNCITRAL (2009a), https://documents-dds-ny.un.org/doc/UNDOC/LTD/V09/808/23/PDF/V0980823.pdf?OpenElement, para. 20. Accessed 16 May 2017.

[24]In each of these five meeting sessions at UNCITRAL, the basic recorded documents are: one General Report and one Draft Supplement (also known as "Note by the Secretariat"). In the sixteenth session, however, there is one more proposal prepared by the Permanent Bureau of the Hague Conference on Private International Law. All of these documents are of crucial importance for further analysis.

What also deserves attention is that UNCITRAL widely cooperated with other international organizations such as the World Intellectual Property Organization (WIPO) during this discussion, and organized expert group meetings and colloquiums[25] according to WIPO's suggestions.[26] In addition, the Hague Conference on Private International Law (HCCH) was also consulted regarding this very specific issue, and subsequently delivered an important opinion letter, which will also be discussed later in this paper.[27]

The intensive cooperation between UNCITRAL and other divergently specialized organizations also leads to abundant fruits. Following the same approach as before, the alternatives proposed at the sixteenth meeting are summarized as below.

Alternative A:
"The law should provide that the law applicable to the creation, effectiveness against third parties, priority and enforcement of a security in intellectual property is the law of the State in which the intellectual property is protected. [However, subject to recommendation 223, the law applicable to a priority conflict between a secured creditor and the grantor's insolvency representative is the law of the State in which the grantor is located.]"[28]
Alternative B:
"The law should provide that the law applicable to the creation of a security right in intellectual property is the law [of the State in which the grantor is located][chosen by the parties]. However, the law applicable to the effectiveness against third parties, priority and enforcement of a security in intellectual property is the law of the State in which the intellectual property is protected."[29]
Alternative C:
"The law should provide that the law applicable to the creation and enforcement of a security right in intellectual property is the law of the State in which the grantor is located. However, the law applicable to the third-party effectiveness and priority of a security right in intellectual property is the law of the State in which the intellectual property is protected."[30]
Alternative D:

---

[25]See also UNCITRAL Third International Colloquium on Secured Transactions (March 1–3, 2010; Vienna), papers on-line available at http://www.uncitral.org/uncitral/en/commission/working_groups/6Security_Interests.html. Accessed 16 May 2017.

[26]See UNCITRAL (2009e), https://documents-dds-ny.un.org/doc/UNDOC/GEN/V09/877/38/PDF/V0987738.pdf?OpenElement, para. 3. Accessed 16 May 2017.

[27]See UNCITRAL (2009b), https://documents-dds-ny.un.org/doc/UNDOC/LTD/V09/855/76/PDF/V0985576.pdf?OpenElement. Accessed 16 May 2017.

[28]See UNCITRAL (2009c), https://documents-dds-ny.un.org/doc/UNDOC/LTD/V09/855/16/PDF/V0985516.pdf?OpenElement, para. 21. Accessed 16 May 2017.

[29]See UNCITRAL (2009c), https://documents-dds-ny.un.org/doc/UNDOC/LTD/V09/855/16/PDF/V0985516.pdf?OpenElement, pp. 7–8. Accessed 16 May 2017.

[30]See UNCITRAL (2009c), https://documents-dds-ny.un.org/doc/UNDOC/LTD/V09/855/16/PDF/V0985516.pdf?OpenElement, p. 8. Accessed 16 May 2017.

"The law should provide that the law applicable to the creation, third-party effectiveness, priority and enforcement of a security right in intellectual property is the law of the State in which the grantor is located. However, the law applicable to the third-party effectiveness and priority of a security right in intellectual property as against the right of a transferee or licensee of the encumbered intellectual property is the law of the State in which the intellectual property is protected."[31]

If we follow the logic of UNCITRAL Working Group VI sixteenth session's conclusion, the applicable law for perfection or third-party effectiveness under the four proposed conflict-of-laws rules described as above can be determined as:

Under Alternative A: the law of the State in which the intellectual property is protected (i.e. *lex protectionis*; however, the law of the State in which the grantor is located applies when a priority conflict between a secured creditor and the grantor's insolvency representative arise);
Under Alternative B: the law of the State in which the intellectual property is protected, i.e. also *lex protectionis* (the law of the State in which the grantor is located applies exclusively to the creation of a security right in intellectual property; for priority and enforcement, *lex protectionis* principle applies);
Under Alternative C: the law of the State in which the intellectual property is protected, i.e. *lex protectionis* as well (for creation and enforcement, the law of the State in which the grantor is located applies).
Under Alternative D: in principle, the law of the State in which the grantor is located applies. In exceptional cases, namely when a priority conflict arises as against the right of a transferee or licensee of the encumbered intellectual property, *lex protectionis* applies.

The Hague Conference on Private International Law also submitted its own alternative proposal, and as acknowledged in its own language,[32] the approach taken was structurally similar to the previously-mentioned Alternative D brought by UNCITRAL. The only difference is that it added a limitation on the law applicable to the transferability of an intellectual property due to the treatment of this as a preliminary issue.[33]

---

[31]See UNCITRAL (2009c), https://documents-dds-ny.un.org/doc/UNDOC/LTD/V09/855/16/PDF/V0985516.pdf?OpenElement, p. 8. Accessed 16 May 2017.

[32]See UNCITRAL (2009b) https://documents-dds-ny.un.org/doc/UNDOC/LTD/V09/855/76/PDF/V0985576.pdf?OpenElement, para. 14. Accessed 16 May 2017.

[33]Hague Conference addressed their concern on this issue and provided reasoning as below:

"The application of the law of the State in which the grantor is located is nevertheless subject to two important limitations. First, as stated above, the transferability of the intellectual property right is a preliminary issue to be addressed before the creation of a security in intellectual property. Accordingly, it is important to reiterate the importance of the law governing the intellectual property as the legal framework for the creation of a security right in intellectual property [omitted]." See UNCITRAL (2009b), https://documents-dds-ny.un.org/doc/UNDOC/LTD/V09/855/76/PDF/V0985576.pdf?OpenElement, paras. 13–14. Accessed 16 May 2017.

1.2.5 17th Session (8–12 February 2010, New York)

Serving as the last session meeting focusing on intellectual property encumbrances before the IP Supplement was finalized, there was vibrant discussion at UNCITRAL Working Group VI, which also produced appreciable literature for researchers on this subject. Not only did they conclude three main alternatives in their final Recommendation 253,[34] but in the accompanying report,[35] a fourth, fifth and sixth legislative option were also raised and considered by the Group. What is worthy of note is that in this session, proposals were widely debated with numerous hypothetical examples. The six proposals are listed and analyzed as follows:

Alternative A:
"The law should provide that the law applicable to the creation, effectiveness against third parties, priority and enforcement of a security right in intellectual property is the law of the State in which the intellectual property is protected."[36]
Alternative B:
"The law should provide that the law applicable to the creation, effectiveness against third parties, priority and enforcement of a security right in intellectual property that may be registered in an intellectual property registry is the law of the State under whose authority the registry is maintained."[37] Accordingly, the law applicable to those matters with respect to a security right in intellectual property that may not be registered in an intellectual property registry is the law of the State in which the grantor is located.[38]
Alternative C:
"The law should provide that the law applicable to the creation, effectiveness against third parties, priority and enforcement of a security right in intellectual property is the law of the State in which the grantor is located. However, the law applicable to the effectiveness against third parties and priority of a security right in intellectual property as against the right of a transferee or licensee of the encumbered intellectual property is the law of the State in which the intellectual property is protected."[39]

---

[34]See UNCITRAL (2010a), https://documents-dds-ny.un.org/doc/UNDOC/GEN/V10/511/34/PDF/V1051134.pdf?OpenElement, paras. 43, 47 and 49. Accessed 16 May 2017.

[35]See generally, UNCITRAL (2010a), https://documents-dds-ny.un.org/doc/UNDOC/GEN/V10/511/34/PDF/V1051134.pdf?OpenElement. Accessed 16 May 2017.

[36]See UNCITRAL (2009d), https://documents-dds-ny.un.org/doc/UNDOC/LTD/V09/885/80/PDF/V0988580.pdf?OpenElement, paras. 39–40 and below. Accessed 16 May 2017.

[37]See UNCITRAL (2009d), https://documents-dds-ny.un.org/doc/UNDOC/LTD/V09/885/80/PDF/V0988580.pdf?OpenElement, paras. 39–40 and below. Accessed 16 May 2017.

[38]See UNCITRAL (2009d), https://documents-dds-ny.un.org/doc/UNDOC/LTD/V09/885/80/PDF/V0988580.pdf?OpenElement, paras. 39–40 and below. Accessed 16 May 2017.

[39]See UNCITRAL (2009d), https://documents-dds-ny.un.org/doc/UNDOC/LTD/V09/885/80/PDF/V0988580.pdf?OpenElement, paras. 39–40 and below. Accessed 16 May 2017.

Fourth Option:

"Within the limits of the law relating to the transferability of intellectual property, the law should provide that:

(a) Where the intellectual property is registered in a specialized registry, the law applicable to the creation, effectiveness against third parties and priority of a security right in intellectual property is the law of the State under whose authority the registry is maintained. However, the law applicable to the enforcement of such a security right is the law of the State in which the grantor is located; and
(b) Where the intellectual property is not registered in a specialized registry or where no specialized registry exists, the law applicable to issues of creation, effectiveness against third parties and enforcement of a security right in intellectual property is the law of the State in which the grantor is located, whenever possible. However, the law of the State in which the intellectual property is protected is the law applicable to priority as against competing claimants and, in particular, the priority of a security right in intellectual property as against the right of a transferee or a licensee of the encumbered intellectual property."[40]

Fifth Option:
"The creation and enforcement of a security right in intellectual property could be referred to the law of the State in which the intellectual property was protected, unless the parties chose the law of the grantor's location; and the third-party effectiveness and priority of such a security right would be referred to the law of the State in which the intellectual property was protected."[41]

Sixth Option:
"The law should provide that the law applicable to the creation of a security right in intellectual property is the law of the State in which the grantor is located unless the parties to the security agreement select the law of the State in which the intellectual property is protected as the law applicable to such issue.
The law should provide that the law applicable to the effectiveness and priority of a security in intellectual property as against the rights of a transferee, licensee or another secured creditor is the law of the State in which the intellectual property is protected.
The law should provide that the law applicable to the effectiveness and priority of a security in intellectual property as against all other competing claimants is the law of the State in which the grantor is located.
The law should provide that the law applicable to the enforcement of a security right in intellectual property is the law of the State in which the grantor is located

[40]See UNCITRAL (2010a), https://documents-dds-ny.un.org/doc/UNDOC/GEN/V10/511/34/PDF/V1051134.pdf?OpenElement, para. 43. Accessed 16 May 2017.

[41]See UNCITRAL (2010a), https://documents-dds-ny.un.org/doc/UNDOC/GEN/V10/511/34/PDF/V1051134.pdf?OpenElement, para. 47. Accessed 16 May 2017.

unless the parties to the security agreement select the law of the State in which the intellectual property is protected as the law applicable to such issue."[42]

Returning to these proposals and their applicable results, we may find that by following the indicated rules of each proposal, the laws applicable for perfection or third-party effectiveness under the six proposed conflict-of-laws rules are:

Under Alternative A: the law of the State in which the intellectual property is protected, i.e. *lex protectionis*;
Under Alternative B: for IP that is register-able at IP registry, the law of the State under whose authority the registry is maintained applies; for IP that is not register-able at IP registry, Grantor's Location applies.
Under Alternative C: in principle, the law of the State in which the grantor is located applies. In exceptional cases, i.e. when a priority conflict arises as against the right of a transferee or licensee of the encumbered intellectual property, *lex protectionis* applies.

Under 4th Option:
For IP registered in a specialized registry, the law of the State where the registry authority is located applies to a security interest in it[43]; for IP not registered in a specialized registry or where no specialized registry exists, Grantor's Location applies to its SR-in-IP.[44]

Please note that this approach may look similar to many previous ones. But it is in fact different from the other proposal versions. In the previous ones, the benchmark is whether the "SR-in-IP" is register-able, not the register-ability of the "IP" itself.

Under 5th Option: the law of the State in which the intellectual property is protected, i.e. also *lex protectionis* (the law of the State in which the grantor is located applies to the creation and enforcement of a SR-in-IP only when the parties chose them; for priority issue, still it is the *lex protectionis* principle that applies);
Under 6th Option: in principle, the law of the State in which the grantor is located applies. However, the exception is if a third-party effectiveness or priority issue arises as against the rights of a transferee, licensee or another secured creditor of the encumbered intellectual property, then the law of the State in which the intellectual property is protected, i.e. *lex protectionis* also applies in this case.

Please note that in most of the previously reviewed proposals, the exceptions to Principles were also presented in similar wording but in fact, it has never included

[42]See UNCITRAL (2010a), https://documents-dds-ny.un.org/doc/UNDOC/GEN/V10/511/34/PDF/V1051134.pdf?OpenElement, para. 49. Accessed 16 May 2017.

[43]UNCITRAL (2010a), https://documents-dds-ny.un.org/doc/UNDOC/GEN/V10/511/34/PDF/V1051134.pdf?OpenElement, para. 43. Accessed 17 May 2017.

[44]However, if the issue is priority, then one exception exists: *lex protectionis* applies to priority as against competing claimants and; in particular, it applies to the priority of a security right in intellectual property as against the right of a transferee or a licensee of the encumbered intellectual property.

the case of a right against "another secured creditor" (only against a transferee or licensee were mentioned before). When applying these easily-ignored differences in daily transactions, however, these trivial details could play a dominate role in the court' determination of the allocation of rights. Therefore, every proposal is carefully dealt with in the following discussion parts.

1.3 Proposals and Debates from an Academic Perspective: CLIP

Unlike UNCITRAL's semi-official role which comprises representatives from Member States, CLIP ("European Max Planck Group on Conflict of Laws in Intellectual Property") is a group of scholars in the fields of private international law and intellectual property law.[45] Based on its academic character, legal issues related to cross-border dealings of intellectual property are examined and reflected with deliberate reform proposals along with detailed commentary. In CLIP's final work,[46] the issue of security rights in intellectual property is also included. There are three main articles that relate to security interest in IPRs in "Principles on Conflict of Laws in Intellectual Property" (hereafter "CLIP Principles").[47]

Article 3:801 is set to address the issue of "obligation to create or transfer a security right in intellectual property." Paragraph (1) further indicates that it concerns only "the mutual rights and obligations of the parties arising from a contract to create or transfer a security right in intellectual property."[48] The applicable law for mutual obligations is thus preliminarily determined by the law chosen by the parties; this, however, is of course different from the issue of third party effectiveness.

Article 3:802 of CLIP Principles further provides a framework for the proprietary aspect of security interest in IPRs, and puts a special focus on perfection. In Paragraph (1)(b) it is provided that for any registration requirements in general security rights registers, the law applicable to security rights in intellectual property

---

[45]About CLIP, see http://www.cl-ip.eu/_www/en/pub/home.html. Accessed 17 May 2017.

[46]European Max Planck Group on Conflict of Laws in Intellectual Property (2013) (hereafter "CLIP Principles and Commentary").

[47]Latest full text of CLIP Principles can be found on-line.

See CLIP (2011), http://www.cl-ip.eu/_www/files/pdf2/Final_Text_1_December_2011.pdf. Accessed 17 May 2017. However, commentary of the Principles is accessible only through the above-mentioned book. See CLIP (2013).

[48]Paragraph (2) of Article 3:801 further provides that "in the absence of a choice of law the mutual rights and obligations of the parties shall be governed by the law of the State where the grantor of the security has her/his habitual residence at the time of conclusion of the contract. Where it is clear from all the circumstances of the case that the contract is manifestly more closely connected with another State, the law of that other State shall apply." See CLIP (2013), p. 352.

shall be "the law of the State where the grantor has her/his habitual residence at the time of the creation of the security right."[49]

However, if it is "any registration requirements in intellectual property registers the State of protection"[50] and "the effect of registration or non-registration in such register",[51] the law of the State for which protection is sought shall apply. CLIP also defers registration from third-party effectiveness.

Article 3:802 (2)(e) provides that the priority and the third-party effects of security rights in intellectual property is also determined by the law of the State for which protection is sought.[52]

1.4 Comparison Between Various Proposals of UNCITRAL and CLIP

After sorting out the proposals raised by UNCITRAL Working Group VI during its major five meetings, readers may find that both the quantity of the proposals and their detailed provisions constitute appreciable hurdles for researchers exploring this subject. However, this was not the final work.

In addition to the proposed twenty-two legislative choices, the conclusion UNCITRAL reached in its final IP Supplement further raised another possibility, which reads as follows:

Recommendation 248[53]
"Law applicable to a security right in intellectual property
The law should provide that:

(a) The law applicable to the creation, effectiveness against third parties and priority of a security right in intellectual property is the law of the State in which the intellectual property is protected;
(b) A security right in intellectual property may also be created under the law of the State in which the grantor is located and may also be made effective under that law against third parties other than another secured creditor, a transferee or a licensee; and
(c) The law applicable to the enforcement of a security right in intellectual property is the law of the State in which the grantor is located."

[49]See CLIP Principles and Commentary, p. 354.

[50]Paragraph (2) (d) of Article 3:802. See also CLIP (2013), p. 354.

[51]CLIP (2013), p. 354.

[52]Paragraph (2) (e) of Article 3:802. See also CLIP (2013), p. 354.

[53]See UNCITRAL (2011b), http://www.uncitral.org/pdf/english/texts/security-lg/e/10-57126_Ebook_Suppl_SR_IP.pdf, p. 147.

Table 1 UNCITRAL session Proposals & IP Supplement (2008–2010)

1st Meeting i.e. 13th session (19–23 May 2008, New York)	Proposal [1]	*Lex protectionis*
	Proposal [2]	Grantor's Location
	Proposal [3]	Grantor's Location
	Proposal [4]	Register-able SR-in-IP: *Lex protectionis* Non-Register-able SR-in-IP: Grantor's Location
	Proposal [5]	Single IP encumbrance: *Lex protectionis* Multiple encumbrances: Grantor's Location
2nd Meeting i.e. 14th session (20–24 October 2008, Vienna)	Proposal [1]	*Lex protectionis*
	Proposal [2]	Grantor's Location
	Proposal [3]	[SR-in-IP] Subject to registration at IP registry: the law of the State where the registry authority is located [SR-in-IP] Not subject to registration at IP registry: (possibly) Grantor's Location
3rd Meeting i.e. 15th session (27 April–01 May 2009, New York)	Proposal [1]	*Lex protectionis*
	Proposal [2]	*Lex protectionis*
	Proposal [3]	Grantor's Location
4th Meeting i.e. 16th session (2–6 November 2009, Vienna)	Alternative A	*Lex protectionis*
	Alternative B	*Lex protectionis*
	Alternative C	*Lex protectionis*
	Alternative D	Principle: Grantor's Location Exception: *Lex protectionis* (as against the right of a transferee or licensee of the encumbered intellectual property)
	Hague Conference	Preconditioning limitation: transferability Principle: Grantor's Location Exception: *Lex protectionis* (as against the right of a transferee or licensee of the encumbered intellectual property)
5th Meeting i.e. 17th session (8–12 February 2010, New York)	Alternative A	*Lex protectionis*
	Alternative B	[SR-in-IP] Register-able at IP registry: the law of the State under whose authority the registry is maintained [SR-in-IP] Not register-able at IP registry: Grantor's Location
	Alternative C	Principle: Grantor's Location Exception: *Lex protectionis* (as against the right of a transferee or licensee of the encumbered intellectual property)
	4th Proposal	[SR-in-IP] IP registered in a specialized registry: the law of the State where the registry authority is located [SR-in-IP] IP not registered in a specialized registry or where no specialized registry exist: Grantor's Location

(continued)

Table 1 (continued)

	5th Proposal	*Lex protectionis*
	6th Proposal	Principle: Grantor's Location Exception: *Lex protectionis* (as against the rights of a transferee, licensee or another secured creditor of the encumbered intellectual property)
Final Decision	Recommendation 248	Both (*Lex protectionis* & Grantor's Location) Exception: to be effective against the rights of a transferee, licensee or another secured creditor of the encumbered intellectual property, *lex protectionis* is the only law applicable
CLIP Principles (2011)		
Final Text (December 1, 2011)	Article 3:802	(1) registration – any registration requirements in general security rights registers: Grantor's Location (defined as the law of the State where the grantor has her/his habitual residence at the time of the creation of the security right) – any registration requirements in intellectual property registers of the State of protection and the effect of registration or non-registration in such register: *Lex protectionis* (2) Third-party effectiveness: *Lex protectionis*

Source Materials from UNCITRAL and CLIP with comparison made by this research

Therefore, according the final Recommendation 248, to perfect (gain effectiveness against third parties) security interest in intellectual property, the law applicable is, in principal, the law of the state in which the intellectual property is protected. However, if the SR-in-IP is made effective according to the law of the state in which the grantor is located as against any third parties except for (1) another secured creditor, (2) a transferee or (3) a licensee, this right is also lawfully perfected.[54]

To help readers efficiently compare the results of applying those twenty-two-plus-one[55] proposals, a table was made as below. Please note, that to simplify, it aims to focus for the issue of perfection/public notice/third-party effectiveness only (Table 1).[56]

---

[54]The law applicable to priority issue, however, is limited to the law of the state in which the intellectual property is protected (i.e. *lex protectionis*).

[55]This includes the twenty-two proposals and the final Recommendation 248.

[56]Some details of the proposals may require further attention and will be discussed from a more analytical perspective in the coming session. There are underline emphases in this table and these are functioning as careful reminders.

2 Grantor's Location, *Lex Loci Protectionis*, and the Mixed Approaches

In the following session, the focus will be placed on the debates surrounding the major proposals (i.e. the grantor's location vs. *lex protectionis*) of UNCITRAL and, if any, their hybrid forms. Despite certain exceptions, the advantages and disadvantages of various hybrid approaches are reflective of their stemming from the two major proposals (Grantor's Location and *lex protectionis*).

In the following paragraphs, the core rationales as well as the pros and cons of three main different approaches, namely the law of the grantor's location, *lex protectionis*, and the hybrid approaches will be introduced.

2.1 Debating History and Rationales Raised at UNCITRAL

2.1.1 Rationales Raised for and Against the *Lex Loci Protectionis* Approach

According to the *lex loci protectionis* approach, the applicable law will be the law of the protecting state. The pros of the *lex protectionis* approach are:

a. Conformity with the existing (international) norms and practice

The most common argument in favor of the *lex protectionis* approach is that it is derived from international (IP) norms and practice. Supporters of this approach have generally taken the view[57] that "the principle of national treatment embodied in international conventions protecting intellectual property implicitly imposed a universal rule" referring all matters arising with respect to property rights in intellectual property to the law of the State in which the intellectual property was protected (i.e. *lex loci protectionis*).[58]

As a matter of fact, from the perspective of legality, it may not be difficult to find a supporting legal basis for this standing. For example, many arguments refer to article 2(1) of the Paris Industrial Property Convention and Article 5(2) of the Berne Intellectual Property Convention, in this regard.[59]

However, it is the view of this paper, and also one that has been expressed in the commentary of UNCITRAL IP Supplement, that there exists no clear evidence so far proving international conventions which were designed to protect "intellectual

[57]See UNCITRAL (2011b), http://www.uncitral.org/pdf/english/texts/security-lg/e/10-57126_Ebook_Suppl_SR_IP.pdf, para. 298. Accessed 17 May 2017.

[58]See also UNCITRAL (2009e), https://documents-dds-ny.un.org/doc/UNDOC/GEN/V09/877/38/PDF/V0987738.pdf?OpenElement, para. 90.

[59]See UNCITRAL (2011b), http://www.uncitral.org/pdf/english/texts/security-lg/e/10-57126_Ebook_Suppl_SR_IP.pdf, para. 298. Accessed 17 May 2017.

property" expressly addressed the law applicable to issue of "security interest in intellectual property rights".[60] Nevertheless, even when challenged by the literal interpretation of *lex loci protectionis*, supporters of this approach still claim that the principle of territoriality is generally adopted and is the main guidance in this area.[61]

b. Applying the same law to both security rights and ownership rights in intellectual property

It is stressed that the "principal advantage of an approach based on the *lex protectionis* is that, in recognition of the principle of territoriality adopted in international conventions for the protection of intellectual property, its application would result in the same law applying to both security rights and ownership rights in intellectual property."[62]

This advantage could, in return, spare the problem mentioned under the grantor's location approach, i.e. when a priority issue arises against other rights holders such as licensees or transferees. In that case, the *lex protectionis* principle provides the same basis (namely, the same applicable substantive law) to examine both rights of each or all of the competing claimants.

On the other hand, the cons of the *lex protectionis* approach are:

a. Unclear basis and boundaries of *lex protectionis*

Some commentaries have subscribed to the view that the international (IP) norms and practical interpretation of intellectual property conventions have been highly controversial or are still unsettled with regard to whether they reach security interest in IP (not IP itself). It was stated that those conventions simply provided that the

[60]See UNCITRAL (2011b), http://www.uncitral.org/pdf/english/texts/security-lg/e/10-57126_Ebook_Suppl_SR_IP.pdf, para. 297. Accessed 17 May 2017.

[61]"[...] the appropriate connecting factor is the place of protection of the relevant intellectual property right. In other words, according to this view, States parties to any of these international conventions are required to apply the *lex protectionis* to issues arising with respect to security rights in intellectual property." See UNCITRAL (2011b), http://www.uncitral.org/pdf/english/texts/security-lg/e/10-57126_Ebook_Suppl_SR_IP.pdf, para. 298. Accessed 17 May 2017. The only exclusion to *lex loci protectionis* is "purely contractual matters between the grantor and secured creditor," as it is left to *lex contractus*. See UNCITRAL (2011b), http://www.uncitral.org/pdf/english/texts/security-lg/e/10-57126_Ebook_Suppl_SR_IP.pdf, para. 299. Accessed 17 May 2017.

[62]See UNCITRAL (2011b), http://www.uncitral.org/pdf/english/texts/security-lg/e/10-57126_Ebook_Suppl_SR_IP.pdf, para. 299. Accessed 17 May 2017.

extent of protection and the rights of redress of intellectual property owners were subject to the law of the State in which the intellectual property was protected, making no reference to the law applicable to security rights.[63]

On the other hand, "there is very little precedent on the application of the *lex protectionis*"[64] to issues arising with respect to security rights in intellectual property. It was also observed that, even if those conventions provided an applicable law rule for security rights, they did not "cover all property effects contemplated by the Supplement, that is, the creation, effectiveness against third parties", as well as priority and enforcement considerations of a security right in intellectual property.[65]

It is also on the same basis that some commentators have preferred an approach based on the law of the grantor's location but with the exception of "the third-party effectiveness and priority of a security right as against the rights of an outright transferee or licensee"[66] on the encumbered intellectual property, which, in their view, shall be referred to the *lex loci protectionis*.[67]

b. Lack of efficiency

It is argued that "if the *lex loci protectionis* approach is taken, in many transactions, registration in registries located in numerous States would have to take place."[68] It is thus very likely that the cost and complexity of an intellectual property financing transaction would be increased due to multiple registration requirements. Both administrative (registration) cost for IP encumbrance owners and search cost for potential secured creditors may be increased.[69]

To further illustrate the problem, the above-mentioned scenarios will most likely happen in the following situations:

---

[63]See UNCITRAL (2011b), http://www.uncitral.org/pdf/english/texts/security-lg/e/10-57126_Ebook_Suppl_SR_IP.pdf, para. 297. Accessed 17 May 2017.

[64]UNCITRAL (2011b), http://www.uncitral.org/pdf/english/texts/security-lg/e/10-57126_Ebook_Suppl_SR_IP.pdf, at para. 30. Accessed 17 May 2017.

[65]UNCITRAL (2011b), http://www.uncitral.org/pdf/english/texts/security-lg/e/10-57126_Ebook_Suppl_SR_IP.pdf, at para. 30. Accessed 17 May 2017.

[66]UNCITRAL (2011b), http://www.uncitral.org/pdf/english/texts/security-lg/e/10-57126_Ebook_Suppl_SR_IP.pdf, at para. 304. Accessed 17 May 2017.

[67]UNCITRAL (2011b), http://www.uncitral.org/pdf/english/texts/security-lg/e/10-57126_Ebook_Suppl_SR_IP.pdf, at para. 304. Accessed 17 May 2017.

[68]UNCITRAL (2011b), http://www.uncitral.org/pdf/english/texts/security-lg/e/10-57126_Ebook_Suppl_SR_IP.pdf, para. 300. Accessed 17 May 2017. See more in the following "Hybrid Approach" part.

[69]Example (a). See UNCITRAL (2011b), http://www.uncitral.org/pdf/english/texts/security-lg/e/10-57126_Ebook_Suppl_SR_IP.pdf, para. 300. Accessed 17 May 2017.

1. Transactions undertaken in which "a portfolio of intellectual property rights protected under the laws of various States is used as security for credit"[70],
2. Transactions that have taken place when "the encumbered assets are not limited to intellectual property that is used and protected under the law of a single State"[71];
3. Transactions in which "all assets of a grantor are encumbered."[72]

c. Inconsistency with the insolvency proceedings

By adopting *lex loci protectionis*, there would potentially emerge a problem when the grantor is not located in the State in which the law of the encumbered intellectual property is protected. When an insolvency proceeding concerning the grantor is commenced in the State in which it is located, a problem may arise when "referring a security right to the law of the protecting State might lead to the applicable law rule being set aside as contrary to public policy or mandatory law considerations of the *lex fori concursus*."[73]

d. Depriving the choice of secured creditors

Applying *lex protectionis* on every aspect of the secured transactions could result in a binding effect that is criticized as being too inflexible for business practice. It is argued that parties should be able to preserve some autonomy for making choices while still respecting or acknowledging the formal requirements of other social institutions.

For example, it is mentioned that "as long as a secured creditor can always meet the requirements of the *lex protectionis* "by virtue of recommendation 4, subparagraph (b),"[74,75] of the Legislative Guideline, providing for a *lex protectionis* approach may close the possibility of utilizing Grantor's Location or the general security rights registry may thus unnecessarily deprive secured creditors of the

[70]Example (b). See UNCITRAL (2011b), http://www.uncitral.org/pdf/english/texts/security-lg/e/10-57126_Ebook_Suppl_SR_IP.pdf, para. 300. Accessed 17 May 2017.

[71]Example (c). See UNCITRAL (2011b), http://www.uncitral.org/pdf/english/texts/security-lg/e/10-57126_Ebook_Suppl_SR_IP.pdf, para. 300. Accessed 17 May 2017.

[72]See UNCITRAL (2011b), http://www.uncitral.org/pdf/english/texts/security-lg/e/10-57126_Ebook_Suppl_SR_IP.pdf, para. 300. Accessed 17 May 2017.

[73]See UNCITRAL (2011b), http://www.uncitral.org/pdf/english/texts/security-lg/e/10-57126_Ebook_Suppl_SR_IP.pdf, para. 300. Accessed 17 May 2017. See also Recommendation 222 of the Legislative Guideline. UNCITRAL (2010b), https://www.uncitral.org/pdf/english/texts/security-lg/e/09-82670_Ebook-Guide_09-04-10English.pdf, at p. 408. Accessed 22 May 2017.

[74]Subparagraph (b) of Recommendation 4 provides:

"Notwithstanding recommendation 2, the law should not apply to:

[…] (b) Intellectual property in so far as the provisions of the law are inconsistent with national law or international agreements, to which the State is a party, relating to intellectual property." See UNCITRAL (2010b), https://www.uncitral.org/pdf/english/texts/security-lg/e/09-82670_Ebook-Guide_09-04-10English.pdf, at p. 62. Accessed 22 May 2017.

[75]See also UNCITRAL (2011b), http://www.uncitral.org/pdf/english/texts/security-lg/e/10-57126_Ebook_Suppl_SR_IP.pdf, para. 289. Accessed 17 May 2017.

choices of choosing among institutions with the expense of raising transaction costs.[76]

2.1.2 Rationales Raised for and Against the Grantor's Location Approach

This approach applies the grantor's location as the connecting factor for the determination of applicable law in the secured IP transaction. Frequently mentioned pros of the grantor's location approach are:

a. Increasing the availability and lowering the cost of credit

The most substantial advantage of this approach is that it leads to the application of a single law to as many aspects (creation, third-party effectiveness, priority and enforcement) of a security right as possible.[77]

To use an example to advance understanding: under this approach, even if the assets in one transaction may have connections with more than one State, "a secured creditor can obtain a security right in all present and future intangible assets" from a grantor (which includes both intellectual property and other assets) by creating one security right, ascertaining its priority, making it effective against third parties and having it enforced by referring to the law of a single State, i.e. the law of the grantor's location.[78]

What is unique about this approach is that by applying one single law, both registration and searching costs with respect to existence and *erga omnes* validity of security rights could be reduced in a large portion of SR-in-IP cases.[79] The underlying reason is that a secured creditor in most transactions would need to register only in the State in which the grantor was located; meanwhile, a third party or potential transaction participant would also need to search in the register of one single State only.

Needless to say, it is pointed out that this simplified register and search process could dramatically reduce transaction costs resulting from duplicated searches in every single jurisdiction where each IP asset is located.[80]

---

[76]See also UNCITRAL (2011b), http://www.uncitral.org/pdf/english/texts/security-lg/e/10-57126_Ebook_Suppl_SR_IP.pdf, para. 300. Accessed 17 May 2017. Note that the recommendation 4, subparagraph (b) requirement was not included in the final IP Supplement.

[77]See UNCITRAL (2011b), http://www.uncitral.org/pdf/english/texts/security-lg/e/10-57126_Ebook_Suppl_SR_IP.pdf, para. 291. Accessed 17 May 2017.

[78]See also UNCITRAL (2011b), http://www.uncitral.org/pdf/english/texts/security-lg/e/10-57126_Ebook_Suppl_SR_IP.pdf, para. 291. Accessed 17 May 2017.

[79]See also UNCITRAL (2011b), http://www.uncitral.org/pdf/english/texts/security-lg/e/10-57126_Ebook_Suppl_SR_IP.pdf, para. 291. Accessed 17 May 2017.

[80]See also UNCITRAL (2011b), http://www.uncitral.org/pdf/english/texts/security-lg/e/10-57126_Ebook_Suppl_SR_IP.pdf, para. 291. Accessed 17 May 2017.

On the other hand, certainty of secured IP transactions could also be enhanced because fewer applicable laws would be involved and thus the complexity could be logically reduced. This effect would encourage the potential creditors to offer more credits by foreseeing and managing reasonable risks; by so doing, a positive impact on increasing the availability and lowering the cost of credit can also be created.[81]

b. Harmonizing with the conflict-of-laws rules in insolvency procedures

Under the insolvency law, the law of the State in which the main insolvency proceeding is likely to be administered could also be the law of the state of the credit grantor's location.

This is because, the definition of connecting factors under insolvency law[82] is also described as "the place of central administration."[83] Thus, as a logical result, the law applicable to the creation, third-party effectiveness, priority and enforcement of a security right and the law applicable to various insolvency procedures, e.g., "stays, avoidance proceedings, treatment of assets and ranking of claims," will most likely become the law of one and the same State.[84]

Denoting the same definition of "the place of central administration" for both secured transaction law and insolvency law has certain advantages. Even though it is foreseeable that finding the statutory seat in law may be easier than determining the real seat, it must be borne in mind that referring to the statutory seat might create a risk that "the applicable law rule being set aside for reasons of public policy or mandatory law, if the statutory seat and the place of central administration of the grantor are not eventually located in the same State."[85]

This problem may be better understood with the following example. If when the insolvency proceedings start and it is found that the law of the State of the statutory seat provides certain provisions on the priority of a security right, which is also regulated by the insolvency law of the State in which insolvency proceedings are opened (*lex fori concursus*), whenever the two sets of rules collide, the above-mentioned problem will then arise.[86]

---

[81]See also UNCITRAL (2011b), http://www.uncitral.org/pdf/english/texts/security-lg/e/10-57126_Ebook_Suppl_SR_IP.pdf, para. 291. Accessed 17 May 2017.

[82]See UNCITRAL Model Law on Cross-Border Insolvency, Articles 2, Subparagraph (b), and 16, para. 3. http://www.uncitral.org/pdf/english/texts/insolven/1997-Model-Law-Insol-2013-Guide-Enactment-e.pdf. Accessed 17 May 2017.

[83]See also UNCITRAL (2011b), http://www.uncitral.org/pdf/english/texts/security-lg/e/10-57126_Ebook_Suppl_SR_IP.pdf, para. 292. Accessed 17 May 2017.

[84]See also UNCITRAL (2011b), https://www.uncitral.org/pdf/english/texts/security-lg/e/10-57126_Ebook_Suppl_SR_IP.pdf, para. 292. Accessed 17 May 2017.

[85]See also UNCITRAL (2011b), https://www.uncitral.org/pdf/english/texts/security-lg/e/10-57126_Ebook_Suppl_SR_IP.pdf, para. 292. Accessed 17 May 2017.

[86]See UNCITRAL (2011b), http://www.uncitral.org/pdf/english/texts/security-lg/e/10-57126_Ebook_Suppl_SR_IP.pdf, para. 292. Accessed 17 May 2017.

Despite the wide support, there are also cons of the grantor's location approach:

a. The non-avoidance of other rules based on *lex protectionis*

The criticism against applying the law of the state of the grantor's location in a secured IP transaction usually points out the following case illustrating the problems when this approach is mixed with other rights that bear *lex loci protectionis* character in essence.

For example, a secured creditor normally not only has to ensure his or her priority as against other secured creditors, but also to any other competing claimants. In that sense, when the creditor finds it necessary to compete with other right holders whose rights are defined from the *lex loci protectionis* perspective, he or she may have no other choice but to meet the requirements of the law that typically governs ownership in intellectual property, i.e., turn back to the *lex loci protectionis* approach.[87]

Several types of competing claimants in security rights could most likely pose a risk to secured creditors in this regard. They are, among others, the transferee of intellectual property, the exclusive licensee of intellectual property,[88] the secured creditor, who under some traditional IP laws is "treated as an owner or may exercise the rights as an owner,"[89] and also the insolvency representative that is treated as an owner.[90]

To sum up, applying the grantor's location approach is criticized as having ignored the potential ownership aspect of IPRs. Returning the ownership issue back to the debate, however, will inevitably bring that debate to the old road of *lex loci protectionis*, or at least cause serious confusion if the law does not simultaneously deal with other issues of relevance.

It goes without saying that when secured creditors realize the approach of applying the law of the grantor's state would not guarantee any priority against certain potential competing claimants (*inter alia*, transferees or licensees of IPRs), he or she may reasonably decide either not to grant the credit ("decrease the availability of the credit") or to raise the interest rate to balance the unpredictable risks associated with institutional uncertainty ("increase the cost of credit").[91]

---

[87]See UNCITRAL (2011b), http://www.uncitral.org/pdf/english/texts/security-lg/e/10-57126_Ebook_Suppl_SR_IP.pdf, para. 305. Accessed 17 May 2017.

[88]In a commercial IP contract, an exclusive licensee is also very likely to be treated as a transferee, e.g., para. 306 of the UNCITRAL (2011b), https://www.uncitral.org/pdf/english/texts/security-lg/e/10-57126_Ebook_Suppl_SR_IP.pdf, para. 292. Accessed 17 May 2017.

[89]See also UNCITRAL (2011b), https://www.uncitral.org/pdf/english/texts/security-lg/e/10-57126_Ebook_Suppl_SR_IP.pdf, para. 30, 87–88, 222 and 306. Accessed 17 May 2017.

[90]See UNCITRAL (2011b), https://www.uncitral.org/pdf/english/texts/security-lg/e/10-57126_Ebook_Suppl_SR_IP.pdf, para. 315. Accessed 17 May 2017.

[91]See also UNCITRAL (2011b), https://www.uncitral.org/pdf/english/texts/security-lg/e/10-57126_Ebook_Suppl_SR_IP.pdf, para. 312–313. Accessed 17 May 2017.

b. The risk of unenforceability in future defaults

Since the territory principle of IP protection has developed within a relatively short period of time, although there is wide acceptance of this principle in the international society, there is nevertheless no consensus on how broad its applicability or scope should be.

Under this circumstance, if the transaction is completed using the grantor's location approach and the law of the State in which the grantor is located happens to be not the law of the protecting State, the secured creditor will have to face the uncertainty that his or her right may or may not be deemed as effective and enforceable in the court and under the law of the protecting State.[92]

It is also pointed out that, this risk could be more concrete or visualized especially when a certain security right is registered in an intellectual property registry. As more public authority is involved in the process of establishing, granting or acknowledging such a registered security right, when a dispute arises, the applicable law of the State of the grantor's location may be set aside as "fundamentally contrary to the public policy and the internationally mandatory rules of the forum."[93]

c. The cost incurred when determining the location of the grantor

The approach of the grantor's location has a major drawback, i.e. contrary to a right defined with a clear registration or other geographical boundaries (e.g. the targeted market of patent-protected inventions or the place of first publication for copyrighted work), the location of the grantor is undoubtedly more exposed to constant change in today's highly mobile, even globalized world.[94] Therefore, the searching cost for security interest in IP may become incredibly high in cases when the grantor is not a first-hand right holder.[95]

---

[92]See also UNCITRAL (2011b), https://www.uncitral.org/pdf/english/texts/security-lg/e/10-57126_Ebook_Suppl_SR_IP.pdf, para. 312–313. Accessed 17 May 2017.

[93]See Legislative Guideline Recommendation 222, UNCITRAL (2010b), https://www.uncitral.org/pdf/english/texts/security-lg/e/09-82670_Ebook-Guide_09-04-10English.pdf. Accessed 22 May 2017. See also UNCITRAL (2011b), https://www.uncitral.org/pdf/english/texts/security-lg/e/10-57126_Ebook_Suppl_SR_IP.pdf, para. 289. Accessed 17 May 2017.

[94]In a previous seminar discussion, I indicated that only the grantor's location is determined at the time when the security right is to be created "on future IP." Therefore, taking the *lex loci protectionis* may impede the realization of what Lorin Brennan called the "Working Capital Financing" (or the "Fluid IP Financing Model" in the presentation).

While it is true that when creating the SR on future IP, the location of the asset may be undetermined. However, the grantor's location also has its vital disadvantage in that the grantor (or an IP holding company in the previous example) may find it very easy to change its location too. In this way, the applicable law can be way too arbitrary.

[95]To respond to this problem, one way is acknowledging that the IP Supplement proposed to determine the location of the grantor by "the place of central administration (real seat), not where the legal entity is incorporated (statutory seat). Note also, that this is a different approach from the US Uniform Commercial Code Article 9, which stipulates all secured transactions in the US.

The following example is used as an illustration. Assume, for example, a security interest grantor is a transferee who received the asset from some other initial or intermediate owner whose location is in a State other than the State of this current grantor's location. In this case, as a security right may be created when the IP asset is owned by the former right holders, any new potential secured creditor would have, in order to best protect his or her own interest, to search in every security rights registry (and possibly in the relevant intellectual property registry as well, if there exists any) of a State where the former right holder used to reside.[96]

To solve this problem, the IP Supplement provided another set of rules to assist the determination of the law of the State in which the grantor was located. To put it more precisely, it is the "timing" of determining the location of the grantor that matters. In the case described above, under the law recommended in the Legislative Guideline, if the initial or intermediate owner had himself or herself granted a security right that was subject to the law of the location of the initial or intermediate owner, the applicable law would be "the law of the State in which the grantor was located at the time a priority conflict arose."[97]

In other words, the law recommended in the Legislative Guideline provides a distinct set of rules in determining the location of the grantor. Unless in some certain situations, each transferee of an encumbered asset would take the asset subject to a pre-existing security right [except for the "a short period of time" rule].[98] By so doing, each transferee would be subject to a security right created by a prior owner, and thus the problem of expensive and endless checking on the history of the asset could to some extent be resolved.

(Footnote 95 continued)

However, it remains true that it is relatively easier to change the location of the grantor than the IP assets. The problem proposed by this character is how to determine the grantor's location when he/she moves frequently (i.e. the problem of "timing of determination"). The comprised solution of UNCITRAL is determining the location at the time "a priority conflict arose (not when the transaction is completed)." Besides, any following transferee of an encumbered asset would take the asset subject to a pre-existing security right [except for "a short period of time" exception]. See also UNCITRAL (2011b), https://www.uncitral.org/pdf/english/texts/security-lg/e/10-57126_Ebook_Suppl_SR_IP.pdf, para. 260, 263, 274, 276, 294 and 296. Accessed 17 May 2017.

[96]See also UNCITRAL (2011b), https://www.uncitral.org/pdf/english/texts/security-lg/e/10-57126_Ebook_Suppl_SR_IP.pdf, para. 260, 263, 274, 276, 294 and 296. Accessed 17 May 2017.

[97]See Legislative Guideline, recommendations 208 and 220, subpara (b). UNCITRAL (2010b), https://www.uncitral.org/pdf/english/texts/security-lg/e/09-82670_Ebook-Guide_09-04-10English.pdf, pp. 405 and 408. Accessed 17 May 2017.

[98]See Legislative Guideline, recommendations 79–82. UNCITRAL (2010b), https://www.uncitral.org/pdf/english/texts/security-lg/e/09-82670_Ebook-Guide_09-04-10English.pdf, pp. 230 and 231. Accessed 17 May 2017.

2.1.3 Hybrid Approaches and the Underlying Rationales

The first hybrid approach is a combined approach with identification based on the function of registration.

Its definition is given as the approach which makes a distinction between issues arising from a security right in intellectual property that is subject to registration in an intellectual property registry (whether this registry is a national, regional or international system). This kind of SR-in-IP related issue shall be governed by "the law of the State under whose authority the registry is maintained."[99]

However, an exception is also reserved for issues relating to enforcement. It is argued that, for reasons of cost and time-efficiency, the law applicable to enforcement should be referred to "the law of the State in which the grantor was located."[100]

On the other hand, "issues arising with respect to a security right in intellectual property that is not subject to such registration" would be referred to "the law of the State in which the grantor is located."[101]

However, even for such an approach, one more exception is also reserved for "the third-party effectiveness and priority of a security right in intellectual property" because that may be referred to the *lex protectionis*."[102]

The main strength of this approach, it is argued, is that "it takes into account the very existing fact of national, regional or international intellectual property registries."[103] It is also considered under these circumstances that the States that have such registries may be reluctant to adopt a conflict-of-laws rule that would simply ignore the practice of those established registries.[104]

It is well reasoned that to the extent legislation of regional or international organizations provides for registration of rights in intellectual property, member States of these organizations would logically be unwilling to adopt a rule which would be against their obligation to obey their own regional or international legislation.[105]

---

[99] See UNCITRAL (2011b), https://www.uncitral.org/pdf/english/texts/security-lg/e/10-57126_Ebook_Suppl_SR_IP.pdf, para. 307. Accessed 17 May 2017.

[100] See UNCITRAL (2011b), https://www.uncitral.org/pdf/english/texts/security-lg/e/10-57126_Ebook_Suppl_SR_IP.pdf, paras. 307–308. Accessed 17 May 2017.

[101] See UNCITRAL (2011b), https://www.uncitral.org/pdf/english/texts/security-lg/e/10-57126_Ebook_Suppl_SR_IP.pdf, para. 309. Accessed 17 May 2017.

[102] See UNCITRAL (2011b), https://www.uncitral.org/pdf/english/texts/security-lg/e/10-57126_Ebook_Suppl_SR_IP.pdf, para. 310. Accessed 17 May 2017.

[103] See UNCITRAL (2011b), https://www.uncitral.org/pdf/english/texts/security-lg/e/10-57126_Ebook_Suppl_SR_IP.pdf, para. 310. Accessed 17 May 2017.

[104] See UNCITRAL (2011b), https://www.uncitral.org/pdf/english/texts/security-lg/e/10-57126_Ebook_Suppl_SR_IP.pdf, para. 310. Accessed 17 May 2017.

[105] See UNCITRAL (2011b), https://www.uncitral.org/pdf/english/texts/security-lg/e/10-57126_Ebook_Suppl_SR_IP.pdf, para. 310. Accessed 17 May 2017.

To give an example, in the IP Supplement it is argued that member States of the European Union may not be willing to adopt a rule that does not take into consideration that, "under article 16 of the Community Trademark Regulation 207/2009 ("CTM Regulation"), community trademarks are subject primarily to articles 17–24 of the CTM Regulation, and, only if these provisions have no specific rule, the law of the State where the proprietor has his seat, establishment (if inside the EU) or Spanish law (seat of the Office)."[106]

The main disadvantage of this approach, however, lies in the fact that rights on certain types of intellectual property are generally capable of being registered in an intellectual property registry (e.g., patents and trademarks) , while other types of IPRs (i.e. copyrights) are not. It thus unnecessarily results in a differentiated conflict-of-laws treatment for security rights in different types of intellectual property, without an obvious or solid policy reason.[107]

Besides, it is also pointed out that to the extent that the approach to the law applicable to security right in intellectual property is based on the *lex protectionis*", such an approach would create distinctions that are not necessary as "the *lex protectionis* coincides with the law of the State of the registry and should apply to all types of intellectual property."[108]

Due to the fact that this approach tries to embrace both approaches, it would also of necessity be burdened with the disadvantages of both approaches. Therefore, when the second part of such an approach is identical with the grantor's location approach, only with a more limited scope of application, it would have to bear all of its potential pitfalls as well.[109]

Moreover, it is argued that "such an approach may add cost and complexity to outright transfers of intellectual property rights that are not subject to such registration under the *lex protectionis*," the reason being the fact that "an outright transferee of such an intellectual property right would have to investigate the law of the State of the grantor's location to ensure that the transfer was not subject to a prior security right."[110]

Besides, it is also pointed out that applying two different laws to priority and enforcement could create more cost and complexity. For example, it is likely that an issue may be characterized "in one State as an issue of priority and in another State

[106]See UNCITRAL (2011b), https://www.uncitral.org/pdf/english/texts/security-lg/e/10-57126_Ebook_Suppl_SR_IP.pdf, para. 310. Accessed 17 May 2017.

[107]See UNCITRAL (2011b), https://www.uncitral.org/pdf/english/texts/security-lg/e/10-57126_Ebook_Suppl_SR_IP.pdf, paras. 309–310. Accessed 17 May 2017.

[108]See UNCITRAL (2011b), https://www.uncitral.org/pdf/english/texts/security-lg/e/10-57126_Ebook_Suppl_SR_IP.pdf, paras. 309–310. Accessed 17 May 2017.

[109]See also UNCITRAL (2011b), https://www.uncitral.org/pdf/english/texts/security-lg/e/10-57126_Ebook_Suppl_SR_IP.pdf, para. 309. Accessed 17 May 2017.

[110]See also UNCITRAL (2011b), https://www.uncitral.org/pdf/english/texts/security-lg/e/10-57126_Ebook_Suppl_SR_IP.pdf, para. 309. Accessed 17 May 2017.

as an issue of enforcement."[111] Besides, priority may affect enforcement issues such as "who has the right to take over enforcement, distribution of proceeds from a sale, rights acquired by a transferee in an extrajudicial sale."[112]

Finally, and on very practical grounds, it is argued that this approach would require an investigation of the *lex protectionis* of all States concerned besides, otherwise one can't be sure about whether "those States permit registration of a security right in intellectual property in an intellectual property registry."[113]

The other approach is designating creation and enforcement of SR-in-IP to the law of the State of the grantor's location.

For this alternative, definition is given as referring the creation and enforcement of a security right to the law of the State of the grantor's location. The only exception is that the parties can also agree to refer the law of the protecting State.[114]

To make it more specific, under such an approach, the third-party effectiveness and priority of a security right would be referred to the law of the State of the grantor's location, and the only exception is made upon "the third-party effectiveness and priority of a security right as against the rights of a transferee, licensee or another secured creditor."[115] In that case, *lex protectionis* applies.

The advantage of this approach is summarized as follows[116]:

"It admits a limited amount of party autonomy with respect to creation and enforcement; third-party effectiveness and priority areas are reserved to the law of the protecting State," and in addition, "it also allows the third-party effectiveness and priority of a security right as against an insolvency representative to be referred to the law of the State of the grantor's location."[117]

The disadvantages of this approach are also obvious. First, the characterization problem becomes inevitable. When creation and third-party effectiveness are referred to two different laws, only States that treat these two issues as distinct issues (i.e., follow the exact approach as the approach recommended in the Legislative Guideline) could apply such a rule. As a result, there is a chance that

---

[111]UNCITRAL (2011b), https://www.uncitral.org/pdf/english/texts/security-lg/e/10-57126_Ebook_Suppl_SR_IP.pdf, para. 310. Accessed 17 May 2017.

[112]UNCITRAL (2011b), https://www.uncitral.org/pdf/english/texts/security-lg/e/10-57126_Ebook_Suppl_SR_IP.pdf, para. 310. Accessed 17 May 2017.

[113]UNCITRAL (2011b), https://www.uncitral.org/pdf/english/texts/security-lg/e/10-57126_Ebook_Suppl_SR_IP.pdf, para. 310. The example given is that under such a rule, the law applicable to a security right in copyright will have to depend on whether "the copyright may be registered in a copyright registry or not."

[114]See UNCITRAL (2011b), https://www.uncitral.org/pdf/english/texts/security-lg/e/10-57126_Ebook_Suppl_SR_IP.pdf, para. 311. Accessed 17 May 2017.

[115]See UNCITRAL (2011b), https://www.uncitral.org/pdf/english/texts/security-lg/e/10-57126_Ebook_Suppl_SR_IP.pdf, para. 311. Accessed 17 May 2017.

[116]It is literally cited as this approach is influential and constitutes the important part of the final adopted Recommendation 248. See UNCITRAL (2010b), https://www.uncitral.org/pdf/english/texts/security-lg/e/10-57126_Ebook_Suppl_SR_IP.pdf, pp. 147–149. Accessed 17 May 2017.

[117]See also UNCITRAL (2011b), https://www.uncitral.org/pdf/english/texts/security-lg/e/10-57126_Ebook_Suppl_SR_IP.pdf, para. 311. Accessed 17 May 2017.

this rule will never be broadly applied unless there is wide adoption of a law which is in line with the substantive law recommended in the Guide.[118]

Besides, it has been argued that "referring any issue other than the mutual rights and obligations of the parties to party autonomy on only security rights in intellectual property would be a departure from the main approach" adopted in the Legislative Guideline.[119] Furthermore, such as practice is also rarely found in generally adopted or well-established conflict-of-laws principles.[120]

Moreover, as already mentioned, referring two different laws to third-party effectiveness and priority based on the identity of the competing claimant would result in "all secured creditors seeking to meet the third-party effectiveness requirements of both laws in order to ensure priority against all possible competing claimants."[121] In that case, the transaction cost could hardly be reduced.

In addition, referring two different laws to priority and enforcement issues could result in inconsistencies as "one law would apply to priority in one State and another law could apply to priority in another State in which a priority issue is rather characterized as an enforcement issue."[122] Thus, due to the similar problem of characterization, referring priority and enforcement to two different laws might result in circular priority problems.[123]

Finally, it departs from the principal set in the first place, that "to avoid these problems, the Guide has recommended the law applicable to enforcement as the law applicable to the priority of a security right in an intangible asset."[124]

b. Denoting different connecting factors to various legal concepts

Another combination of rules is suggested as the following:

"The *lex protectionis* applies to the creation, third-party effectiveness and priority of a security right in intellectual property;"[125]

"However, the law of the State in which the grantor was located could govern the third-party effectiveness and priority of such a security right as against judgment

---

[118]UNCITRAL (2011b), https://www.uncitral.org/pdf/english/texts/security-lg/e/10-57126_Ebook_Suppl_SR_IP.pdf, para. 311. Accessed 17 May 2017.

[119]UNCITRAL (2011b), https://www.uncitral.org/pdf/english/texts/security-lg/e/10-57126_Ebook_Suppl_SR_IP.pdf, para. 312. Accessed 17 May 2017.

[120]See Legislative Guideline, recommendation 10, which does not provide any party autonomy for applicable law issues other than for the mutual rights and obligations of the parties. UNCITRAL (2010b), https://www.uncitral.org/pdf/english/texts/security-lg/e/09-82670_Ebook-Guide_09-04-10English.pdf, p. 63. Accessed 17 May 2017.

[121]See also UNCITRAL (2011b), https://www.uncitral.org/pdf/english/texts/security-lg/e/10-57126_Ebook_Suppl_SR_IP.pdf, para. 313. Accessed 17 May 2017.

[122]UNCITRAL (2011b), https://www.uncitral.org/pdf/english/texts/security-lg/e/10-57126_Ebook_Suppl_SR_IP.pdf, para. 313. Accessed 17 May 2017.

[123]UNCITRAL (2011b), https://www.uncitral.org/pdf/english/texts/security-lg/e/10-57126_Ebook_Suppl_SR_IP.pdf, para. 313. Accessed 17 May 2017.

[124]See the Legislative Guideline, recommendation 218.

[125]UNCITRAL (2011b), https://www.uncitral.org/pdf/english/texts/security-lg/e/10-57126_Ebook_Suppl_SR_IP.pdf, para. 314. Accessed 17 May 2017.

creditors and the grantor's insolvency representative;"[126] "In addition, the law of the State in which the grantor was located could govern the enforcement of such a security right."[127]

The advantage of this approach is that the importance of the *lex protectionis* would be properly recognized. On the other hand, it is also consistent with the insolvency procedure[128] since assigning grantor's location as the connecting factor would be in line with the international insolvency law.

In the end, UNCITRAL adopted the interim conclusion: Recommendation 248. This is the language in the UNCITRAL document (IP Supplement):

Recommendation 248

Law applicable to a security right in intellectual property
The law should provide that:

(a) The law applicable to the creation, effectiveness against third parties and priority of a security right in intellectual property is the law of the State in which the intellectual property is protected;
(b) A security right in intellectual property may also be created under the law of the State in which the grantor is located and may also be made effective under that law against third parties other than another secured creditor, a transferee or a licensee; and
(c) The law applicable to the enforcement of a security right in intellectual property is the law of the State in which the grantor is located."

2.2 *Evaluating UNCITRAL's Achievements Vis-à-Vis the Unanswered Questions*

As the comparative table in the previous section shows, during the drafting process, UNCITRAL reviewed more than twenty legislative proposals. However, since there were divergent opinions and very lively debates, even though Recommendation 248 was reached in the end, it apparently cannot answer all the questions that have been posed in the discussions.

For instance, after comparison, readers may come with the first question: why in some proposed alternatives, when Grantor's Location is assigned as being the connecting factor for the perfection of security right in intellectual property, an

---

[126]UNCITRAL (2011b), https://www.uncitral.org/pdf/english/texts/security-lg/e/10-57126_Ebook_Suppl_SR_IP.pdf, para. 314. Accessed 17 May 2017.

[127]UNCITRAL (2011b), https://www.uncitral.org/pdf/english/texts/security-lg/e/10-57126_Ebook_Suppl_SR_IP.pdf, para. 314. Accessed 17 May 2017.

[128]UNCITRAL (2011b), https://www.uncitral.org/pdf/english/texts/security-lg/e/10-57126_Ebook_Suppl_SR_IP.pdf, para. 315. Accessed 17 May 2017.

exception is opened to third-party effectiveness as against the right of a transferee or licensee of the encumbered intellectual property; in other proposals, however, asserting third-party effectiveness against "other secured creditor" is also included in the *lex protectionis* domain. If the reason behind the *lex protectionis* is sovereignty, then what makes the right of a transferee or licensee different from another secured creditor?

The other example is: as highlighted in the comparative table, four of the proposals made a distinction among the laws applicable with the classification of "registry". However, even though the wordings of these proposals may look similar, putting them under the application of substantive laws could bring very divergent results.[129] Why, in some cases, is the criterion the IP itself which has to be registered (and registered in an IP registry), while in other scenarios it depends on whether it is SR-in-IP that is subject to registration?

In practical situations, for example, under the US copyright law, the IP (copyright) itself is not required to be registered. Interestingly, however, when a security interest in copyright is to be created *erga omnes*, it has to be registered in the US Copyright Office or follow the Uniform Commercial Code (hereafter, "UCC") Article 9 state filing regime.[130] Therefore, differences of the wordings in UNCITRAL proposals may need further justification regarding why various results are created and whether they provide socially desirable outcomes.

Furthermore, one institutional problem that UNCITRAL may have to examine is why the registry system matters. From the five meetings and the documented literature, we can find that only reference to the *lex loci protectionis* was made. However, at the local level, comparative substantive law study shows in most of the countries where dual SR-in-IP registration systems exist, conflicts of institutions are also unavoidable.[131] In those countries, however, the problem may take place in the form of "preemption debate"[132] or "special versus general rule"[133] debates, depending on whether there is a federal or unitary system. From this regard, it is the economics or logics of two institutions (property-indexed registry and person-indexed registry) that matters, not merely a designated applicable law.

The other confusion which UNCITRAL may have to further examine is, it only discussed the conflict-of-laws rule that indicates where to register in order to ascertain third-party effectiveness, but ignored the fact that the problem is not just which country's law should be applicable, but also in that country, the multiple

[129]For example, at the 13th session it was described as "register-able SR-in-IP"; at the 14th session it became "SR-in-IP which is subject to registration at IP registry"; as to the last meeting, it is "SR-in-IP register-able at IP registry", and "IP registered in a specialized registry" (there are two proposals in this meeting).

[130]Nat'l Peregrine, Inc. v. Capitol Fed. Savs. & Loan Ass'n, 116 B.R.194 (Bankr. C.D. Cal. 1990); In re Avalon Software, 209 B.R. 517 (Bankr. D. Ariz. June 6, 1997); World Auxiliary Power Co. v. Silicon Valley Bank, 303 F.3d 1120 (B.A.P. 9th Cir. 2002).

[131]See Nat'l Peregrine, Inc., In re Avalon Software and World Auxiliary Power Co., id.

[132]Preemption debate is more common in federal countries.

[133]"Special versus general rule" is the main issue in the unitary countries.

choices (or in some cases, no choice available) between specialized registry and general registry. Most importantly, it did not consider the problem that not every registry indicated by the conflict-of-laws rule can accept the registration of a SR in foreign IPRs.

Another aspect which UNCITRAL left unresolved is in the discussions, references are often made to the grantor's location under the US law (i.e. UCC). In the US, however, it is more of a mixed picture. Under the US law, grantor's location only partially applies because in some cases, the federal preemption rule requires a registration in the US Patent & Trademark Office or Copyright Office, even if it is a purely domestic case.[134] Therefore, it is a *lex loci protectionis* or mixed approach that the US is taking, not a purely grantor's location approach.

The above lack of clarifications thus reveal a methodological gap: that there is no concrete methodology or benchmark in arguments being raised during the discussion. There is little reference to conflict-of-laws theories either. Besides, there is limited reference to existing conflict-of-laws in various countries, even though the problem in need of resolution is a conflict-of-laws issue. That is to say comparative study of private international law analysis is missing in the debating process. Therefore, the following section is an initial attempt to bridge this gap.

3 Conceptualizing SR-in-IP: Pledge, Mortgage, or a Third-Type?

Since what remains unanswered after UNCITRAL is an academic inquiry rooted in a conflict-of-laws context, this paper takes another route to analyze this dilemma. Instead of following the pros-and-cons approach to evaluate the costs and benefits of two main-stream camps of UNCITRAL, it is the established conflict-of-laws rules in different countries that will be examined in the following section.

Theoretically, when a cross-border IP secured transaction case is brought to any court and if a jurisdiction problem is not argued by both parties, the next step for the court is to look for the applicable law from its country's existing private international law rules. In a common situation such as this, what would be the doctrinal rules? Whether that application result can be justified by legal reasoning should be of interest for both scholars and practitioners. This approach is also valuable since it provides at least a bridging opportunity between the established conflict-of-laws jurisprudence, linking it to the current emerging, new issue.

In the following section, a comparative survey on the applicable law in various countries (i.e. the United States, Japan, China and Taiwan) will thus be introduced and analyzed to build the theoretical connections.

[134]For more of this feature of the US law, see Haemmerli (1996), Nguyen (2002), Lui (2011).

3.1 *Classic Conflict-of-Laws Theories Regarding Characterization*

To determine the law applicable for secured interest in IP, firstly it is necessary to "characterize" the nature of the to-be addressed issue. This is because, for choice-of-law problems, judicial concepts, categories and local elements as well as connecting factors are employed to deal with the specific case at hand.[135] Following that, a certain conflict-of-law rule can then be identified.

To give an example, under the English conflict of laws jurisprudence, it is generally accepted that "the formal validity of a marriage is governed by the law of the place of celebration (*lex loci celebrationis*)."[136] There are other established rules for the English conflict-of-laws analysis, e.g. "capacity to marry is governed by the law of the parties' domicile."[137] Also, succession to immovables under the English system is governed by the law of the *situs*.[138]

From the previous illustrations, formal validity of marriage, capacity to marry, and succession to immovables can be deemed as different "categories" or "classes", which, together with accompanying connecting factors, further indicate applicable laws of place of celebration, domicile and *situs*, composed the choice-of-law function system.[139]

The problem, however, lies in the fact that cross-border disputes by nature involve laws of more than one country; thus it is an initial issue regarding which country's law shall be applied to characterize the dispute. There are at least three main theories illustrating such a problem, i.e. how a legal problem should be characterized: the *lex fori*, *lex causae* and comparative law theory.

3.1.1 Lex Fori

In most countries' judicial practice, the conflict rules of the *lex fori* (the domestic law of the court hearing the case) are usually applied to determine the characterizing issue. The reason raised to support *lex fori* is that in principal, the purpose of characterization is to (re)formulate conflict-of-laws rules of the domestic court; it is thus contrary to this principle to turn to foreign law for the answer.[140]

This principle has been well-recognized. In UK, in the leading Macmillan Inc. v Bishopsgate Investment Trust plc case, Auld LJ. has reconfirmed that the proper

[135]See Collins et al. (2006), p. 37.
[136]See Collins et al. (2006), p. 37.
[137]See Collins et al. (2006), pp. 37–38.
[138]See Collins et al. (2006), p. 37.
[139]See Collins et al. (2006), p. 38.
[140]See Collins et al. (2006), p. 48.

approach is to look beyond the formulation of the claim and to identify according to the *lex fori* the true issue or issues brought up by the claim and the defence."[141]

3.1.2 Lex Causae

Applying *lex causae* means to characterize the dispute according to the law identified in the later choice-of-law analysis stage, and use it as the same legal standard to be applied to determine the case.[142]

Lex causae, however, has been criticized as problematic because even if it may appear logical to apply the *lex causae* to the whole case, including for the characterization stage, in reality, it may produce a circular way of legal reasoning. To put it another way, the *lex causae* is to apply to the process of characterization before the process of characterization has led to the choice of the relevant *lex causae*. When circular in nature, *lex causae* theory could be impractical as it may not provide any concrete guiding rule.

3.1.3 Comparative Law

A third way that can avoid the rigid thinking of *lex fori* and the circular result of *lex causae* is to apply a neutral comparative law perspective. The comparative law approach takes into consideration of the legal concepts in different jurisdictions. However, even if the advantage of this theory is to accommodate as much diversity as possible, it has been severely criticized as purely ideal and unrealistic since judges who have only been trained from a domestic legal background cannot be expected to make a sound judgment regarding a delicate and even complicated foreign law.[143]

3.2 Characterizing SR-in-IP

Even though there are multiple theories (*lex fori*, *lex causae*, and comparative law) explaining how a dispute involving foreign elements may be characterized by judges, *lex fori* is still the most widely-adopted method in the courtrooms of most countries.

---

[141]MacMillan v. Branch Banking & Trust Co., 221 N.C. 352 (N.C. 1942).

[142]See Japan METI Intellectual Property Policy Office (2009), http://www.meti.go.jp/policy/intellectual_assets/english.html. Accessed 18 May 2017.

[143]See Japan METI Intellectual Property Policy Office (2009), http://www.meti.go.jp/policy/intellectual_assets/english.html. Accessed 18 May 2017.

Following this approach, the next section's analysis would use the characterization rule of where the court is as a default reference. This could avoid the problem of open-ended and inconclusive pursuit of an "objectively defined meaning"[144] of security interest in IP, which in reality, may lead to a result of "mere conceptualism."[145]

3.3 *Comparative Choice-of-Law Perspective: The Law Applicable for Pledge and/or SR in Movables*

3.3.1 The United States: Grantor's Location (But for IPR—Mixed)

Before determining the applicable law, how security interest in IPRs shall be characterized under the American conflict-of-laws rules is the first issue that has to be tackled. Fortunately, in the United States this issue is much clearer than it may appear in other countries. The reason is because the United States has a unique system of integrated secured transaction law, i.e. UCC Article 9.[146]

Since UCC Article 9 covers comprehensively the definition of security interest financing tools, including "pledge, assignment, chattel mortgage, chattel trust, trust deed, factor's lien, equipment trust, conditional sale, trust receipt, other lien or title retention contract and lease or consignment intended as security"[147] in the past, the characterization problem in the United States would be less troublesome and could be examined under the UCC Article 9's general framework. The other unique feature of the US system is that the choice-of-law clause is also covered by UCC Article 9,[148] which is unusual compared to other civil issues (e.g. real property), as the latter appears much more frequently in pure conflict-of-laws stipulations.[149]

One of the reasons for UCC Article 9 to adopt its own conflict-of-laws rule is due to the US federal system—when conducting secured transactions in the US, it is very likely that the parties involved (the debtor, secured party, and/or any third persons) may have domiciles in different states in the US. In addition, the collateral attached in the transaction could also be located in a further different state. As a result, in order to reduce the uncertainty and cost of making multi-state secured transactions, a set of conflict-of-law rules is necessary. For instance, parties should be informed in advance with regard to questions such as where do they perfect the

---

[144]See also Collins et al. (2006), p. 48.

[145]See Collins et al. (2006), p. 48.

[146]Due to space constraint, for a more general understanding of the US secured transaction law structure, please see Whaley and McJohn (2014).

[147]Whaley and McJohn (2014). See also § 9-102 & § 9-109 of Uniform Commercial Code (2010).

[148]Part 3. Perfection and Priority, Subpart 1: Law Governing Perfection and Priority. See U.C.C. §§ 9-301 ~ 9-316 (amended 1999).

[149]See American Law Institute (1988).

security interest in personal property (and obtain the third-party effectiveness), or what would the governing law be should a dispute arise in the future.

UCC provides the law applicable for conflicts arising from multi-state secured transactions. Firstly, the rule of thumb is party autonomy. Parties may choose the governing law for their domestic/international transaction, whether or not the transaction bears a relation to the State or country designated.[150] Secondly, the exception is if one of the parties is a consumer, the transaction must bear a reasonable relation to the law of the State or country designated,[151] and it may not deprive the consumer of the benefits of consumer protection law.[152]

However, all of the above conditions are subject to the "fundamental policy" (public policy) restriction.[153] In the absence of an agreement specifying the law of a particular state, the rights and obligations of the parties are determined by the law that would be selected by application of this State's conflict of laws principles.[154]

On the principle of autonomy, there are several points that can be addressed. First of all, this conflict-of-laws rule is in line with most proposed approaches of UNCITRAL (except the most territorial ones for intellectual property rights). Second, it has limited application[155]: as disputes concerning collateral involve not only the debtor and the secured party, but rights and obligations of third parties as well. In that case, questions regarding where to perfect a security interest or how the priority rule follows are separately regulated by the UCC, as follows.

The second rule UCC provides is that the governing Law is based on: (1) the location of collateral, and (2) the debtor's location.

Regarding Possessory Security Interest: for possessory security interest, the governing law of perfection and the priority on a security interest is the law of the state in which the collateral is located (§9-301 (1)[156])[157];

---

[150]Please see U.C.C. §1-301 (d).

[151]Please see U.C.C. §1-301 (e) (1).

[152]Please see U.C.C. §1-301 (e) (2).

[153]Please see U.C.C. §1-301 (f).

[154]Please see U.C.C. §1-301 (d).

[155]Please see U.C.C. §1-301 (g).

[156]U.C.C. § 9-301 is titled as "Law Governing Perfection and Priority of Security Interests" and provides:

"(1) Except as otherwise provided in this section, while a debtor is located in a jurisdiction, the local law of that jurisdiction governs perfection, the effect of perfection or nonperfection, and the priority of a security interest in collateral.

(2) While collateral is located in a jurisdiction, the local law of that jurisdiction governs perfection, the effect of perfection or nonperfection, and the priority of a possessory security interest in that collateral."

[157]As to why UCC chooses such an approach as the indication for law applicable in a multi-state transaction or conflict-of-laws situation, reasons are provided that:

"Documents, instruments, and ordinary goods are physical objects that have identifiable geographic locations. In this respect, they are unlike accounts and general intangibles. Further, they are inherently less mobile than motor vehicles, airplanes, shipping containers and the other

Regarding Non-Possessory Security Interest: for non-possessory security interest, the governing law of perfection and the priority on a security interest is the law of the location of the debtor (including the conflict of laws rules) (UCC Article 9, Secured Transactions (1999) §9-103 (3)[158];

This style of law-making is very similar to the dual-approach (i.e. law of the location of the encumbered asset for tangibles (*lex situs* or *lex rei sitae*) versus law of the location of the grantor for intangibles)[159,160] taken by UNCITRAL,[161] as elaborated previously.

There are, however, some important variations that deserve further attention:

The UNCITRAL Legislative Guide makes distinctions by categorizing tangibles and intangibles, while the UCC basically relies on the differentiation between possessory and non-possessory collateral. It is indeed a common practice that security interest in tangible assets used to be perfected by possession, and the other way works for intangibles. However, it is not always the case.

For example, a secured creditor today may choose to file a financing statement over a tangible collateral under the UCC (equivalent to registering in a general or specialized security rights registry as provided by the UNCITRAL), rather than taking possession and risking the loss of better use by the debtor/grantor who supposedly has advanced skills or knowledge regarding how to exploit the collateral fully.

(Footnote 157 continued)

certificate-of-title and mobile goods that are covered by 9-103(2) and (3)." See Nordstrom et al. (1987), p. 199.

[158]Please note the reason stated below as to why the UCC 1999 version started to take a different approach (i.e. shifted to a central filing system) regarding where the place of filing a financing statement should be determined: "Former Article 9 afforded each State three alternatives approaches, depending on the extent to which the State desires central filing (usually with the Secretary of State), local filing (usually with a county office), or both. … Local filing increases the net costs of secured transactions … by increasing uncertainty and the number of required filing." See Comment 2 to 1999 § 9-501, extracted from Hagedorn (2007), p. 159. The reasons provided for central filing (i.e. duplicated registrations and multiple costs) under UCC, though only at a nation-wide level, serves as an importance reference for this international secured transaction law reform undertaken at UNCITRAL.

[159]It is not from the beginning when UCC was firstly drafted that its conflict-of-laws rules were designed this way. Scholars have indicated that throughout the historical exploration, it can be found that the 2001 version of UCC brought a major change in philosophy from its earlier 1972 version. "While the 1972 version generally looked to the law of the state of the *situs* of the collateral, the 2001 version looks to the debtor's "location" for nonpossessory security interests. For possessory security interests (i.e. those security interests that are perfected by the creditor taking possession of the collateral), the 2001 version retains the *situs nexus*." See Hay et al. (2009), p. 824.

[160]To examine how the UCC conflict-of-laws section moves from the law of the state of the *situs* of the collateral ("*lex situs*") to a debtor-location nexus and, most importantly, its implications for international transactions, see Borchers (1998).

[161]See Session 1.2 (analysis of UNCITRAL proposals) and footnotes 2–44.

In the previous situation, the governing law would be the law of the debtor's location under UCC, in contrast to the law of the location of the encumbered asset under UNCITRAL Legislative Guideline. Therefore, a "conflict" exists and could cause future problems for international secured financing practice unless the US changes the UCC to be compatible with the UNCITRAL Legislative Guideline.

Regarding intellectual property rights—UCC does not specify any applicable law for intellectual property rights serving as collateral, but however does tag them under the general "non-possessory" category. UNCITRAL Legislative Guideline nevertheless treats intellectual property rights differently from any other collateral asset. Note, however, that collateralized intellectual property rights are subject to the registration requirement of US federal law. Since in this case it is regulated on the federal (and hence unitary) level, there is no conflict among different states. However, it still remains as a valid and complicated issue when being further raised to the international level.

Another difference exists in the definition of grantor or debtor's location. When it comes to legal entities, UCC determines its location by looking at "the place of business"[162] while UNCITRAL Legislative Guideline uses "the place of central administration" as the connecting factor. If the grantor's location approach is adopted and if the intellectual property rights are held by legal entities, this divergence would cause conflicts and inconsistencies.

The third conflict-of-laws rule UCC provides concerns certificate of Titles. The problem, however, is whether it has particular implication for IPRs is still unclear.

UCC special provision for security interest on certificate of titles provides that for security interest attached on certificate of titles, the governing law of the perfection and priority matters on a security interest is the law "under whose certificate of title the goods are covered governs perfection, the effect of perfection or non-perfection, and the priority of a security interest in goods covered by a certificate of title from the time the goods become covered by the certificate of title until the goods cease to be covered by the certificate of title."[163]

What deserves further attention is that under both UCC and UNCITRAL Legislative Guideline[164] the governing law for "certificate of titles" or "collateral being listed in specialized registries" would be the law (including the conflict of laws rules) of the jurisdiction issuing the certificate.

There are mainly two reasons for this. First, it applies basically to highly-mobile assets such as motor vehicles. The location of this kind of asset is difficult to determine, or changes too easily and too frequently. Second, it is also emphasized that the registry must be maintained, and/or the title certificate is issued according to

---

[162]Please see U.C.C. §9-307 (2010). Besides, in the older version, UCC Article used to phrase this as "(where the organization) is incorporated." For states that has not yet adopted the latest U.C.C. §9 (2010), this could cause further serious conflicts.

[163]Please see U.C.C. §9-303 (c) (2010).

[164]See Legislative Guideline, UNCITRAL (2010b), https://www.uncitral.org/pdf/english/texts/security-lg/e/09-82670_Ebook-Guide_09-04-10English.pdf, at pp. 391–392. Accessed 22 May 2017.

"national law" or "international convention." Hence, the role of public authority is to some extent emphasized again.

Intellectual property rights, although not currently falling into UCC or UNCITRAL Legislative Guideline's definition of certificate of titles, have very similar nature in common, i.e. unidentifiable location and public authority involvement in registries. Whether or not that could be utilized—as an argument in support of assigning the law of the state where intellectual property rights are granted—is a question that needs to be carefully examined.

In conclusion, UCC of the United States is a model law that has been widely adopted[165] by all of its 50 states.[166] It took an unprecedentedly integrated and functional approach which managed to create a single and comprehensive security right in movable assets, unifying numerous and diverse possessory and non-possessory rights in tangible and intangible assets.

UCC also significantly increased its comprehensiveness by including transfer-of-title and retention-of-title arrangements existing in both state statutes and common-law traditions. By explicitly mentioning the innovativeness and world-wide spread of the UCC model, the UNCITRAL Legislative Guideline on Secured Transactions has acknowledged the strong impact of UCC on its legislation as well.[167] UCC's provision is thus particularly worth study.

What is even more important is that the UCC contains not only a substantive law provision, but due to the United States' heavily-federalized character, a set of conflict-of-law rules. The reason is, of course, to facilitate the completion of multiple-state transactions. As the most well-known multi-jurisdictional State, the path United States has taken also shaped the conflict-of-law chapter of the UNCITRAL Legislative Guideline.

On the practical level, although the UCC itself deals only with the United States' domestic conflict-of-law issues (i.e. instead of addressing multiple-country secured transactions happening all over the world, it copes preliminarily with problems

[165]While employing a not so precise term of "uniform," two things have to be brought up as reminders in advance.

One, the meaning of "uniform" under UCC is a relative rather than an absolute feature. For examples, scholars have indicated earlier that "Article 9 is still in force in its 1962 version in seven states, and only a minority of the states has adopted the new (1977) version of Article 9." See Nordstrom et al. (1987), p. 9.

Even in States that have adopted the same version of the UCC, variations may still be existent. See Legislative Guideline. UNCITRAL (2010b), https://www.uncitral.org/pdf/english/texts/security-lg/e/09-82670_Ebook-Guide_09-04-10English.pdf, at pp. 391–392. Accessed 22 May 2017.

[166]The other thing is: in addition to the fact that different states may modify the language of their promulgated versions of secured transaction law, even if the uniform statutory language were adopted, it does not automatically leads to uniformity in judicial interpretation. See Nordstrom et al., p. 9.

[167]See UNCITRAL Legislative Guideline, UNCITRAL (2010b), https://www.uncitral.org/pdf/english/texts/security-lg/e/09-82670_Ebook-Guide_09-04-10English.pdf, at p. 56. Accessed 22 May 2017.

arising from multiple-state secured transactions happening within the United States). Nonetheless, it serves as a sensible reference point or "mini-analogy" of the larger but to some extent, similar problem in the international arena.[168] Hence, this section's analysis provides not only the specific provisions or legal techniques of the UCC-regime, but tries to ask and answer the same series of questions encountered by any conflict-of-laws lawyers, not only in the US, but globally as well.

3.3.2 Japan: The Law of the Place Where the Subject Property Is Located

According to Article 13 of the Act on General Rules for Application of Laws[169] (Rights *in Rem* and Rights Requiring Registration), it is provided that "(1) Rights *in rem* and other rights requiring registration with regard to movables or immovables shall be governed by the law of the place where the subject property is located;"[170] and (2) "Notwithstanding the preceding paragraph, the acquisition and loss of the rights provided for in the preceding paragraph shall be governed by the law of the place where the subject property is located at the time when the events causing the acquisition or loss are completed."[171]

The other Article that calls for further attention is Article 23 (Assignment of Receivables) which provides that "the effect of an assignment of a receivable in relation to a debtor and other third parties shall be governed by the law applicable to the receivable which is to be assigned."[172]

What also makes a difference is the timing issue. According to Japan's Act on General Rules for Application of Laws,[173] the timing to determine the applicable law shall be governed by "the law of the place where the subject property is located at the time when the events causing the acquisition or loss are completed."[174] The US conflict-of-law rule, on the other hand, determines by when the last event occurs.

---

[168]It, however, needs to be pointed out that some issues that exist in one category may be found in another. For example, UCC may not be 100% applicable to intellectual property-related collaterals in the US since federal law dominates some aspects of it and due to the preemption principle rooted in the US Constitution. Therefore, this vacancy may be left out in UCC, but nonetheless has to be addressed in the international level.

[169]Act on General Rules for Application of Laws, Act No. 78 of 2006. Entry into force on January 1, 2007.

[170]This English translation was made by Masato Dogauchi et al. See Dogauchi et al. (2007). I would like to express my sincere gratitude here. The translation is also available in Asian-Pacific Law & Policy Journal. See Anderson and Okuda (2006).

[171]See Dogauchi et al. (2007). See also Anderson and Okuda (2006).

[172]See Dogauchi et al. (2007). See also Anderson and Okuda (2006).

[173]Act on General Rules for Application of Laws, Act No. 78 of 2006. Entry into force on January 1, 2007.

[174]Act No. 78 of 2006, Entry into force on January 1, 2007.

Since the applicable law for rights *in rem* in Japan is very clear and strict, it is necessary to give a clearer definition of these rules to allow them to be further informative and well understood. When defining the rights *in rem*, scholarly opinions generally deem it as "a right that allows the right holder to directly control the property.[175]"

As to what is "other rights requiring registration with regard to movables or immovables," Article 581 of Japanese Civil Code (regarding Perfection of Special Agreement on Redemption)[176] and Article 605 of Civil Code (regarding Perfection of Leasehold)[177] are commonly raised as typical examples—yet not exclusive ones—to explain the latter half of this Article's applicable scope.[178] Among various definitions of "registration," for private international law studies the most widely accepted feature is generally determined as: through registration, this right would be effective against any third party.[179]

From this perspective, since the security right in intellectual property is perfected only after being registered in the respective registries, it falls within the category of Article 13 of Japanese private international law (i.e. Act on General Rules for Application of Laws).

The other issue concerns the distinction between what is a movable right and what is an immovable right. Although the two concepts served as different connecting factors, they are assigned the same applicable law ("the law of the place where the subject property is located"). Therefore, scholars and judicial opinions thus do not frequently make a distinction and tend to classify both of them under an overarching umbrella concept called "rights *in rem*."

In other words, no matter whether the security right of intellectual property is classified as a movable right or immovable right under the Japanese Civil Code, since the private international law of Japan (i.e. Act on General Rules for Application of Laws) has already added a third independent connecting factor, that is, "other rights requiring registration," security right in intellectual property automatically falls into this category, and the governing law would thus be the law of the place where the subject property is located.

The applicable scope of Article 13 is generally acknowledged as covering the "acquisition, transfer and loss of the right, as well as defining the specific scope of the right."[180] Therefore, even if this paper touches mainly upon the registration

---

[175]See Kanzaki et al. (2006), p. 200. Other scholars also argue that this control has to be exclusive for anyone who wishes to exercise the same right, see e.g. Matsuoka and Kougi (2008), p. 149.

[176]Article 581 of Japanese Civil Code: If the special agreement on redemption is registered simultaneously with the contract for sale, the redemption shall also be effective against third parties.

[177]Article 605 of Japanese Civil Code: A lease of immovable property, when registered, shall also be effective against a person who subsequently acquires real rights with respect to the immovable property.

[178]See Kanzaki et al. (2006), p. 200. See also Matsuoka and Kougi (2008), p. 153.

[179]See Kanzaki et al. (2006), p. 200.

[180]See Kanzaki et al. (2006), p. 200. See also Matsuoka and Kougi (2008), p. 153.

issue, or more precisely the perfection part of security interest in intellectual property, Article 13 and its *les res situs* principle doubtless applies to and shall also be considered when determining the creation, priority or enforcement aspects of SR-in-IP.

3.3.3 China: The Law of the Place Where the Security Interest Is Created

Compared to other jurisdictions, the law of China is relatively young in terms of its development in the area of conflict-of-laws. Only until very recently, the "Law of the Application of Law for Foreign-related Civil Relations" (中华人民共和国涉外民事关系法律适用法)[181] was promulgated in the People's Republic of China (hereafter "China"). The purpose of the law is to consolidate the divergent Chinese conflict of laws regulations and take a step forwards towards a unified and comprehensive codification of civil law in China.[182]

The law's drafting process started in the early 1990s and the final work is an academic model law which appeared in the year 2000.[183] Chinese legislators were reviewing the first draft in 2002. However, due to other legislative priorities, it was as late as the beginning of 2010 that conflict of laws finally reached the top of the legislative agenda.[184] As a result, it is not surprising that the law contains many omissions and has certain other deficiencies as well. Chinese scholars have welcomed it with mixed feelings since they only had limited influence in the last stage of the drafting process.[185]

This newly promulgated law adopted party autonomy and the closest connection as the main principles. The law furthermore replaces nationality with habitual residence functioning as the principal connecting factor for personal matters in Chinese private international law. However, some omissions still remain and new questions are raised when applying the law.[186] There have been legislative gaps that concern "the form of legal acts, the maintenance duties after divorce as well as the assignment and transfer of rights and duties in general."[187]

With special regard to the SR-in-IP issue and another point of uncertainty concerning rights in movable property, surprisingly, free choice of law is provided by the Chinese private international law. Article 37 may be particularly

[181]The law is passed on October 28, 2010 and effective since April 1, 2011.

[182]So far, there is limited literature written in non-Chinese language on the legislative history and legal interpretation of the new Chinese private international law. For readers who can read German, this article may provide much information. See Pissler (2012).

[183]See Pissler (2012).

[184]See Pissler (2012).

[185]See Pissler (2012). See also Lee (2011), pp. 87–89.

[186]See Pissler (2012). See also Lee (2011), pp. 87–89.

[187]See Pissler (2012). See also Lee (2011), pp. 87–89.

questionable because it is unclear how the rights of any third parties may be protected, when such choice of law is not even publicized, nor third parties provided with vital legal information in general.

The new Chinese private international law grants the parties the right to choose the applicable law for the real rights of chattel.[188] In the absence of applicable law chosen by the parties, the law of the locality of the chattel where the dispute originates shall apply.[189] Besides this, the parties are also free to choose the applicable law for a change of the real rights of chattel in transit; in the absence of a chosen applicable law, the law at the transport destination shall apply.[190] For security interest in rights (pledges of right), the Act provides that the law of the place where the security interest is created applies.[191]

In addition, there are still other provisions that may be applied for intellectual property rights. It is specified that the applicable law for the ownership and content of intellectual property rights is the law at the locality where protection is claimed.[192] Nevertheless, what may draw certain attention is another provision which says that the parties are entitled to the right to choose the applicable law for assignment or license of intellectual property rights.[193] In the absence of such a chosen law, however, the law that applies shall be decided based on Article 41 of the same provision of contract matters of Application of Law for Foreign-related Civil Relations.

The last thing that has to be borne in mind is that, the Supreme People's Court has issued some judicial interpretations which relate to international contract law and tort law in the past to solve certain questions. It nevertheless still remains uncertain whether these interpretations still may apply since the enactment of the new law. Most importantly, it is widely expected that in the near future, the Chinese Supreme People's Court will issue a further judicial interpretation on private international law to assist Chinese courts in applying the new law.[194]

3.3.4 Taiwan: The Law of the Place Where the (Security) Right Is Created (or *Lex Loci Protectionis* for IPRs)

Taiwan also has a private international law ("Act Governing the Choice of Law in Civil Matters Involving Foreign Elements"; "涉外民事法律適用法") which is modified on May 26, 2010.

---

[188]See Article 37 of Law of the Application of Law for Foreign-related Civil Relations.
[189]See Article 37 of Law of the Application of Law for Foreign-related Civil Relations.
[190]See Article 38 Law of the Application of Law for Foreign-related Civil Relations.
[191]See Article 40 Law of the Application of Law for Foreign-related Civil Relations.
[192]See Article 48 Law of the Application of Law for Foreign-related Civil Relations.
[193]See Article 49 Law of the Application of Law for Foreign-related Civil Relations.
[194]See Lee (2011).

The problem with the SR-in-IP issue for Taiwan is perhaps how in fact does the Court characterize "security interest in intellectual property." Shall it be deemed as a general type of rights *in rem*, or shall it be seen as a pledge of right? Moreover, there are also special provisions about intellectual property rights that may be applicable.

Article 38 of the Act Governing the Choice of Law in Civil Matters Involving Foreign Elements provides that the law applicable for *rights in rem* is the law where the property is located (Paragraph 1). The law applicable for *rights in rem* that is created on a right is the law where the right is created (Paragraph 2).[195]

The majority of the scholarly opinions interpreted paragraph 2 of Article 38 as quasi-property and pledges of right.[196] It is hence advised that intellectual property rights or other intangible rights may not be automatically covered in this section.[197]

Article 42 of the Act Governing the Choice of Law in Civil Matters Involving Foreign Elements further illustrates that "the law applicable for a right that is created on intellectual property right is the law where the right is protected." The problem with regard to the interpretation of this article is how to define "the law applicable for a right that is created on intellectual property right." Does it mean intellectual property rights only, or does it extend to any rights that can be created or arise from intellectual property? If the answer is the latter, then the security interest in intellectual property of course falls within it.

Therefore, the law applicable for security interest in intellectual property could be decided either by the law where the security interest is created[198] (Article 38, Paragraph 2) or the law where the collateralized intellectual property right is protected (Article 42, Paragraph 1). In other words, the *lex loci protectionis* principle may or may not apply in the SR-in-IP case in Taiwan, depending on how the two articles are interpreted in court.

3.4 Comparative Choice-of-Law Perspective: The Law Applicable for Mortgage and/or SR in Immovables

3.4.1 The United States: *Lex Loci Rei Sitae*

According to the American Law Institute's authoritative Restatement (First) of Conflict of Laws (1934), it was provided that the validity and effect of a mortgage

---

[195]Paragraph 3 also provides a provision on when the location of a *right in rem* is changed. Paragraph 4, on the other hand, is about the applicable for rights in rem for ships and aircrafts.

[196]Ke (2010), p. 250

[197]See also Article 42, Act Governing the Choice of Law in Civil Matters Involving Foreign Elements.

[198]Another issue here would be "how do we define where the right is created?" Does it refer to the IP registry or the general secured transaction registry?

on land is determined by the law of the state where the land is.[199] Besides, the validity and effect of an assignment of a mortgage on land are determined by the law of the state where the land is.[200] In addition, the method and effect of the foreclosure of a mortgage on land are determined by the law of the state where the land is.[201]

All these rules have been tested in the US courts and were seldom challenged or changed. In the leading case *Burr v. Beckler*,[202] for instance, it is reconfirmed that "the validity, construction, force, and effect of instruments affecting the title to land depend upon the law of the state where the land lies." In other words, it is widely accepted that the *lex loci rei sitae* principle applies to the immovable property and rights emerging from it in the United States.

3.4.2 Japan: Lex Loci Rei Sitae

Since the applicable law rules regarding rights *in rem* are stipulated by the same article, which makes no distinction between movable and immovable property, readers are kindly advised to refer to the previous section which focused on movable property.

In sum, since according to Article 13 of the Act on General Rules for Application of Laws[203] (Rights *in Rem* and Rights Requiring Registration), the first paragraph provides that "rights *in rem* and other rights requiring registration with regard to movables or immovables shall be governed by the law of the place where the subject property is located,"[204] there is no doubt that the *lex loci rei sitae* principle applies to the immovable property rights in Japan.

3.4.3 China: *Lex Loci Rei Sitae*

Article 36 of Law of the Application of Law for Foreign-related Civil Relations of China provides that the law applicable for rights in immovable property is the law where the property is located. In other words, the *lex loci rei sitae* principle applies and determines the applicable law for immovable property in China.

---

[199]See Restatement (First) of Conflict of Laws § 225 (Am. Law Inst. 1934).

[200]See Restatement (First) of Conflict of Laws § 226 (Am. Law Inst. 1934).

[201]See Restatement (First) of Conflict of Laws § 227 (Am. Law Inst. 1934).

[202]Burr v. Beckler, 106 N.E. 206 (Ill. 1914).

[203]Act No. 78 of 2006, Entry into force on January 1, 2007.

[204]This English translation was made possible by Dogauchi et al. (2007). I would like to express my sincere gratitude here. The translation is also available in Asian-Pacific Law & Policy Journal. See Anderson and Okuda (2006).

3.4.4 Taiwan: Lex Loci Rei Sitae

Article 38 of the Act Governing the Choice of Law in Civil Matters Involving Foreign Elements provides that the law applicable for *rights in rem* is the law where the property is located (Paragraph 1). Therefore, the *lex loci rei sitae* principle clearly applies.

4 Concluding Remarks

4.1 The Economics of SR-in-IP

One of the most persuasive rationales that have been raised at UNCITRAL and CLIP favoring the Grantor's Location approach is that it avoids fragmentation of secured transactions and hence lowers the costs of duplicated registration and search.[205] However, this claim is based on two assumptions: (1) the transaction is employing "a portfolio of IPRs" as encumbered assets, so that the cost of perfecting one single security right requires "a portfolio of registrations in separated IPRs registries"; (2) the corresponding relationship of applicable law and designated registry is linear and clear.

However, in reality it is not uncommon that a portfolio of other tangible or intangible assets is also employed as collateral in secured transactions. Why then should IPRs be treated differently from other assets that can be employed as collateral? Put another way, what makes the case of SR-in-IP more controversial than others?

This article starts with this academic curiosity. One possible explanation we provisionally provide is that IP is a unique right that is created to protect a unique asset, i.e. information. Unlike other assets, information has a border-less character in nature. One may create a valuable invention at home and by disseminating the information on internet, it becomes ubiquitous immediately. However, to have this invention protected in the form of property, the current *lex loci protectionis* regime requires patent applications in essentially every jurisdiction in the world. This hence created the unique "self-duplicating" problem of IPRs: namely, the collision between border-less information and territorial IPRs. When a house is built and protected by law, there exists only one right for one property. For IPRs, the number of rights depends on how many markets (jurisdictions) the invention is connected to. Therefore, there can be dozens or hundreds of patents being granted in different countries in order to protect one and the same invention. This "self-duplicating"

[205]See CLIP (2013), p. 35. See also UNCITRAL (2011b), http://www.uncitral.org/pdf/english/texts/security-lg/e/10-57126_Ebook_Suppl_SR_IP.pdf, para. 298. Accessed 17 May 2017.

Rationales raised for and against the Grantor's Location approach and its accompanying footnotes 77–128.

problem affects every aspects of IPRs enforcement on the global level; security interest is merely a piece of the bigger picture.

On the other hand, it is also necessary to distinguish the economic roles of IPRs in different industries. For some, it is common that one single patent or copyright or trademark may play a crucial role in revenue-generating; for others, it is a "combination of IPRs" that actually leads to a final product.[206] When considering using these different assets for secured transaction, it is logical that some IP financers may choose the "single-asset model" while other prefer the "portfolio of assets model," depending on how much value a single IP holds for all the parties concerned. If a single IP is so valuable that even a tiny risk would have to be insured, the secured creditor would want to register in each and every IPR registry. The reason is obvious: because it allows sequent transferees or licensees of this single IP to access the public security interest recordation information, and hence helps establish third-party effectiveness.

The disadvantage, however, is that in most countries, specialized security right in intellectual property registry is indexed against property (IPRs) and is thus available only to "domestic" IPRs. The problem of self-duplication of IPRs and the accompanying security interest registration problem cannot be solved under this current regime, even though it can work well for the "single-asset model".

Grantor's Location is an additional choice that may solve the problem of the inefficient "self-duplication problem" of IPRs, because either the nationality or the habitual residence of a security right holder shall be singular. However, it has to be feasible on the institutional level: that domestic IPR registry takes SR recordation of foreign IPRs. Before that is achieved, two things may have to co-exist and both be acknowledged.

Firstly, not every country has a general secured transaction system, e.g., China. Therefore, adopting a US UCC Article 9 or Japanese *joutotanpo-* type of general secured transaction law is the pre-condition for sound conflict-of-laws rule to work. Second, this general secured transaction system must allow a foreigner (foreign company) to register, so that the singular applicable law (Grantor's Location) approach can be realized.

To sum it up, the transaction cost is at the discretion of parties involved. That transaction cost may also legitimate itself by bringing greater benefits (e.g. wider third-party effectiveness or priority protection) that offset costs from complicated transactions such as registering in every IP registry. Through preserving both choices (the "*Lex Loci Protectionis* plus Specialized Registry"and "Grantor's

[206]"Many people assume that a patented medicine is protected by one particular patent. Unfortunately, it is not as straight-forward as that. Patents do not protect medicines as such, but "inventions". In the pharmaceutical sector, such an invention may for example relate to a product (e.g. a specific molecule), a process (e.g. the process to manufacture this molecule), a medical indication (e.g. the effect of this molecule on a human body), or a combination of products (e.g. a fixed dose combination of two molecules.)" See e.g. Boulet et al. (2003), http://apps.who.int/medicinedocs/en/d/Js4913e/, p. 40. Accessed 18 May 2017.

Location plus General Registry"), a multi-dimensional, "Each-Takes-What-He-Needs" SR-in-IP system can then be realized.

4.2 *Aftermath of UNCITRAL: Registry Guide, Technical Legislative Guide on Implementation, Model Law and the Guide to Enactment*

As previously mentioned, this paper has mainly dealt with the IP Supplement, as it serves as the most extensively discussed document so far, and insofar as it has a spotlight focus on SR-in-IP. After the IP Supplement was published in 2010, however, UNCITRAL made consequent efforts and brought forth new legislative guides, including the following: (1) Draft Security Rights Registry Guide ("Registry Guide"),[207] (2) Draft Technical Legislative Guide on the Implementation of a Security Rights Registry ("Technical Legislative Guide on Implementation"),[208] (3) Draft Model Law on Secured Transactions ("Model Law")[209] and (4) Draft Guide to Enactment of the Draft Model Law on Secured Transactions ("Guide to Enactment").[210] Their applicability and impact on SR-in-IP, however, requires further elaboration.

There are several issues that become noted in these documents. For example, a registry for SR-in-IP is crucial because of the physical limitation of traditional possessory pledges.[211] Some assets, including IPRs, are however subject to specialized registration.[212] General registry and specialized movable property registry thus require proper coordination.[213] Nevertheless, exactly as to how the cross-referencing of these two registries can be made possible, especially when it

---

[207]See UNCITRAL (2011a), https://documents-dds-ny.un.org/doc/UNDOC/LTD/V11/859/00/PDF/V1185900.pdf?OpenElement. Accessed 18 May 2017.

[208]See UNCITRAL (2013), https://documents-dds-ny.un.org/doc/UNDOC/LTD/V13/803/11/PDF/V1380311.pdf?OpenElement. Accessed 18 May 2017.

[209]See UNCITRAL (2015b), https://documents-dds-ny.un.org/doc/UNDOC/LTD/V15/080/04/PDF/V1508004.pdf?OpenElement. Accessed 18 May 2017.

[210]See UNCITRAL (2015a), https://documents-dds-ny.un.org/doc/UNDOC/LTD/V15/083/78/PDF/V1508378.pdf?OpenElement. Accessed 18 May 2017.

[211]See UNCITRAL (2011a), https://documents-dds-ny.un.org/doc/UNDOC/LTD/V11/859/00/PDF/V1185900.pdf?OpenElement, para. 18. Accessed 18 May 2017.

[212]See UNCITRAL (2011a), https://documents-dds-ny.un.org/doc/UNDOC/LTD/V11/859/00/PDF/V1185900.pdf?OpenElement, para. 21. Accessed 18 May 2017.

[213]See UNCITRAL (2011a), https://documents-dds-ny.un.org/doc/UNDOC/LTD/V11/859/00/PDF/V1185900.pdf?OpenElement, para. 52. Accessed 18 May 2017.

comes to the issue of intellectual property licensing,[214] UNCITRAL has yet to provide a concrete answer.

UNCITRAL, however, did indicate priority position when two registries are competing: the registration made in the specialized registry trumps the other.[215] In addition, the Model Law will also defer to any State law relating to intellectual property.[216] Therefore, it is in line with our prior conclusion that at current stage, both choices (the "*Lex Loci Protectionis* plus Specialized Registry" and "Grantor's Location plus General Registry") shall be preserved. Under the current legal regime, participants of secured transactions involving IPRs are advised to take careful consideration of the third-party effectiveness of singular registration. They may have to carefully calculate the enormous cost of global IPR-indexed registrations, and weigh that against its strong effectiveness over future licensees, transferees and/or other competing claimants.

References

American Law Institute (1934) Restatement of law, first, conflict of laws. American Law Institute, Washington DC

American Law Institute (1988) Restatement of law, second, conflict of laws. American Law Institute, Washington DC

Anderson K, Okuda Y (2006) Translation of Japan's private international law: act on the general rules of application of laws [Ho no Tekiyo ni Kansuru Tsusokuho], Law No. 10 of 1898 (as newly titles and amended 21 June 2006). APLPJ 8:138

Borchers PJ (1998) Choice of law relative to security interest and other liens in international bankruptcies. Am J Comp Law Suppl 46:165

Boulet P, Garrison C, Hoen ET (2003) Drug patents under the spotlight: sharing practical knowledge about pharmaceutical patent. http://apps.who.int/medicinedocs/en/d/Js4913e/. Accessed 18 May 2017

CLIP (2011) Principles on conflict of laws in intellectual property. http://www.cl-ip.eu/_www/files/pdf2/Final_Text_1_December_2011.pdf. Accessed 17 May 2017

CLIP (2013) Conflict of laws in intellectual property: the CLIP principles and commentary. Oxford University, Oxford

Collins L, Briggs A, Harris J, McClean JD, McLachlan C, Morse CGJ (2006) Dicey, Morris and Collins on the conflict of laws. Sweet & Maxwell, London

Dogauchi M, Kanzaki T, Hayakawa Y, Nishitani Y, Nakanishi Y, Kitazawa A (2007) New private international law of Japan. Jpn Annu Int Law 50:3–87

[214]At Preface. See UNCITRAL (2011a), https://documents-dds-ny.un.org/doc/UNDOC/LTD/V11/859/00/PDF/V1185900.pdf?OpenElement, p. 3. Security interest of intellectual property licensing is nevertheless included in the Draft Model Law. See UNCITRAL (2015b), https://documents-dds-ny.un.org/doc/UNDOC/LTD/V15/080/04/PDF/V1508004.pdf?OpenElement, p. 4 and Article 13-4(b), p. 11. Accessed 18 May 2017.

[215]See UNCITRAL (2013), https://documents-dds-ny.un.org/doc/UNDOC/LTD/V13/803/11/PDF/V1380311.pdf?OpenElement, para. 38. Accessed 18 May 2017.

[216]See UNCITRAL (2015a), https://documents-dds-ny.un.org/doc/UNDOC/LTD/V15/083/78/PDF/V1508378.pdf?OpenElement, para. 36. Accessed 18 May 2017.

Haemmerli A (1996) Insecurity interests: where intellectual property and commercial law collide. Columbia Law Rev 96:1645–1752
Hagedorn RB (2007) Secured transaction in a nutshell. West, St Paul
Hay P, Weintraub R, Borchers P (2009) Conflict of Laws, Foundation Press, New York
Kanzaki T, Hayakawa Y, Motonaga K (2006) Ko ku sai shi hou (Private international law). Yuhikaku, Tokyo
Ke ZD (2010) Guo ji si fa (Private international law). Angel, Taipei
Lee SY (2011) Guo ji si fa xue (Private international law). Peking University Press, Beijing
Lu ZY (2007) Zhuan li quan zhi ya rong zi xian zhuang fen xi (Analysis of the state of patent pledge financing). China Invention Pat 6:45–47
Lui C (2011) Navigating through the legal minefield of state and federal filing for perfecting security interests in intellectual property. Santa Clara Law Rev 51:705
Matsuoka H (2008) Gen dai ko ku sai shi hou kou gi (Lectures on private international law). Houritsubunkasha, Kyoto
Nguyen XT (2002) Commercial law collides with cyberspace: the trouble with perfection—insecurity interests in the new corporate asset. Wash Lee Law Rev 59(1):37
Nordstrom RJ, Murray JE Jr, Clovis AL (1987) Problems and materials on secured transactions. West, St Paul
Pissler KB (2012) Das neue internationale privatrecht der volksrepublik China: nach den steinen tastend den fluss überqueren (The new private international law of the People's Republic of China: cross the river by feeling the stones). Rabels Zeitschrift fuer auslaendisches und internationales Privatrecht 76(1):1–46
SIPO (2007) China intellectual property yearbook 2006. Knowledge Press, Beijing
UNCITRAL (1997) Model law on cross-border insolvency. http://www.uncitral.org/uncitral/en/uncitral_texts/insolvency/1997Model.html. Accessed 22 May 2017
UNCITRAL (2002) Report of Working Group VI (Security Interests) on the work of its first session. https://documents-dds-ny.un.org/doc/UNDOC/GEN/V02/549/74/PDF/V0254974.pdf?OpenElement. Accessed 16 May 2017
UNCITRAL (2007) Report of Working Group VI (Security Interests) on the work of its twelfth session. https://documents-dds-ny.un.org/doc/UNDOC/GEN/V07/810/60/PDF/V0781060.pdf?OpenElement. Accessed 16 May 2017
UNCITRAL (2008a) Annex to the UNCITRAL legislative guide on secured transactions dealing with security rights in intellectual property (Part 2). https://documents-dds-ny.un.org/doc/UNDOC/LTD/V08/562/95/PDF/V0856295.pdf?OpenElement. Accessed 16 May 2017
UNCITRAL (2008b) Report of Working Group VI (Security Interests) on the work of its fourteenth session. https://documents-dds-ny.un.org/doc/UNDOC/GEN/V08/577/88/PDF/V0857788.pdf?OpenElement, para 124. Accessed 16 May 2017
UNCITRAL (2008c) Report of Working Group VI (Security Interests) on the work of its thirteenth session. https://documents-dds-ny.un.org/doc/UNDOC/GEN/V08/539/36/PDF/V0853936.pdf?OpenElement. Accessed 16 May 2017
UNCITRAL (2008d) Security rights in intellectual property rights. https://documents-dds-ny.un.org/doc/UNDOC/LTD/V08/521/28/PDF/V0852128.pdf?OpenElement. Accessed 16 May 2017
UNCITRAL (2009a) Draft annex to the UNCITRAL legislative guide on secured transactions dealing with security rights in intellectual property. https://documents-dds-ny.un.org/doc/UNDOC/LTD/V09/808/23/PDF/V0980823.pdf?OpenElement. Accessed 16 May 2017
UNCITRAL (2009b) Draft supplement to the UNCITRAL legislative guide on secured transactions dealing with security rights in intellectual property: proposal by the Permanent Bureau Of The Hague Conference on private international law. https://documents-dds-ny.un.org/doc/UNDOC/LTD/V09/855/76/PDF/V0985576.pdf?OpenElement. Accessed 16 May 2017
UNCITRAL (2009c) Draft supplement to the UNCITRAL legislative guide on secured transactions dealing with security rights in intellectual property. https://documents-dds-ny.un.org/doc/UNDOC/LTD/V09/855/16/PDF/V0985516.pdf?OpenElement. Accessed 16 May 2017

UNCITRAL (2009d) Draft supplement to the UNCITRAL legislative guide on secured transactions dealing with security rights in intellectual property. https://documents-dds-ny.un.org/doc/UNDOC/LTD/V09/885/80/PDF/V0988580.pdf?OpenElement. Accessed 16 May 2017

UNCITRAL (2009e) Report of Working Group VI (Security Interests) on the work of its sixteenth session. https://documents-dds-ny.un.org/doc/UNDOC/GEN/V09/877/38/PDF/V0987738.pdf?OpenElement. Accessed 16 May 2017

UNCITRAL (2010a) Report of Working Group VI (Security Interests) on the work of its seventeenth session. https://documents-dds-ny.un.org/doc/UNDOC/GEN/V10/511/34/PDF/V1051134.pdf?OpenElement. Accessed 16 May 2017

UNCITRAL (2010b) UNCITRAL legislative guide on secured transactions. https://www.uncitral.org/pdf/english/texts/security-lg/e/09-82670_Ebook-Guide_09-04-10English.pdf. Accessed 22 May 2017

UNCITRAL (2011a) Draft security rights registry guide. https://documents-dds-ny.un.org/doc/UNDOC/LTD/V11/859/00/PDF/V1185900.pdf?OpenElement. Accessed 18 May 2017

UNCITRAL (2011b) UNCITRAL legislative guide on secured transactions: supplement on security rights in intellectual property. http://www.uncitral.org/pdf/english/texts/security-lg/e/10-57126_Ebook_Suppl_SR_IP.pdf. Accessed 16 May 2017

UNCITRAL (2013) Draft Technical Legislative Guide on the Implementation of a Security Rights Registry. https://documents-dds-ny.un.org/doc/UNDOC/LTD/V13/803/11/PDF/V1380311.pdf?OpenElement. Accessed 18 May 2017

UNCITRAL (2015a) Draft guide to enactment of the draft model law on secured transactions. https://documents-dds-ny.un.org/doc/UNDOC/LTD/V15/083/78/PDF/V1508378.pdf?OpenElement. Accessed 18 May 2017

UNCITRAL (2015b) Draft model law on secured transactions. https://documents-dds-ny.un.org/doc/UNDOC/LTD/V15/080/04/PDF/V1508004.pdf?OpenElement. Accessed 18 May 2017

Whaley DJ, McJohn SM (2014) Problems and materials on secured transactions. Wolters Kluwer, Alphen aan den Rijn

UNCITRAL's Contribution to Intellectual Property Financing Law

Spyridon V. Bazinas

Abstract The UNCITRAL Legislative Guide on Secured Transactions (the "Guide") and the Supplement on Security Rights in Intellectual Property (the "Supplement") are intended to provide guidance to legislators on issues relating to the creation, third-party effectiveness, priority and enforcement (even in the grantor's insolvency) of a security interest in intellectual property, as well as on the law applicable to such matters. The commentary of the Supplement explains how the legislative recommendations of both the Guide and the Supplement apply in the context of an intellectual property financing transaction. With the same goal in mind, the recommendations of the Supplement modify the general legislative recommendations of the Guide as they apply to security interests in intellectual property. The Supplement breaks new ground by: (a) suggesting new ways to improve the coordination between secured transactions and intellectual property law; (b) introducing a regime that facilitates the use of intellectual property as security for credit, including secured credit to be used for the acquisition of intellectual property; (c) suggesting ways in which the investment of intellectual property licensors or licensees in developing and marketing a licensed product may be protected in the case of insolvency; and (d) recommending a a conflict-of-laws rule dealing with the law applicable to security interests in intellectual property.

Senior Legal Officer, International Trade Law Division, Office of Legal Affairs (which serves as the Secretariat of UNCITRAL). The views expressed in this article are the personal views of the author and do not necessarily represent the views of the United Nations or UNCITRAL. This article is based on a presentation made at an International Symposium on Intellectual Property and Venture Capital: The Secrets to Building Innovation Ecosystems, which was held at the University of Tokyo on 4 and 5 September 2014 and an article by the same author published in the Uniform Commercial Code Law Journal, vol. 43 # 2, Fall 2010, 601.

S.V. Bazinas (✉)
Vienna Int'l Centre, Vienna, Austria
e-mail: spiros.bazinas@uncitral.org

T. Kono (ed.), *Security Interests in Intellectual Property*, Perspectives in Law, Business and Innovation, DOI 10.1007/978-981-10-5415-0_4

1 Introduction

To a large extent, economic development depends on innovation which, typically requires expensive and extensive research and development activities, and is generally protected through intellectual property rights.[1] Yet, all over the world, the law relating to financing with intellectual property as collateral ("intellectual property financing")[2] is either underdeveloped or not sufficiently well-coordinated with the laws governing secured financing and insolvency.[3] Thus, great uncertainty prevails as to the law applicable to security interests in intellectual property which is bound to have a negative impact on the cost and the availability of credit to intellectual property right holders.[4]

The Supplement on Security Rights in Intellectual Property (hereinafter referred to as the "Supplement"), which the United Nations Commission on International Trade Law ("UNCITRAL") adopted in July 2010,[5] provides guidance to States that wish to facilitate intellectual property financing by adopting a secured financing regime along the lines of the regime recommended in the UNCITRAL Legislative Guide on Secured Transactions (hereinafter referred to as the "Guide"), which UNCITRAL adopted in December 2007.[6]

The overall objective of the Supplement is to promote the availability of secured credit to intellectual property right holders at more affordable rates, thus enhancing the value of intellectual property as security for credit.[7] At the same time, the Supplement seeks to achieve this objective without interfering with fundamental State policies of intellectual property law,[8] taking intellectual property as it is defined by, and if it may be encumbered under, law relating to intellectual property.[9]

---

[1]This article is not intended to address the questions of whether an idea is really innovative and, if so, whether it should be protected by an intellectual property right.

[2]This article is not intended to discuss intellectual property financing through participation in the equity of start-ups, intellectual property licensing or securitization of royalties.

[3]See Philips (2008), http://www.wipo.int/wipo_magazine/en/2008/05/article_0002.html. Accessed 19 May 2017.

[4]For a comparative examination of intellectual property finance issues, see Knopf (2002).

[5]UNCITRAL (2010a), https://documents-dds-ny.un.org/doc/UNDOC/GEN/V10/556/48/PDF/V1055648.pdf?OpenElement, para. 227. Accessed 19 May 2017.

[6]UNCITRAL (2007), https://documents-dds-ny.un.org/doc/UNDOC/GEN/V07/857/09/PDF/V0785709.pdf?OpenElement, paras. 99 and 100. Accessed 19 May 2017.

[7]UNCITRAL (2011), https://www.uncitral.org/pdf/english/texts/security-lg/e/10-57126_Ebook_Suppl_SR_IP.pdf, paras. 46–47. See also recommendation 1 (a), at UNCITRAL (2010d), https://www.uncitral.org/pdf/english/texts/security-lg/e/09-82670_Ebook-Guide_09-04-10English.pdf, p. 30. Accessed 19 May 2017.

[8]UNCITRAL (2011), https://www.uncitral.org/pdf/english/texts/security-lg/e/10-57126_Ebook_Suppl_SR_IP.pdf, para. 1. Accessed 19 May 2017. See also recommendation 4 (b), at UNCITRAL (2010d), https://www.uncitral.org/pdf/english/texts/security-lg/e/09-82670_Ebook-Guide_09-04-10English.pdf, p. 62. Accessed 19 May 2017.

[9]UNCITRAL (2011), https://www.uncitral.org/pdf/english/texts/security-lg/e/10-57126_Ebook_Suppl_SR_IP.pdf, para. 55. Accessed 19 May 2017. See also recommendation 18, at

The purpose of this article is to briefly explain the salient features of intellectual property financing under the Supplement and in particular, the Supplement's innovative approaches to coordination between security interests and intellectual property law (Sect. 1), acquisition financing in an intellectual property context (Sect. 2), the law applicable to security interests in intellectual property (Sect. 3) and the impact of insolvency of a licensor or licensee on a security interest in that party's rights (Sect. 4).

2 Coordination Between Security Interests and Intellectual Property Law

As already mentioned, the overall objective of the Guide is to the availability of secured credit at more affordable rates. To achieve this objective, the Guide formulates a number of objectives, such as predictability, transparency, equal treatment of the various sources of credit, as well as balancing the interests of all affected persons.[10] The Guide also reflects certain fundamental policies, including the functional, unitary and comprehensive approach to secured transactions.[11] All these key objectives and fundamental policies apply equally to an intellectual property context.[12] This means that the overall objective of the Supplement is to facilitate the extension of credit to intellectual property owners and other right holders, enhancing the value of intellectual property rights as security for credit.

The Supplement, however, seeks to achieve this objective in a way that does not interfere with the rights of intellectual property owners and other right holders under law relating to intellectual property, contract law or general property law. This means, for example, that the Supplement does not affect the content or impede the protection of an intellectual property right. It also means that nothing in the Supplement diminishes the value of intellectual property rights or causes confusion as to the source of products or services. Furthermore, it means that nothing in the Supplement affects the terms and conditions of licence agreements.[13]

(Footnote 9 continued)

UNCITRAL (2010d), https://www.uncitral.org/pdf/english/texts/security-lg/e/09-82670_Ebook-Guide_09-04-10English.pdf, p. 98. Accessed 19 May 2017.

[10]See recommendation 1 (d), (f), (g) and (j), at UNCITRAL (2010d), https://www.uncitral.org/pdf/english/texts/security-lg/e/09-82670_Ebook-Guide_09-04-10English.pdf, p. 30. Accessed 19 May 2017.

[11]UNCITRAL (2010d), https://www.uncitral.org/pdf/english/texts/security-lg/e/09-82670_Ebook-Guide_09-04-10English.pdf, paras. 60–72 and p. 62. Accessed 19 May 2017.

[12]UNCITRAL (2011), https://www.uncitral.org/pdf/english/texts/security-lg/e/10-57126_Ebook_Suppl_SR_IP.pdf, paras. 80–81. Accessed 19 May 2017.

[13]UNCITRAL (2011), https://www.uncitral.org/pdf/english/texts/security-lg/e/10-57126_Ebook_Suppl_SR_IP.pdf, paras. 49–52. Accessed 19 May 2017.

by both asset description and grantor identifier. Such a coordination of registries would certainly require that States review and revise not only their secured transactions laws but also their intellectual property laws.

Another way of coordination of registries discussed in the Guide and the Supplement is to link registries electronically in such a way that information entered in one registry will appear as well in the others, so that wherever a party searches it will be able to discover all security interests relating to certain assets or assets of a certain debtor (however, to achieve such a purpose both asset- and debtor-based indices would be necessary).[24] This is a matter discussed further in the UNCITRAL Guide on the Implementation of a Security Rights Registry (2013; the "Registry Guide").[25]

3 Acquisition Financing

3.1 *The Need for a Special Treatment of Intellectual Property Acquisition Financing*

The idea of a special regime for security interests securing the price for the acquisition of intellectual property or rights of a licensee under an intellectual property licence agreement is in principle not unknown. However, according to empirical evidence, its application has been rather limited. By establishing such a regime, the Supplement is intended to facilitate the extension of credit to persons that create and acquire intellectual property rights and rights of a licensee under an intellectual property licence agreement.[26]

The basic idea is that a lender providing the funds for the acquisition of intellectual property or for obtaining a licence of intellectual property deserves to be treated in the same way as a lender providing the funds for the acquisition of goods. The main reasons are that: (a) without those funds, the buyer may not be able to acquire the goods; and (b) with those funds the estate of the buyer is enriched to the benefit of all creditors.

In essence, the Supplement implements in an intellectual property context the super-priority given to a retention-of-title seller or an acquisition-secured creditor. This approach is intended to support the acquisition of intellectual property rights, as well as of licensee rights under an intellectual property licence agreement.

[24]UNCITRAL (2011), https://www.uncitral.org/pdf/english/texts/security-lg/e/10-57126_Ebook_Suppl_SR_IP.pdf, para. 140. Accessed 19 May 2017.

[25]UNCITRAL (2014a), http://www.uncitral.org/pdf/english/texts/security/Security-Rights-Registry-Guide-e.pdf, paras. 64–70. Accessed 19 May 2017.

[26]Brennan (2008), http://www.wipo.int/wipo_magazine/en/2008/05/article_0004.html. Accessed 19 May 2017.

The purpose of this article is to briefly explain the salient features of intellectual property financing under the Supplement and in particular, the Supplement's innovative approaches to coordination between security interests and intellectual property law (Sect. 1), acquisition financing in an intellectual property context (Sect. 2), the law applicable to security interests in intellectual property (Sect. 3) and the impact of insolvency of a licensor or licensee on a security interest in that party's rights (Sect. 4).

2 Coordination Between Security Interests and Intellectual Property Law

As already mentioned, the overall objective of the Guide is to the availability of secured credit at more affordable rates. To achieve this objective, the Guide formulates a number of objectives, such as predictability, transparency, equal treatment of the various sources of credit, as well as balancing the interests of all affected persons.[10] The Guide also reflects certain fundamental policies, including the functional, unitary and comprehensive approach to secured transactions.[11] All these key objectives and fundamental policies apply equally to an intellectual property context.[12] This means that the overall objective of the Supplement is to facilitate the extension of credit to intellectual property owners and other right holders, enhancing the value of intellectual property rights as security for credit.

The Supplement, however, seeks to achieve this objective in a way that does not interfere with the rights of intellectual property owners and other right holders under law relating to intellectual property, contract law or general property law. This means, for example, that the Supplement does not affect the content or impede the protection of an intellectual property right. It also means that nothing in the Supplement diminishes the value of intellectual property rights or causes confusion as to the source of products or services. Furthermore, it means that nothing in the Supplement affects the terms and conditions of licence agreements.[13]

(Footnote 9 continued)

UNCITRAL (2010d), https://www.uncitral.org/pdf/english/texts/security-lg/e/09-82670_Ebook-Guide_09-04-10English.pdf, p. 98. Accessed 19 May 2017.

[10]See recommendation 1 (d), (f), (g) and (j), at UNCITRAL (2010d), https://www.uncitral.org/pdf/english/texts/security-lg/e/09-82670_Ebook-Guide_09-04-10English.pdf, p. 30. Accessed 19 May 2017.

[11]UNCITRAL (2010d), https://www.uncitral.org/pdf/english/texts/security-lg/e/09-82670_Ebook-Guide_09-04-10English.pdf, paras. 60–72 and p. 62. Accessed 19 May 2017.

[12]UNCITRAL (2011), https://www.uncitral.org/pdf/english/texts/security-lg/e/10-57126_Ebook_Suppl_SR_IP.pdf, paras. 80–81. Accessed 19 May 2017.

[13]UNCITRAL (2011), https://www.uncitral.org/pdf/english/texts/security-lg/e/10-57126_Ebook_Suppl_SR_IP.pdf, paras. 49–52. Accessed 19 May 2017.

by both asset description and grantor identifier. Such a coordination of registries would certainly require that States review and revise not only their secured transactions laws but also their intellectual property laws.

Another way of coordination of registries discussed in the Guide and the Supplement is to link registries electronically in such a way that information entered in one registry will appear as well in the others, so that wherever a party searches it will be able to discover all security interests relating to certain assets or assets of a certain debtor (however, to achieve such a purpose both asset- and debtor-based indices would be necessary).[24] This is a matter discussed further in the UNCITRAL Guide on the Implementation of a Security Rights Registry (2013; the "Registry Guide").[25]

3 Acquisition Financing

3.1 The Need for a Special Treatment of Intellectual Property Acquisition Financing

The idea of a special regime for security interests securing the price for the acquisition of intellectual property or rights of a licensee under an intellectual property licence agreement is in principle not unknown. However, according to empirical evidence, its application has been rather limited. By establishing such a regime, the Supplement is intended to facilitate the extension of credit to persons that create and acquire intellectual property rights and rights of a licensee under an intellectual property licence agreement.[26]

The basic idea is that a lender providing the funds for the acquisition of intellectual property or for obtaining a licence of intellectual property deserves to be treated in the same way as a lender providing the funds for the acquisition of goods. The main reasons are that: (a) without those funds, the buyer may not be able to acquire the goods; and (b) with those funds the estate of the buyer is enriched to the benefit of all creditors.

In essence, the Supplement implements in an intellectual property context the super-priority given to a retention-of-title seller or an acquisition-secured creditor. This approach is intended to support the acquisition of intellectual property rights, as well as of licensee rights under an intellectual property licence agreement.

---

[24]UNCITRAL (2011), https://www.uncitral.org/pdf/english/texts/security-lg/e/10-57126_Ebook_Suppl_SR_IP.pdf, para. 140. Accessed 19 May 2017.

[25]UNCITRAL (2014a), http://www.uncitral.org/pdf/english/texts/security/Security-Rights-Registry-Guide-e.pdf, paras. 64–70. Accessed 19 May 2017.

[26]Brennan (2008), http://www.wipo.int/wipo_magazine/en/2008/05/article_0004.html. Accessed 19 May 2017.

The purpose of this article is to briefly explain the salient features of intellectual property financing under the Supplement and in particular, the Supplement's innovative approaches to coordination between security interests and intellectual property law (Sect. 1), acquisition financing in an intellectual property context (Sect. 2), the law applicable to security interests in intellectual property (Sect. 3) and the impact of insolvency of a licensor or licensee on a security interest in that party's rights (Sect. 4).

2 Coordination Between Security Interests and Intellectual Property Law

As already mentioned, the overall objective of the Guide is to the availability of secured credit at more affordable rates. To achieve this objective, the Guide formulates a number of objectives, such as predictability, transparency, equal treatment of the various sources of credit, as well as balancing the interests of all affected persons.[10] The Guide also reflects certain fundamental policies, including the functional, unitary and comprehensive approach to secured transactions.[11] All these key objectives and fundamental policies apply equally to an intellectual property context.[12] This means that the overall objective of the Supplement is to facilitate the extension of credit to intellectual property owners and other right holders, enhancing the value of intellectual property rights as security for credit.

The Supplement, however, seeks to achieve this objective in a way that does not interfere with the rights of intellectual property owners and other right holders under law relating to intellectual property, contract law or general property law. This means, for example, that the Supplement does not affect the content or impede the protection of an intellectual property right. It also means that nothing in the Supplement diminishes the value of intellectual property rights or causes confusion as to the source of products or services. Furthermore, it means that nothing in the Supplement affects the terms and conditions of licence agreements.[13]

(Footnote 9 continued)

UNCITRAL (2010d), https://www.uncitral.org/pdf/english/texts/security-lg/e/09-82670_Ebook-Guide_09-04-10English.pdf, p. 98. Accessed 19 May 2017.

[10]See recommendation 1 (d), (f), (g) and (j), at UNCITRAL (2010d), https://www.uncitral.org/pdf/english/texts/security-lg/e/09-82670_Ebook-Guide_09-04-10English.pdf, p. 30. Accessed 19 May 2017.

[11]UNCITRAL (2010d), https://www.uncitral.org/pdf/english/texts/security-lg/e/09-82670_Ebook-Guide_09-04-10English.pdf, paras. 60–72 and p. 62. Accessed 19 May 2017.

[12]UNCITRAL (2011), https://www.uncitral.org/pdf/english/texts/security-lg/e/10-57126_Ebook_Suppl_SR_IP.pdf, paras. 80–81. Accessed 19 May 2017.

[13]UNCITRAL (2011), https://www.uncitral.org/pdf/english/texts/security-lg/e/10-57126_Ebook_Suppl_SR_IP.pdf, paras. 49–52. Accessed 19 May 2017.

by both asset description and grantor identifier. Such a coordination of registries would certainly require that States review and revise not only their secured transactions laws but also their intellectual property laws.

Another way of coordination of registries discussed in the Guide and the Supplement is to link registries electronically in such a way that information entered in one registry will appear as well in the others, so that wherever a party searches it will be able to discover all security interests relating to certain assets or assets of a certain debtor (however, to achieve such a purpose both asset- and debtor-based indices would be necessary).[24] This is a matter discussed further in the UNCITRAL Guide on the Implementation of a Security Rights Registry (2013; the "Registry Guide").[25]

3 Acquisition Financing

3.1 The Need for a Special Treatment of Intellectual Property Acquisition Financing

The idea of a special regime for security interests securing the price for the acquisition of intellectual property or rights of a licensee under an intellectual property licence agreement is in principle not unknown. However, according to empirical evidence, its application has been rather limited. By establishing such a regime, the Supplement is intended to facilitate the extension of credit to persons that create and acquire intellectual property rights and rights of a licensee under an intellectual property licence agreement.[26]

The basic idea is that a lender providing the funds for the acquisition of intellectual property or for obtaining a licence of intellectual property deserves to be treated in the same way as a lender providing the funds for the acquisition of goods. The main reasons are that: (a) without those funds, the buyer may not be able to acquire the goods; and (b) with those funds the estate of the buyer is enriched to the benefit of all creditors.

In essence, the Supplement implements in an intellectual property context the super-priority given to a retention-of-title seller or an acquisition-secured creditor. This approach is intended to support the acquisition of intellectual property rights, as well as of licensee rights under an intellectual property licence agreement.

---

[24]UNCITRAL (2011), https://www.uncitral.org/pdf/english/texts/security-lg/e/10-57126_Ebook_Suppl_SR_IP.pdf, para. 140. Accessed 19 May 2017.

[25]UNCITRAL (2014a), http://www.uncitral.org/pdf/english/texts/security/Security-Rights-Registry-Guide-e.pdf, paras. 64–70. Accessed 19 May 2017.

[26]Brennan (2008), http://www.wipo.int/wipo_magazine/en/2008/05/article_0004.html. Accessed 19 May 2017.

The purpose of this article is to briefly explain the salient features of intellectual property financing under the Supplement and in particular, the Supplement's innovative approaches to coordination between security interests and intellectual property law (Sect. 1), acquisition financing in an intellectual property context (Sect. 2), the law applicable to security interests in intellectual property (Sect. 3) and the impact of insolvency of a licensor or licensee on a security interest in that party's rights (Sect. 4).

2 Coordination Between Security Interests and Intellectual Property Law

As already mentioned, the overall objective of the Guide is to the availability of secured credit at more affordable rates. To achieve this objective, the Guide formulates a number of objectives, such as predictability, transparency, equal treatment of the various sources of credit, as well as balancing the interests of all affected persons.[10] The Guide also reflects certain fundamental policies, including the functional, unitary and comprehensive approach to secured transactions.[11] All these key objectives and fundamental policies apply equally to an intellectual property context.[12] This means that the overall objective of the Supplement is to facilitate the extension of credit to intellectual property owners and other right holders, enhancing the value of intellectual property rights as security for credit.

The Supplement, however, seeks to achieve this objective in a way that does not interfere with the rights of intellectual property owners and other right holders under law relating to intellectual property, contract law or general property law. This means, for example, that the Supplement does not affect the content or impede the protection of an intellectual property right. It also means that nothing in the Supplement diminishes the value of intellectual property rights or causes confusion as to the source of products or services. Furthermore, it means that nothing in the Supplement affects the terms and conditions of licence agreements.[13]

(Footnote 9 continued)

UNCITRAL (2010d), https://www.uncitral.org/pdf/english/texts/security-lg/e/09-82670_Ebook-Guide_09-04-10English.pdf, p. 98. Accessed 19 May 2017.

[10]See recommendation 1 (d), (f), (g) and (j), at UNCITRAL (2010d), https://www.uncitral.org/pdf/english/texts/security-lg/e/09-82670_Ebook-Guide_09-04-10English.pdf, p. 30. Accessed 19 May 2017.

[11]UNCITRAL (2010d), https://www.uncitral.org/pdf/english/texts/security-lg/e/09-82670_Ebook-Guide_09-04-10English.pdf, paras. 60–72 and p. 62. Accessed 19 May 2017.

[12]UNCITRAL (2011), https://www.uncitral.org/pdf/english/texts/security-lg/e/10-57126_Ebook_Suppl_SR_IP.pdf, paras. 80–81. Accessed 19 May 2017.

[13]UNCITRAL (2011), https://www.uncitral.org/pdf/english/texts/security-lg/e/10-57126_Ebook_Suppl_SR_IP.pdf, paras. 49–52. Accessed 19 May 2017.

According to the principle enshrined in recommendation 4, subparagraph (b), the Guide and the Supplement defer to intellectual property law (defined in a broad way to include national law and international treaties) if an issue is addressed in that law in an asset-specific rule that is different way from the rule recommended in the Guide. For example, the Guide and the Supplement defer to intellectual property law as to the registration of a security interest in an intellectual property registry but do not defer with respect to a transfer of title in intellectual property for security purposes, which they treat as a security device.

Deference to the State's intellectual property-specific rules dealing with security interests in intellectual property rights is certainly a limitation to the Supplement and its harmonization effect, but it is necessary in view of the need to facilitate the extension of credit to intellectual property right holders, without interfering with the fundamental policies of law relating to intellectual property. This limitation, however, relates only to matters with respect to which an overlap and/or conflict between secured transactions and intellectual property law is possible: that is, matters relating to the creation, third-party effectiveness, priority and enforcement of a security interest in an intellectual property right. Issues relating to the creation, effectiveness, priority and protection of an intellectual property right are exclusively matters of intellectual property law.

To the extent that issues of coordination between secured transactions and intellectual property law arise as a result of the "principle of deference to intellectual property law" (for example, whether a notice of a security interest may be registered in an intellectual property rights registry to make the security interest effective against third parties), the Supplement deals with them with modest suggestions in its commentary as to how States enacting a secured transactions law based on the recommendations of the Guide and the Supplement might amend their intellectual property law.[14]

Moreover, the terminological clarifications made in the Supplement are also important for the coordination of security interests and intellectual property laws, as some of the key common terms are understood differently in a secured transactions context from that of an intellectual property context. For example, under secured transactions law, the term "secured creditor" means a person who is not the owner unless it acquires the encumbered asset in the context of enforcement. To the contrary, under intellectual property law, the term "secured creditor" may include the owner or a person with the rights of an owner, such as the right to renew registrations and pursue infringements.[15]

Another such example is the term "encumbered asset". In a secured transactions context, an intellectual property right is just another intangible asset, provided that it

[14]UNCITRAL (2011), https://www.uncitral.org/pdf/english/texts/security-lg/e/10-57126_Ebook_Suppl_SR_IP.pdf, paras. 135–140. Accessed 19 May 2017.

[15]UNCITRAL (2011), https://www.uncitral.org/pdf/english/texts/security-lg/e/10-57126_Ebook_Suppl_SR_IP.pdf, paras. 29–30. Accessed 19 May 2017.

has economic value. Whether an asset has economic value is a practical and not a legal issue. Thus, it is discussed in the Supplement,[16] but no rule is recommended in the Supplement for inclusion in secured transactions law.

In an intellectual property context, an intellectual property right is the heroic expression of intellectual effort and as such has to be handled with care and caution.[17] The Supplement simply recognizes that the determination of what exactly the asset is and whether it may be encumbered, is a matter of intellectual property law, not of secured transactions law.[18]

Coordination is also achieved between the security interest registry and a specialized registry (e.g., a patent or trademark registry), if a State has such a specialized registry. The Supplement does not, however, recommend the creation of specialized registries for States that do not have such a specialized registry.[19]

The Guide and the Supplement address this issue in three ways: (a) by way of a hierarchy rule, according to which, if intellectual property law provides that a security interest in intellectual property has to be registered in an intellectual property registry or has other provisions that are inconsistent with the registration-related provisions of the Guide,[20] intellectual property law will prevail[21]; (b) by way of a priority rule, according to which a security interest made effective against third parties by registration in an intellectual property registry has priority over a security interest registered in the security interest registry[22]; and (c) by way of coordination of registries so that the different types of registry will be compatible or linked with each other.[23] For example, an intellectual property registry system could allow the registration of notices relating to possible security interests in present or future intellectual property rights with third-party effects, establish and maintain both asset-based and name-based indices and allow searches

[16]UNCITRAL (2011), https://www.uncitral.org/pdf/english/texts/security-lg/e/10-57126_Ebook_Suppl_SR_IP.pdf, paras. 33–34. Accessed 19 May 2017.

[17]At one of the initial informal meetings, an intellectual property law expert remarked: "You cannot give a secured lender an intellectual property right as collateral. It is like giving a Stradivarius violin to a gorilla. The gorilla can only destroy it!".

[18]UNCITRAL (2011), https://www.uncitral.org/pdf/english/texts/security-lg/e/10-57126_Ebook_Suppl_SR_IP.pdf, paras. 13–16. Accessed 19 May 2017.

[19]UNCITRAL (2011), https://www.uncitral.org/pdf/english/texts/security-lg/e/10-57126_Ebook_Suppl_SR_IP.pdf, para. 135. Accessed 19 May 2017.

[20]Recommendation 38. See UNCITRAL (2010d), https://www.uncitral.org/pdf/english/texts/security-lg/e/09-82670_Ebook-Guide_09-04-10English.pdf, p. 144. Accessed 19 May 2017.

[21]Recommendation 4, subparagraph (b). UNCITRAL (2010d), https://www.uncitral.org/pdf/english/texts/security-lg/e/09-82670_Ebook-Guide_09-04-10English.pdf, p. 62. Accessed 19 May 2017.

[22]Recommendation 77, subparagraph (a). See UNCITRAL (2010d), https://www.uncitral.org/pdf/english/texts/security-lg/e/09-82670_Ebook-Guide_09-04-10English.pdf, p. 230. Accessed 19 May 2017.

[23]See UNCITRAL (2011), https://www.uncitral.org/pdf/english/texts/security-lg/e/10-57126_Ebook_Suppl_SR_IP.pdf, para. 138. Accessed 19 May 2017.

by both asset description and grantor identifier. Such a coordination of registries would certainly require that States review and revise not only their secured transactions laws but also their intellectual property laws.

Another way of coordination of registries discussed in the Guide and the Supplement is to link registries electronically in such a way that information entered in one registry will appear as well in the others, so that wherever a party searches it will be able to discover all security interests relating to certain assets or assets of a certain debtor (however, to achieve such a purpose both asset- and debtor-based indices would be necessary).[24] This is a matter discussed further in the UNCITRAL Guide on the Implementation of a Security Rights Registry (2013; the "Registry Guide").[25]

3 Acquisition Financing

3.1 The Need for a Special Treatment of Intellectual Property Acquisition Financing

The idea of a special regime for security interests securing the price for the acquisition of intellectual property or rights of a licensee under an intellectual property licence agreement is in principle not unknown. However, according to empirical evidence, its application has been rather limited. By establishing such a regime, the Supplement is intended to facilitate the extension of credit to persons that create and acquire intellectual property rights and rights of a licensee under an intellectual property licence agreement.[26]

The basic idea is that a lender providing the funds for the acquisition of intellectual property or for obtaining a licence of intellectual property deserves to be treated in the same way as a lender providing the funds for the acquisition of goods. The main reasons are that: (a) without those funds, the buyer may not be able to acquire the goods; and (b) with those funds the estate of the buyer is enriched to the benefit of all creditors.

In essence, the Supplement implements in an intellectual property context the super-priority given to a retention-of-title seller or an acquisition-secured creditor. This approach is intended to support the acquisition of intellectual property rights, as well as of licensee rights under an intellectual property licence agreement.

---

[24]UNCITRAL (2011), https://www.uncitral.org/pdf/english/texts/security-lg/e/10-57126_Ebook_Suppl_SR_IP.pdf, para. 140. Accessed 19 May 2017.

[25]UNCITRAL (2014a), http://www.uncitral.org/pdf/english/texts/security/Security-Rights-Registry-Guide-e.pdf, paras. 64–70. Accessed 19 May 2017.

[26]Brennan (2008), http://www.wipo.int/wipo_magazine/en/2008/05/article_0004.html. Accessed 19 May 2017.

The Supplement provides specifically that an "acquisition security interest" in intellectual property rights used or intended to be used by the grantor in the operation of its business should be treated in the same way as an "acquisition security interest" in equipment; such a security interest in intellectual property used or intended to be used by its grantor for the sale or lease in its ordinary course of business should be treated in the same way as an "acquisition security interest" in inventory; and such a security interest in intellectual property used or intended to be used by the grantor for its personal, family or household purposes should be treated in the same way as an "acquisition security interest" in consumer goods.[27]

As a result, an "acquisition security interest" in equipment-equivalent intellectual property or licence rights, has priority over a "non-acquisition security right" in those rights, provided that within a short period of time (20 or 30 days) after the agreement for the sale or licence of intellectual property has been entered into, a notice is registered with respect to the "acquisition security interest" in the security interest registry.[28]

In addition, an "acquisition security interest" in inventory-equivalent intellectual property or licensee rights under a licence agreement has priority over a non-acquisition security interest in those rights, provided that before the agreement for the sale or licence of intellectual property has been entered into, a notice is registered with respect to the "acquisition security interest" in the general security interest registry, and additionally a notice is sent to secured creditors with an earlier-registered "non-acquisition security interest".[29]

Moreover, an "acquisition security interest" in consumer goods-equivalent intellectual property or licensee rights under a licence agreement, upon its creation, has priority over a "non-acquisition security interest" in those rights.[30]

3.2 Priority of an Acquisition Security Interest Registered in an Intellectual Property Registry

To avoid interfering with specialized registration regimes, the Guide and the Supplement do not give the "acquisition security interest"-priority super-priority

---

[27]Recommendation 247, subparagraph (a). See UNCITRAL (2011), https://www.uncitral.org/pdf/english/texts/security-lg/e/10-57126_Ebook_Suppl_SR_IP.pdf, p. 124. Accessed 19 May 2017.

[28]Recommendation 180, alternative A, subparagraph (a). See UNCITRAL (2010d), https://www.uncitral.org/pdf/english/texts/security-lg/e/09-82670_Ebook-Guide_09-04-10English.pdf, p. 375. Accessed 19 May 2017.

[29]Recommendation 180, alternative A, subparagraph (b). See UNCITRAL (2010d), https://www.uncitral.org/pdf/english/texts/security-lg/e/09-82670_Ebook-Guide_09-04-10English.pdf, p. 375. Accessed 19 May 2017.

[30]Recommendation 179. See UNCITRAL (2010d), https://www.uncitral.org/pdf/english/texts/security-lg/e/09-82670_Ebook-Guide_09-04-10English.pdf, p. 375. Accessed 19 May 2017. For a discussion of the various alternatives or the unitary and non-unitary approach to acquisition financing, see the Supplement, chapter IX.

over acquisition security interests registered in an intellectual property registry. As already mentioned, such a security interest has priority over a security interest made effective against third parties by registration in the security interest registry, irrespective of the time of registration.[31]

However, in many situations, the secured creditor of an owner of intellectual property that is subject to specialized registration will in essence have the priority position of an acquisition secured creditor. Where, for example, the intellectual property regime does not permit the registration of a security interest in future intellectual property, the secured creditor of a transferee or licensee of intellectual property can only register after the transfer has been made or the licence has been granted. As a result, the owner's secured creditor will always have priority over the transferee's or licensee's secured creditor.

3.3 *Priority of an Acquisition Security Interest in Proceeds of Intellectual Property*

In line with the relevant rules that apply to "acquisition security interests" in proceeds of tangible assets, the Supplement provides that an "acquisition security interest" in the proceeds of equipment-equivalent intellectual property or licensee rights under a licence agreement has the same super-priority as the "acquisition security interest" in the originally encumbered intellectual property rights[32]; and an "acquisition security interest" in the proceeds of inventory-equivalent intellectual property or licensee rights under a licence agreement has the same super-priority as the "acquisition security interest" in the originally encumbered intellectual property rights, except where the proceeds take the form of receivables, negotiable instruments, rights to payment of funds credited to a bank account or rights to receive the proceeds under a stand-by letter of credit or an independent guarantee. The reason for the extension of the security interest in an asset to the proceeds of that asset (and the extension of the super-priority of an acquisition security interest in an asset to a security interest in the proceeds of that asset) is to ensure that the secured creditor is sufficiently secured, which is likely to have a positive impact on the availability and the cost of credit. The parties can always agree otherwise.[33]

[31]Recommendation 181. See UNCITRAL (2010d), https://www.uncitral.org/pdf/english/texts/security-lg/e/09-82670_Ebook-Guide_09-04-10English.pdf, p. 376. Accessed 19 May 2017.

[32]Recommendation 185, Alternative A, subparagraph (a). See UNCITRAL (2010d), https://www.uncitral.org/pdf/english/texts/security-lg/e/09-82670_Ebook-Guide_09-04-10English.pdf, p. 376. Accessed 19 May 2017.

[33]Recommendation 185, Alternative A, subparagraph (b). See UNCITRAL (2010d), https://www.uncitral.org/pdf/english/texts/security-lg/e/09-82670_Ebook-Guide_09-04-10English.pdf, p. 376. Accessed 19 May 2017.

4 Law Applicable to Security Interests in Intellectual Property

4.1 Property Matters

The Guide and the Supplement do not deal with the law applicable to ownership in intellectual property. They deal though with the law applicable to the creation, third-party effectiveness, priority and enforcement of a security interest in intellectual property.

This is an issue with respect to which great uncertainty prevails.[34] At the time UNCITRAL was preparing the Supplement, there was no generally acceptable uniform applicable law rule concerning security interests in intellectual property at all,[35] or at least with respect to some matters.[36] Thus, UNCITRAL took the time to discuss this issue at length and in depth.[37] Various alternatives were considered and their comparative advantages and disadvantages were discussed.[38] The outcome, which was considered to be a significant success, in particular, as it was agreed upon after a long and well-informed discussion by consensus, may be briefly described as follows.

The Supplement discusses various options with their comparative advantages and disadvantages.[39] One option is based on the law applicable to ownership in intellectual property rights. Under this approach, the law applicable to a security interest in intellectual property should be the law of the State in which the intellectual property is protected (*lex protectionis* or *lex loci protectionis*). The main arguments in favour of this approach are that it would be consistent with the

[34]Baratiti (2010).

[35]The European Max-Planck-Group had not completed its work on the Conflict of Laws in Intellectual Property (CLIP), The CLIP Principles and Commentary, Oxford University Press, 2013.

[36]The American Law Institute (2008) publication of the Principles Governing Jurisdiction, Choice of Law, and Judgments in Transnational Disputes does not deal with the law applicable to the perfection, priority and enforcement of a security interest in intellectual property, but refers that matter to the work of international organizations, such as UNCITRAL and the Hague Conference on Private International Law. See American Law Institute (2008), pp. 150–151.

[37]The discussions included a representative of the Bureau of the Hague Conference on Private International Law, who also submitted a proposal. See UNCITRAL (2009), https://documents-dds-ny.un.org/doc/UNDOC/LTD/V09/855/76/PDF/V0985576.pdf?OpenElement. Informal discussions also took place with the European Max-Planck-Group for Conflict of Laws in Intellectual Property (CLIP), at http://www.ip.mpg.de/ww/de/pub/mikroseiten/cl_ip_eu/home.cfm.

[38]See UNCITRAL (2010b), https://documents-dds-ny.un.org/doc/UNDOC/GEN/V10/519/95/PDF/V1051995.pdf?OpenElement. See UNCITRAL (2010a), https://documents-dds-ny.un.org/doc/UNDOC/GEN/V10/556/48/PDF/V1055648.pdf?OpenElement, paras. 210–223. Accessed 19 May 2017. See also Addenda 1–7 UNCITRAL (2010c), https://documents-dds-ny.un.org/doc/UNDOC/GEN/V10/520/01/PDF/V1052001.pdf?OpenElement. Accessed 19 May 2017.

[39]See UNCITRAL (2011), https://www.uncitral.org/pdf/english/texts/security-lg/e/10-57126_Ebook_Suppl_SR_IP.pdf, paras. 284–339. Accessed 19 May 2017.

approach followed in many intellectual property law conventions and would result in the application of one and the same law to transfers of ownership and to security interests in intellectual property.[40]

Another option is based on the law applicable in the Guide to security interests in intangible assets, that is, the law of the grantor's location (the grantor's principal place of business and, if there are multiple places of business, the grantor's place of central administration (the real seat), and, if there is no place of business, the grantor's habitual residence).[41] The main arguments in favour of this approach are that it would result in the application of a single law, which, in the case of a security interest in a portfolio of intellectual property rights protected under the laws of several States, would result in significant time and cost savings to create and enforce a security interest, and a law that would usually coincide with the law governing matters in the grantor's insolvency (*lex fori concursus*).[42]

A third option is based on a combination of the first two options referring some issues to the law of the grantor's location and other issues to the law of the State in which the intellectual property right is protected. The main argument for this approach is that it maximizes the advantages of both options and minimizes their disadvantages. More concretely, this approach allows parties to choose either the law of the protecting State or the law of the grantor's location as the law applicable to creation (effectiveness between the parties, not affecting third parties).[43]

It refers third-party effectiveness and priority to the law of the protecting State, giving appropriate recognition to the principle of territoriality and the need to refer security interests in registrable intellectual property rights to the law of the State of registration. It also permits third-party effectiveness as against "judgment creditors" and insolvency administrators to be achieved under a single law (the law of the State of the grantor's place of central administration, which is generally understood to be the grantor's centre of main interests). Furthermore, this option refers enforcement (which involves several acts) to a single law (the law of the grantor's location), subject, of course, to the principle of the application of the *lex fori* to procedural matters and the *lex fori concursus* to certain insolvency-related matters (avoidance, ranking of claims and distribution of proceeds).[44] This is the approach recommended in the Supplement.[45]

[40]See UNCITRAL (2011), https://www.uncitral.org/pdf/english/texts/security-lg/e/10-57126_Ebook_Suppl_SR_IP.pdf, paras. 297–300. Accessed 19 May 2017.

[41]Recommendation 208 and 219. See UNCITRAL (2010d), https://www.uncitral.org/pdf/english/texts/security-lg/e/09-82670_Ebook-Guide_09-04-10English.pdf, pp. 405 and 406. Accessed 19 May 2017.

[42]See UNCITRAL (2011), https://www.uncitral.org/pdf/english/texts/security-lg/e/10-57126_Ebook_Suppl_SR_IP.pdf, paras. 290–296. Accessed 19 May 2017.

[43]See UNCITRAL (2011), https://www.uncitral.org/pdf/english/texts/security-lg/e/10-57126_Ebook_Suppl_SR_IP.pdf, paras. 301–317. Accessed 19 May 2017.

[44]Recommendation 223. See UNCITRAL (2010d), https://www.uncitral.org/pdf/english/texts/security-lg/e/09-82670_Ebook-Guide_09-04-10English.pdf, p. 408. Accessed 19 May 2017.

[45]Recommendation 248. See UNCITRAL (2011), https://www.uncitral.org/pdf/english/texts/security-lg/e/10-57126_Ebook_Suppl_SR_IP.pdf, p. 147. Accessed 19 May 2017.

4.2 Contractual Matters

The Guide provides that the law applicable to the mutual rights and obligations of the parties arising from their security agreement is the law chosen by the parties. In the absence of a choice of law by the parties, the applicable law is the law governing the security agreement as determined by the conflict-of-law provisions generally applicable to contractual obligations,[46] such as, for example, the Principles on Choice of Law in International Commercial Contracts. The same law applies to the mutual (or contractual) rights and obligations of the parties to an intellectual property agreement.[47]

5 The Impact of the Insolvency of a Licensor or a Licensee on a Security Interest in that Party's Rights

5.1 General

The UNCITRAL Legislative Guide on Insolvency Law (the "Insolvency Guide") deals with all issues that are typically dealt with in insolvency law, including the treatment of security interests in insolvency proceedings. The Guide in chapter XII includes a comprehensive, self-contained summary of the discussion in the Insolvency Guide of the treatment of security interests in insolvency proceedings.

Both Guides generally deal also with security interests in intellectual property, without placing much emphasis on all relevant issues at the intersection of secured transactions and insolvency law, on the one hand, and intellectual property law, on the other hand. The emphasis on those issues is given in the Supplement. Thus, chapter XII of the Supplement complements chapter XII of the Guide and deals with the impact of insolvency of a licensor or a licensee on a security interest in that party's rights under a licence agreement in a way that is consistent with the Insolvency Guide.

More concretely, the Insolvency Guide contains extensive discussion and recommendations with regard to the impact of insolvency proceedings on contracts that have not been fully performed by both parties. A licence agreement could fall in that category and the insolvency administrator may continue or reject it in order to maximize the value of the insolvency estate to the benefit of all creditors.[48] The Supplement discusses ways in which the counterparty of the insolvent debtor and secured creditors may protect their interests (in line with the Insolvency Guide).

---

46 Recommendation 216. See UNCITRAL (2010d), https://www.uncitral.org/pdf/english/texts/security-lg/e/09-82670_Ebook-Guide_09-04-10English.pdf, p. 407. Accessed 19 May 2017.

47 See https://www.hcch.net/en/instruments/conventions/full-text/?cid=135. Accessed 19 May 2017.

48 Insolvency Guide, recommendations 72 and 73. See UNCITRAL (2005), https://www.uncitral.org/pdf/english/texts/insolven/05-80722_Ebook.pdf, pp. 132–133.

The Insolvency Guide also discusses at length contractual automatic termination clauses upon the occurrence of an event (such as insolvency) and provides that they should be unenforceable as against the insolvency administrator and the insolvent debtor.[49] The Supplement includes references contained in the Insolvency Guide to systems that uphold automatic termination clauses for creators of intellectual property to be able to control their property, for example, in situations where insolvency may affect not only the value of trademarked goods but also of the trademark itself.

5.2 Insolvency of the Licensor

Typically, under insolvency law, when a licensor becomes insolvent, the insolvency administrator may reject any contract that may not have been fully performed by both the insolvent debtor and its counterparty in order to be able to re-negotiate these agreements and maximize the value of the insolvency estate to the benefit of all creditors. If a licence agreement falls into that category and the licensor's insolvency administrator rejects it, a licensee and/or any sub-licensee will lose their rights.

In addition, a secured creditor of the licensor or licensee (or any sub-licensee) will lose its security. In the case of a chain of licensees who have invested in further developing and marketing the licensed products (in particular where there are cross-licensing arrangements and each licensee is also a licensor), this result can be catastrophic for a whole sector of a country's economy.[50] To address this problem, the Supplement includes some points of discussion and makes modest suggestions as to how secured creditors and licensees may be protected by referring to approaches taken in various States (a supplement to a guide on secured transactions cannot resolve this issue, which is an issue of insolvency law).[51]

For example, the secured creditor of the licensor may take a security interest in the intellectual property itself and, if the licensor's insolvency administrator rejects the licence agreement, the licensor's secured creditor may seek to enforce its security right in the intellectual property itself. Of course, as the intellectual

[49]Insolvency Guide, recommendation 71. See UNCITRAL (2005), https://www.uncitral.org/pdf/english/texts/insolven/05-80722_Ebook.pdf, p. 132.

[50]A good example of this situation is the Qimonda case. See In re Qimonda AG Bankr. Litig., 433 B. R. 547 (E.D. Va.2010). It went up to the Supreme Court of the United States. See Jaffe v. Samsung Elecs. Co., 135 S. Ct. 66 (2014).

[51]The matter was discussed during the Fourth UNCITRAL International Insolvency Law Colloquium, held in Vienna from 16 to 18 December 2013. For a presentation by the author, see Bazinas (2013), http://www.uncitral.org/pdf/english/colloquia/insolvency-2013/B5_IP_Bazinas.pdf/. Accessed 19 May 2017. For the results of the colloquium with respect to this matter, see UNCITRAL (2014b), https://documents-dds-ny.un.org/doc/UNDOC/GEN/V14/027/42/PDF/V1402742.pdf?OpenElement, paras. 27–30. Accessed 19 May 2017. However, at its session in 2014, the Commission did not treat this as a matter of priority, see UNCITRAL (2014c), https://documents-dds-ny.un.org/doc/UNDOC/GEN/V14/053/54/PDF/V1405354.pdf?OpenElement, paras. 151–159. Accessed 19 May 2017.

property will be part of the estate, the security interest will be subject to the stay and other limitations imposed in the case of insolvency proceedings (for example, avoidance, preferences).[52]

Similarly, to protect itself from the consequences of a rejection of the licence agreement by the licensor's insolvency administrator, the licensee's secured creditor may refuse to extend credit to the licensee unless the licensee obtains a security interest in the licensed intellectual property. In such a case, if the licensor's insolvency administrator rejects the licence agreement, the licensee can enforce its security interest in the licensed intellectual property (subject, of course, to the limitations on the enforcement of security interests imposed by insolvency law).

Some States have introduced legislation to protect investments of licensees in the case of the licensor's insolvency. For example, in some States, a licensee may be given the right to continue to use the licensed intellectual property right even after rejection of the licence agreement by the licensor's insolvency administrator, provided that the licensee continues paying royalties and otherwise performing the licence agreement. This approach balances the interests of the insolvent licensor to avoid burdens under the licence agreement and the interest of the licensee to protect its investment in the licensed intellectual property.

In addition, in other States, licence agreements may not be subject to rejection under insolvency law because: (a) they are excluded from the list of contracts that may be rejected; (b) exclusive licences are treated as property rights that are not subject to rejection; (c) licence agreements are not executory contracts subject to rejection as the licensor has performed its obligation by granting the licence; or (d) they are registered in the relevant intellectual property registry.

In yet other States, a licence does not depend on the effectiveness of the underlying licence agreement (according to the so-called "abstraction principle"). Thus, the licensee may retain the right to use the licensed intellectual property right at least until the insolvency administrator withdraws the licence based on the principles of unjust enrichment.[53]

5.3 *Insolvency of the Licensee*

If a licensee becomes insolvent and the insolvency administrator decides to continue the licence, the licensee may retain the licence provided that it continues paying royalties as agreed and otherwise duly performs the licence agreement; and, if the licensor has granted a security interest in its right to payment of royalties, the licensor's secured creditor will be entitled to keep that security interest.

[52]Chapter XII of the Guide and the treatment of secured creditors under the Insolvency Guide, Annex I. See UNCITRAL (2005), https://www.uncitral.org/pdf/english/texts/insolven/05-80722_Ebook.pdf.

[53]See UNCITRAL (2011), https://www.uncitral.org/pdf/english/texts/security-lg/e/10-57126_Ebook_Suppl_SR_IP.pdf, paras. 359–361. Accessed 19 May 2017.

If the licensee's insolvency administrator decides to reject the licence agreement and the licensee has granted a security interest in its rights under the licence agreement, the licence will cease to exist, the licensee will lose its right to use the licensed intellectual property right and the licensee's secured creditor will lose its security. If the licensor has also granted a security interest in its right to payment of royalties, the licensor's secured creditor will also lose its security. The secured creditor of the licensor or the licensee may protect itself by taking measures described above (see Sect. 5.3. above on the insolvency of the licensor).

The licensor needs either to receive its royalties and see the licence agreement performed or, otherwise, at least, to be able to terminate the licence agreement. If the licence agreement is continued and the licensee defaults, the licensor may exercise its rights under insolvency law related to remedy the default. In addition, if a secured creditor of the insolvent licensee claims and obtains payment of the sub-royalties with which the licensee pays royalties to the licensor, it is, moreover, important that the licensor has the right to terminate the licence agreement. The Supplement discusses the right of the licensor to seek relief from the insolvency court where there is discontinuation of payment of royalties because of priority given to secured creditors or other relief to protect the intellectual property right.[54]

6 Conclusions

The Guide and the Supplement are designed to facilitate intellectual property financing, without interfering with intellectual property law. This result is achieved by commentary and recommendations that deal with the creation, third-party effectiveness, priority and enforcement (even in the grantor's insolvency) of a security interest in intellectual property, as well as with the law applicable to such matters.

The commentary of the Supplement explains how the recommendations of the Guide and the Supplement would apply in the context of an intellectual property financing transaction. They do so in a way that ensures better coordination between secured transactions and intellectual property law. With the same goal in mind, the recommendations of the Supplement modify the general recommendations of the Guide as they apply to security interests in intellectual property.

The Supplement is intended to provide guidance to States as to issues relating to security interests in intellectual property.[55] It is not intended to deal with purely intellectual property law issues. However, it includes modest suggestions as to how States that may wish to enact the Guide and the Supplement could coordinate their intellectual property laws with their enactment of the Guide and the Supplement.

[54]See UNCITRAL (2011), https://www.uncitral.org/pdf/english/texts/security-lg/e/10-57126_Ebook_Suppl_SR_IP.pdf, paras. 363–366. Accessed 19 May 2017.

[55]Tosato (2011), p. 102.

The integrity of intellectual property law is preserved through a general hierarchy rule that gives precedence to intellectual property law where it deals in an asset-specific and different way with a matter addressed in the Guide and the Supplement. Coordination between secured transactions and intellectual property law is also achieved by way of coordination of intellectual property registries with security interest registries through priority rules and various practical measures aimed at linking those registries.

The Supplement also breaks new ground by: (a) introducing a regime of intellectual property acquisition financing that should have a beneficial impact on the availability and cost of credit to intellectual property right holders and licensors of intellectual property; (b) suggesting ways in which the investment of licensors or licensees in intellectual property may be protected in the case of insolvency; and (c) dealing with applicable law issues in a practical way that is also consistent with intellectual property law.

References

American Law Institute (2008) Principles governing jurisdiction, choice of law, and judgments in transnational disputes. Executive Office, American Law Institute, Washington DC, pp 150–151

Bariatti S (2010) The law applicable to security interests in intellectual property rights. J Private Int Law 6(2):395–416

Bazinas SV (2013) http://www.uncitral.org/pdf/english/colloquia/insolvency-2013/B5_IP_Bazinas.pdf. Accessed 21 May 2017

Brennan L (2008) The impact of insolvency on IP licenses in the work of UNCITRAL. http://www.wipo.int/wipo_magazine/en/2008/05/article_0004.html. Accessed 19 May 2017

Conflict of laws in intellectual property, The CLIP principles and commentary, European Max Planck group on conflict of laws in intellectual property, Oxford University, Oxford

Hague Conference on Private International Law (2015) Principles on choice of law in international commercial contracts. https://www.hcch.net/en/instruments/conventions/full-text/?cid=135. Accessed 19 May 2017

Knopf HP (ed) (2002) Security interests in intellectual property. Carswell Legal, Toronto

Philips J (2008) IP Financing: the ten commandments. http://www.wipo.int/wipo_magazine/en/2008/05/article_0002.html. Accessed 19 May 2017

Tosato A (2011) Security interests over intellectual property. J Intellect Property Law & Pract 6 (2):93–104

UNCITRAL (2005) Legislative guide on insolvency law. https://www.uncitral.org/pdf/english/texts/insolven/05-80722_Ebook.pdf. Accessed 19 May 2017

UNCITRAL (2007) Report of the United Nations Commission on international trade law on the work of its fortieth session. https://documents-dds-ny.un.org/doc/UNDOC/GEN/V07/857/09/PDF/V0785709.pdf?OpenElement. Accessed 19 May 2017

UNCITRAL (2009) Draft Supplement to the UNCITRAL legislative guide on secured transactions dealing with security rights in intellectual property: proposal by the permanent Bureau of the Hague conference on private international law. https://documents-dds-ny.un.org/doc/UNDOC/LTD/V09/855/76/PDF/V0985576.pdf?OpenElement. Accessed 19 May 2017

UNCITRAL (2010a) Report of the United Nations Commission on international trade law forty-third session. https://documents-dds-ny.un.org/doc/UNDOC/GEN/V10/556/48/PDF/V1055648.pdf?OpenElement. Accessed 19 May 2017

UNCITRAL (2010b) Draft supplement to the UNCITRAL legislative guide on secured transactions dealing with security rights in intellectual property. https://documents-dds-ny.un.org/doc/UNDOC/GEN/V10/519/95/PDF/V1051995.pdf?OpenElement. Accessed 19 May 2017

UNCITRAL (2010c) Draft supplement to the UNCITRAL legislative guide on secured transactions dealing with security rights in intellectual property addendum 1. https://documents-dds-ny.un.org/doc/UNDOC/GEN/V10/520/01/PDF/V1052001.pdf?OpenElement. Accessed 19 May 2017

UNCITRAL (2010d) UNCITRAL legislative guide on secured transactions. https://www.uncitral.org/pdf/english/texts/security-lg/e/09-82670_Ebook-Guide_09-04-10English.pdf. Accessed 19 May 2017

UNCITRAL (2011) UNCITRAL legislative guide on secured transactions: supplement on security rights in intellectual property. https://www.uncitral.org/pdf/english/texts/security-lg/e/10-57126_Ebook_Suppl_SR_IPpdf. Accessed 19 May 2017

UNCITRAL (2014a) UNCITRAL guide on the implementation of a security rights registry. http://www.uncitral.org/pdf/english/texts/security/Security-Rights-Registry-Guide-e.pdf. Accessed 19 May 2017

UNCITRAL (2014b) Report of the fourth international insolvency law colloquium. https://documents-dds-ny.un.org/doc/UNDOC/GEN/V14/027/42/PDF/V1402742.pdf?OpenElement. Accessed 19 May 2017

UNCITRAL (2014c) Report of the United Nations Commission on international trade law forty-seventh session. https://documents-dds-ny.un.org/doc/UNDOC/GEN/V14/053/54/PDF/V1405354.pdf?OpenElement. Accessed 19 May 2017

Functional Analysis of Private International Law Rules for Security Interests in Intellectual Property

Toshiyuki Kono and Kazuaki Kagami

Abstract This article aims at contributing to academic debates on PIL rules on security interest in IP using functional analysis. Functional analysis here means a method to take a legal rule as a mechanism which brings about certain effects, to analyze conditions under which the effects would be produced, and to seek possible directions to improve the legal rule. Security interests in IP represent a convergence of three fields of law, i.e. IP, PIL and security interest law. Therefore, an integral platform where these three fields could be analyzed on an equal level would be needed. Functional analysis provides such a platform. For this purpose, this article first clarified the functions of security interest and its conditions, then identified which option as a PIL rule would be appropriate for each condition of the individual function of security interest in IP. Perspectives from both states' and parties' interests should be properly integrated in the analytical process. Lastly, the scope and conditions of party autonomy as well as objective connecting factors were identified. The outcome of this analysis provides tools to clarify not fully conceived parts of previous discussions. The CLIP Principles were compared with our proposals from this perspective.

1 Introduction

This chapter aims at analyzing possible options for private international law (PIL) rules concerning security interest in intellectual property (IP), paying attention to their functions. We consider this a functional analysis of PIL rules. Functional

This article is a part of outcomes of Kakenhi Grant Type S, "Research on International Security Interest in IP by the method of Law and Economic" (2012–2016) (Principal investigater: Toshiyuki Kono).

T. Kono (✉)
Kyushu University, Fukuoka, Japan
e-mail: konoto@law.kyushu-u.ac.jp

K. Kagami
Toyo University, Tokyo, Japan
e-mail: kagami@toyo.jp

T. Kono (ed.), *Security Interests in Intellectual Property*, Perspectives in Law, Business and Innovation, DOI 10.1007/978-981-10-5415-0_5

analysis here means a method to take a legal rule as a mechanism which brings about certain effects, to analyze conditions under which the effects would be produced, and to seek possible directions to improve the legal rule. Since security interests in IP represent a crossing area of three fields of law, i.e. IP, PIL and security interest law, an integral platform where three fields could be analyzed on an equal level would be needed. Functional analysis provides such a platform.

2 Functions of Security Interest and PIL

A traditional definition of security interest would be for example a "means for the preferred collection of debt" or a "way to secure the satisfaction of a creditor".[1] Such a definition focuses on one an anticipated effect only, but there are multiple effects of security interest.[2] In addition, this definition does not pay attention to the mechanism nor the conditions under which its effects would be produced. We therefore suggest a revisit of the concept of security interest and offer the following[3]:

> Security interest is a scheme with a mechanism which transfers debtor's specific asset (whole or a part of his/her ownership or right to use) to a specific creditor, depending upon the circumstances (e.g. debtor's default)[4]

As long as this mechanism is integrated, security interest is not limited to statutory collateral. Non-statutory collateral such as certain types of contract or corporate organizations could be classified as security interest.[5]

The law of security interest is a legal institution which validates and effectuates functions of security interest by regulating the contents of security interest and its conditions. Appropriate validation and effectuation with less costs should be the goal of the security interest law.[6]

The implementation of social institutions is usually not a one-time event, but a process. Things may change in the course of this process. In the case of security interest, the smooth and effective execution of collateral would be desired by stakeholders, because smooth and effective execution would facilitate the

[1]For example, UCC (Uniform Commercial Code) provides a similar definition: "'Security interest' means an interest in personal property or fixtures which secures payment or performance of an obligation." See U.C.C § 1–201(2001).

[2]For example, see Baird (2004), pp. 1789–1800.

[3]In this context, see Baird et al. (1994), p. 314.

[4]This definition does not depend upon legal system in a specific State, so that it would be easier to link with discussions on PIL rule.

[5]On varieties of security interest, see Mann (1997), pp. 625–683.

[6]Legal rules on security interest in a broader sense, includes not only functions to promote, but also to restrict collateral. Thus an approach to integrating the mechanism of security interest can be found other fields of law, such as contract law, trust law, and corporate law.

procurement of funds. However, after a debtor's default, restricting the execution might become desirable, since such restriction could enable the insolvent debtor's rehabilitation. In other words, effects expected *ex ante* and effects desired *ex post* would not be identical.

Inconsistency between *ex ante* and *ex post* stages matters especially for PIL.[7] It is impossible to predict what kind of cross-border cases would occur. It would be too costly to investigate what kinds of laws exist in the world and what functions they have.[8] But in order to set up legal rules, the lawmaker should anticipate in advance what possible effects applicable law would bring about. The widely adopted PIL rules can be understood as such a mechanism, which connects and adapts *ex ante* policy considerations and *ex post* effects: the PIL rules determine applicable law (*ex-post* effect) in accordance with the nature of cross-border legal relationships such as tort, contract, product liability etc. (*ex-ante* decision).

Since this article aims at analyzing possible options of PIL rules concerning security interest in IP, we should analyze the functions of security interest as *ex-post* functions first. Then we try to integrate such functions into the structure of PIL.

3 Critical Analysis of Traditional Explanation on the Functions of Security Interest[9]

3.1 Function 1: Ensuring Debt Collection[10]

3.1.1 Ensuring Debt Collection and Its Conditions

Security interest has traditionally been explained as a legal institution by which a creditor can ensure his/her debt collection. As a result of this function, the business conditions of a transaction could be relaxed by providing collateral, and it would lead to expansion and a smoother transaction. We should identify under what conditions this function could show its best performance.[11]

---

[7]See Kagami (2006).

[8]By introducing a uniform law, the costs to understand various national laws could be reduced. However the introduction of a uniform law itself is costly. Also fitness of rules would be lowered. See Kono and Kagami (2013), pp. 314–337.

[9]Critical analysis on the traditional explanation, besides Baird (2004), see the following literature: Schwartz (1981), pp. 1–37, Bebchuck and Fried (1996), pp. 857–934. As comprehensive discussions on security interest, see the following: Scott (1997), pp. 1436–1465, Adler (1998), pp. 405–410, Flint (1999), pp. 363–405, Bowers (2000), pp. 90–128, Coco (2000), pp. 191–214.

[10]Naming of three functions to be analyzed in this chapter is inspired by Baird (2004).

[11]If all stakeholders' judgments and actions are doable without costs, and if market mechanism functions effectively, introducing collateral does not affect efficiency. Hence significance of collateral presumes imperfect market mechanism. See Schwartz (1981).

First, the probability of a debtor's insolvency should be high. The transaction costs to measure the probability of insolvency should be high as well. Under these conditions, the utility of security interest would be enhanced to avoid insolvency risk or high transaction costs. Second, foreclosure and execution could be made promptly and smoothly, i.e. costs of foreclosure, relevant legal judgments and execution should be low. Third, both disposition and use of collateral should be easy, i.e. the marketability of collateral should be high and transaction costs of finding buyers and of negotiations should be low. Fourth, the price and value of collateral should remain high. This means not only high value at a specific timing, but also no loss of value throughout the process from the time of the debtor's default until the time of sales of collateral.

Whether these conditions would be met or not, depends upon various factors, which include legal systems, the nature and state of collateral, creditor's capability, market trend and transaction costs to understand and use such information. The law of security interest should arrange the environment where these conditions could be met. For instance, the law should facilitate the acquisition of information on debtor and collateral, so that evaluation, use and deposition of collateral could become simple and easy. In addition, requirements under the law and its mechanism should be clear and strict. Legislative security interest satisfies this condition, but the limits of legislative security interest has been widely recognized. Hence the types of collateral has become diverse, covering movable properties as well as intangible assets.[12]

3.1.2 Criticism and Answers

The function to ensure debt collection could be questioned as follows: Suppose that a debtor A sets up collateral for creditor B. Accordingly creditor B will relax conditions for transaction and expand the transaction with A. As its reverse effect, conditions for creditor C's transaction would be worsened and creditor C will tighten conditions for his transactions. As a whole, the effects of security interest would be worse off. Under this circumstance, should we still consider the function to ensure debt collection as convincing?[13]

There would be two ways to react to this fundamental question. One way is to analyze other functions as justification. This analysis will be made in the following sections. Second, even if the function to ensure debt collection should be supported

[12]On diversification of collateral and security interest right, see U.C.C. § 9 (2001); UNCITRAL (2011), https://www.uncitral.org/pdf/english/texts/security-lg/e/09-82670_Ebook-Guide_09-04-10English.pdf; Castellano (2015), pp. 611–640. Overviews of recent developments of security interest and amendments of relevant laws. Armour (2008), pp. 3–29 discusses on policy designs based on preceding theoretical works and empirical analysis.

[13]See Schwartz (1981), Schwartz (1984), pp. 1051–1069.

as a justification of security interest, conditions and mechanisms which make such function happen should be analyzed in a more detailed manner.[14] Let us begin with the latter.

In the same hypothetical case, we suppose that debtor A holds assets X and Y. Creditor B can obtain information on asset X (e.g. the state of the asset, its disposability etc.) with little costs, while such information on asset Y is costly. Taking asset X ensures creditor B's debt collection, but taking asset Y is less effective. On the other hand, the situation for creditor C is exactly the opposite, i.e. taking asset Y is effective for creditor C, but not asset X. The reason why the debtor sets up a security interest is to improve conditions of the transaction. Hence creditor B will take asset X as collateral, while creditor C takes asset Y.

This could be explained well, if we replace B with a bank, C with venture capital, asset X with immovable property, and asset Y with IP. A bank which has no capacity to evaluate IP would not appreciate IP as collateral, so that loan conditions would not change against IP as collateral, while the bank would be willing to take immovable property and reflect its value into loan conditions. This is because the bank has sufficient experience and know-how on evaluation and disposability of immovable properties. On the other hand, venture capital which is capable of evaluating IP and holds the data of potential IP users who would provide credits against IP as collateral, but would not appreciate immovable property, because the venture capital would have to outsource to other institutions the evaluation of the property and its market, which would raise additional costs. Thus each institution takes the appropriate asset for it, taking transaction costs into consideration, and this facilitates debtor's procurement as a whole.

This hypothetical case explains well how the function to ensure debt collection should be analyzed: recognizing that transaction costs could differ, depending upon the nature of collateral and parties, the law should facilitate parties' information collection, negotiations, and agreements.[15] To be noted however is that transaction costs should remain within a certain range since excessive costs would make security interest dysfunctional, while too low costs would make collateral unnecessary.

The above-explained conditions as activating conditions of debt collection function can be summarized as follows:

	Conditions	Affecting factors
1	High probability of debtor's default	Debtor's business situations and environment; Other parties' interests
2	High possibility of collateral execution	Law (concerning the use and execution of collateral) The nature of collateral

(continued)

[14]For example, see Harris and Mooney (1994), pp. 2021–2072.

[15]Costs in this context occur exogenously.

(continued)

	Conditions	Affecting factors
3	High possibility of use or disposal of collateral	Law (concerning assistance of transactions and disposal) The nature of collateral debtor's capacity, effective market
4	High value of collateral	Law (to maintain assets value) The nature of collateral The nature of end users
5	Diverse transaction costs for assets and parties	Law (concerning information collection, negotiations) The nature of collateral The nature of parties

3.2 *Function 2: Insulating Assets*

One of the other functions of security interest is insulating assets. This aims at protecting a debtor's specific asset from business conditions or the state of other assets by insulating the specific asset from other assets, and satisfying a specific creditor with the insulated asset.[16] As a result, such creditor does not have to obtain information on the debtor's other assets, as long as the insulated asset could fully satisfy his credit, and such creditor could reduce costs, so that the creditor could relax conditions of the transaction. For the debtor, as long as he/she holds assets with stable value, the debtor could enter into business with better conditions, by using such assets as insulated specific assets. For example, debtor A holds assets X and Y. The value of X is stable in the market and foreseen as stable in the future (e.g. value is 200). The market value of asset Y on the other hand may vary and could be 300 with the probability of 50%, but might be minus 300 with the probability of 50%. If assets X and Y would be combined, the value of the entire collateral would be either 500 with 50% probability or minus 100 with 50% probability. Under this circumstance, if the debtor wants to procure 200, the creditor has to take the risk not to get paid with 50% probability. This risk would be reflected in a higher interest rate. If asset X would be the sole collateral, it would lead to more favorable conditions for the debtor's procurement.[17]

[16]"'Insulation' is a word to describe the ways in which a secured creditor can minimize the indirect costs associated with bankruptcy." See Baird (2004), p. 1789. But we avoid using the terms "insolvency" or "bankruptcy" and defining in a more general form in order to connect this function with analysis on the level of PIL at a later stage.

[17]As an empirical analysis on insulation and its conditions: Feng et al. (2009), pp. 1833–1876.

In the reality, however, this function is often restricted from the following considerations:

First, this insulation function may work well for a specific creditor. But if other creditors could not know about the insulation and it is difficult to obtain information about it, the insulation may turn out to be an unexpected and unfair surprise for other creditors. To avoid such a situation, the institutionalization of a notification system and the dissemination of relevant information may be needed, but it could be costly. These costs would be reflected in the conditions of the transaction. To avoid such negative impacts, the execution of security interest may have to be restricted in advance. To be noted that such *ex ante* restriction of the execution could collide with the above-explained function to ensure the debt collection.

Second, if assets with a stable value are used as collateral despite the fact that such use of assets is rare in the debtor's region, the use of assets as collateral may work as a negative sign of a debtor's assets or business management in the region. It may cause detriment to his/her business and set benefits brought about by insulating assets off against such an unintended negative sign.[18] What sort of signal would be produced depends upon business practices or social thought patterns in the region.

Third, insulation may be restricted by other legal mechanisms or policies, especially by insolvency law. Suppose that a debtor is insolvent, but the debtor wants rehabilitation of his/her business. A creditor with collateral may prefer executing his/her security interest instead of abandoning his/her security interest for the sake of an uncertain future of the debtor's business. A well-functioning security interest may terminate the debtor's business. Hence, if rehabilitation of the debtor's business should be encouraged, executing security interest should be restricted under certain circumstances. Japanese law is no exception of such consideration (e.g. Art 104 of Corporate Reorganization Act; Art. 148 of Civil Rehabilitation Act).

Fourth, insulation functions may be overwritten by alternative means which have similar functions, such as division of organization, co-ownership, trust, or contract with repurchase agreement. Clarification of advantages and disadvantages of security interest against these other institutions is needed. Security interest may need to be restricted in cases where one of other institutions should be preferred.

Activating conditions to use the insulation function could be summarized as below:

[18]Using the building as debtor's principal place of business as collateral could mean more than collateral.

	Conditions	Affecting factors
1	Insulation of assets is advantageous; Risk of each asset differs; Save costs to obtain information	The nature of asset Capacity and nature of parties
2	No restriction on insulation (1) • Costs to obtain information is small • No influence on other parties	Law (concerning dissemination of information on security interest and its credibility
3	No restriction on insulation (2) • Legal separation of assets • No overwriting by superior goals	Law (law of security interest in broader sense)
4	No restriction of insulation (3) • Signaling effect is ignorable	Business customs Social thought patterns
5	No restriction of insulation (4) • No overwriting by alternative institutions	Law (laws with similar functions) Business practice

3.3 *Function 3: Control Function*

This function means to control a debtor's or creditor's decision-making with collateral and to manage relevant assets. Economists' focus has been placed on this aspect.[19] This function should be analyzed in each bilateral relationship.

3.3.1 Control Function in the Relationship Between Debtor and Creditor

Suppose that a debtor takes a certain amount of credit from a creditor. For the creditor to obtain information on the debtor's business efforts and probability of the debtor's success is usually costly. Therefore the creditor would try to control the debtor and the probability of success by taking collateral. As we defined above, security interest is an institution that causes the transfer of specific assets from the debtor to a creditor. It means that security interest not only enables the creditor to hold the value of a specific asset, but also lets the debtor lose the assets under certain circumstances. Hence collateral could work as a means of sanction against the debtor. Therefore, the debtor would try to make his/her best efforts to avoid loss

[19]As a survey, see Adler (1998), Bowers (2000), and Coco (2000), pp. 191–214. From a legal approach, see Mann (1997), pp. 625–83.

as sanction, by, for instance, continuing business efforts without creditor's supervision. A debtor who is aware of his low probability of success would not provide collateral, avoiding sanction, and accept less favorable loan conditions. On the other hand, a debtor who is confident about the success of his/her business would not be concerned about losing collateral, so that he/she would offer collateral and obtain favorable conditions. Thus by using this function, the creditor could control a debtor's efforts properly and reduce transaction costs.

The conditions to make this function properly work are as follows: First, a debtor's behavioral patterns (e.g. business activities) should affect conditions to execute security interest (e.g. default). Second, when such conditions to execute security interest are fulfilled, execution should certainly take place. This incentivizes the creditor to execute. Third, collateral should have a high subjective value for debtor. In other words, the debtor's subjective value matters. If the debtor would lose collateral for a much lower price than subjective value for him/her, this function would not work. Fourth, ways and possibilities to deviate from this mechanism should be restricted. Fifth, the involved parties have predictability in this mechanism and in these circumstances.

3.3.2 Relationship Between Creditors

Security interest may work to solve issues despite imperfect information between creditors or externalities, but it may cause troubles to creditors as well.[20]

Suppose that debtor A owes creditors B1 and B2. Neither creditor B1 nor creditor B2 has collateral. The debtor A holds assets 6, but his/her business situation is almost precarious in day-to-day management, so that he/she tends to delay payment to his/her creditors. If the debtor cannot pay anymore, and if one of the creditors opts for debt collection, the debtor A's business would completely go bankrupt. If, however, the debtor A would be allowed to continue his/her business, the debtor would manage to pay a creditor, but would have difficulties to pay another creditor. And it is difficult to predict when such a situation would end.

Under this hypothetical case, let us assume that when creditor B1 opts for debt collection, creditor B1 could obtain 5 as a first-mover advantage. If creditor B1 opts for debtor A's continuation, but another creditor B2 chooses debt collection, creditor B1 could get only 1. On the other hand, if both creditors opt for debtor A's continuation, they would get 6. This means that if creditors cooperate and support the debtor, they would get bigger benefits in the long term. Such conditions however would not be easily met and rather unstable, since any creditor may suddenly change his/her mind.

---

[20]Jackson and Kronman (1979), pp. 1143–1182, Jackson (1982), pp. 857–907.

On the other hand, if creditor B1 holds a security interest, in the case of the debtor A's insolvency, creditor B1 could always get 5 with his collateral, while creditor B2 would get only 1 as the rest. If both creditors would choose the debtor A's continuation, they would get 6. When collateral would be introduced, there would be no first-mover advantage, so that creditor B1 might not be incentivized to opt for debt collection. If creditor B2 would hear that creditor B1 is reluctant to opt for debt collection, creditor B2 could be incentivized to support the debtor's continuation. Thus collateral would change the rules of the game which was based on the first-mover advantage. It would lead to cooperative and collaborative relationships between creditors. The debtor would then gain time to ameliorate his/her business conditions.

This scenario would change in the following case. Creditor B1 would get 5 by executing his/her collateral. But if creditor B1 would support the debtor's continuation and the debtor could get rehabilitated, creditor B1 could get 8, while creditor B1 would get only 1 in the case of the debtor's failure. Creditor B1 might be incentivized to support the debtor's continuation, but, to be safe, creditor B1 might rather opt for debt collection. In this case, the debtor A's rehabilitation would be stopped. Hence, to avoid the debtor's bankruptcy, the information on the debtor's business management and the state of his assets should not be difficult to obtain, especially information on how much debt the creditors could collect in both bankruptcy and rehabilitation cases. Second, obtaining information on collateral, i.e. which creditor has collateral and on which specific asset he/she has the collateral, should not be costly. This condition could be satisfied to a large extent by a registration system. Third, there must be an environment where parties' collaboration would be encouraged. This is because multi-party collaboration would depend upon not only their interests and reasons, but also external factors such as social situations. Fourth, the law of security interest should be so designed as to enable the control of specific issues between parties.

3.3.3 Analysis

Even if the involved parties may want to use security interest, the conditions and effects of security interest that each party expects may differ. Therefore to single out general conditions to make the control function work is not possible, but at least the following conditions can be pointed out: First, the parties should understand how the control function works. Second, the parties should be incentivized to act as expected without raising costs. Third, the effects of a control function should be positive, i.e. not only having an effect in each relationship, but also the effects for each party should be positive. For example, if a creditor has to pay substantial costs to control his/her debtor, the advantage of security interest would be lost. Last, but not least, the mechanism of security interest should not be restricted by external circumstances. If a party could circumvent its mechanism by using alternative means, the control function would not work properly. In reality however, to fully exclude external circumstances, such as the market situation, would be impossible.

Thus, the certainty of the mechanism of security interest despite possible external circumstances would be at stake.

Activating conditions of the control function can be summarized as follows:

	Conditions	Affecting factors
1	Parties understand the conditions and the mechanism of security interest	Parties' capacity Costs to obtain information
2	Appropriate incentives to parties	The nature of parties, collateral and parties' relationships; Social environment
3	Bigger benefits than costs	The nature of parties, collateral and parties' relationships; Social environment
4	Certainty of the mechanism of security interest	Legal systems; Business customs

4 Methodological Approach for Security Interest and Private International Law

4.1 Matrix as an Analytical Tool of Private International Law[21]

Flexibility and legal certainty are often cited to analyze PIL rules. However this flexibility vs. legal certainty test does not develop detailed analysis. Literature does not specify "certainty" for example in such a way for whom it is certain, or in what aspect of a legal relationship it is certain. Instead, we propose to use two thresholds to analyze PIL rules, i.e. beneficiary and interests.

Beneficiary could be differentiated as party and state: Parties of cross-border legal relationships are usually the center of the focus to determine applicable law and its results. In certain PIL rules, however, state emerges as the main stakeholder. Examples are Art. 24 para.3 second sentence or Art. 26 second sentence in the Act on General Rules for Application of Laws (Japanese PIL), according to which Japanese law shall be always applicable. This rule is based on the consideration that the practice of the personal status registration system in Japan shall not be affected by applying foreign applicable law. In summary, the key consideration here is whose interest matters, and in this case it is the state's.[22]

Second threshold, interests could be distinguished as effectiveness and fitness. Effectiveness means the possibility of making expected results of certain acts happen. For example, when predictability for relevant parties is low, the expected results of

[21] Recently, especially since 2000, methodology of PIL has been discussed. For example, see Whincop and Keyes (2001), Guzman (2001), pp. 883–940, Basedow et al. (2006), Ruhl (2006), pp. 801–841, Michaels (2008), pp. 1607–1644.

[22] Similar view is stressed in O'Hara and Ribstein (2000), pp. 1151–1232.

certain acts would not be achievable. In this case, effectiveness for the involved parties is low. When the means for the state to intervene is limited or when the state's intervention or involvement cannot be justified, it would be difficult to make expected results of certain acts happen. As a result, effectiveness for the state is low.

Fitness, on the other hand, functions as the test to judge if expected results of certain acts are appropriate for such issues that the acts tackle. For example, the best fitness for policy goals of a specific state would be brought about by laws of that state.

Justification of most of PIL rules can be analyzed by applying these factors, i.e. we could create a matrix to analyze the rules of PIL by combining these factors. Let us elaborate on each element in this matrix further:

First, effectiveness for participant parties means that criterion to judge whether these parties have high possibilities to materialize the results of certain acts. In other words, if this effectiveness is high, transaction costs for these parties are small.

Second, fitness for parties is a criterion according to which the involved parties' decision on the level of PIL fits their relationships and controls their interests properly.

Third, effectiveness for the state means that there exist legal and political reasons as well as physical means to support certain legal judgments, and that these reasons as well as means are in harmony with the judgments. Typical examples of this criterion are the state's intervention based on sovereignty or enforceability of judgments.

Last, but not least, fitness for the state means that certain legal judgments fit the legal system, policy goals and/or values for the state, and that these judgments do not collide with other stakeholders' interests or legal relationships. Government interest or public interest are good examples of this criterion. Exactly speaking, however, public interest could mean social welfare that reflects the intention of members of the state, but it could also mean rulers' goals only. These two must be clearly differentiated.

In addition, by adding different perspectives, i.e. *ex ante* and *ex post*, analysis could be further elaborated. For example, when a specific law such as "the law of the place of occurrence of causal events" is provided for in a pre-determined PIL rule, due care required by that applicable law would influence parties' behaviors. However, if that applicable law and the level of due care could be changed *ex post* by taking the effectiveness and fitness for specific parties into consideration, it would affect the parties' behavior *ex ante*, if they know in advance that applicable law could be changed afterwards. This would affect the society to which the parties belong as well.

4.2 Territoriality

Discussions related to PIL on IP tend to be bound by territoriality. The territoriality is also a widely shared concept concerning PIL on property issues, which include security interest. On the other hand, strictly exclusive territoriality would not be welcomed in modern PIL. Therefore it seems crucial to elaborate the notion. In addition, it should be analyzed under what conditions and to what extent the territoriality appropriately functions.[23]

Although the territoriality has been rarely defined with clarity, such an idea seems to be widely shared that focus is placed on a specific state or society. So it could be understood as a criterion which emphasizes the state's interests rather than parties' interests, but there are some varieties:

The first type of understanding of territoriality is that effectiveness for the state is the absolute stake. Under this understanding, State A should govern cases in which State A should have effectiveness. On the other hand, State A should not intervene in such cases where State B should have effectiveness. As long as State B follows the same principle, States A and B would not cause conflict to each other. As a result, with this understanding, there would be no room to discuss the possibility of choosing applicable law. This view has been traditionally supported concerning IP.

The second type of understating on territoriality is that the choice of applicable law is necessary, but the state's interests should be emphasized. *Lex fori* should be then the applicable law. This view focuses on fitness for the state rather than effectiveness for the state. Because the reason to choose *lex fori* is not that the forum state has effective tools, but that the law of the forum state could materialize the goal of the state better than other laws.

The third type of understanding on territoriality emphasizes strong ties with a specific place, but it could be different from *lex fori*. This approach is based on the idea that the law of such state should be applicable in that it provides IP with real effects of right. Effectiveness for the state is at stake, but it is incorporated in the mechanism of the choice of law (connecting factor). This is described *lex fori protectionis* in the case of IP.

This law is applicable not only in the state which granted the IP, but also in other fora.

Among these views, the first one has been dominant in the field of IP, but the situation has been changing. Supreme Courts in some countries such as Japan and UK took deviating stances from this type of territoriality and applied foreign IP laws.

The first type of territoriality seems to presume certain conditions in order to be functional: First, territorial areas where a state governs effectively and areas where that state should govern must be identical. But this condition could not always be fulfilled. For example, a state where legal or enforcement systems are underdeveloped does not have effective tools to govern and solve disputes within its territory, although it should have it. Thus that state may not provide appropriate solutions in its territory. On the other hand, a huge market state which has historically and politically been influential could be effective even outside of its territory. Second, the first type of territoriality presumes that there would be no lacuna

[23]Some authors analyze whether territoriality should be followed to choose applicable law on IP issues even in the era of globalization and IT. See, for example: Bradley (1997), pp. 505–586; Buxbaum (2009), pp. 631–676; Dinwoodie (2009), pp. 711–800, Metzger (2010), Cook (2014) pp. 293–297, Treppoz (2014), pp. 557–571, Torremans (2013).

or overlapping of areas where states govern effectively. However, due to the expansion of virtual environments and the spread of cloud computing, this condition has been becoming quite unstable. Third, the first type of territoriality links a specific place and goods strongly, but it may sometimes be difficult due to the nature of goods. A classical case is how to identify law applicable to goods in transit. In the case of intangible goods, a connecting factor based on fiction would be inevitable, for example a receivable would be deemed as located in the place of creditor's domicile. Such fiction could be even impossible in the case of public goods or information goods. Fourth, absolute territoriality means that the link with the state could be justified even by excluding other thresholds. But neglecting other interests would need more careful analysis for justification.

This article does not take the first type of territoriality which excludes other considerations than effectiveness for the state. But this article considers the states' and parties' interests on an equal level in order to determine applicable law.

As we saw in the previous section, the matrix to analyze PIL rules is the combination of four elements which the choice of applicable law would affect, i.e. parties and state as beneficiaries and effectiveness and fitness as interests. In order to simplify this analysis, we put effectiveness and fitness together and call them "interests".

		Impact on state's interests	
Impact on parties' interests		Positive	Negative
	Positive	I	II
	Negative	III	IV

Impacts on parties' or state's interests can be illustrated as above. Needless to say, I in this chart would be the most desirable outcome, but at the same time the most difficult to achieve, while IV must be avoided. To be noted is that all these are continuously connected, so this is not a black-and-white-type of decision. As I and IV should be excluded, a real consideration is how to take an appropriate balance between II and III.

Traditional views of PIL on IP or security interest tends to emphasize the state's interests, especially its effectiveness, while party interests are supplementary. According to this view, III should be the core in the chart above. The reason to emphasize the state's effectiveness concerning IP is that legal and relevant systems in the state are the premises of the existence and validity of IP in the country. But no explanation is provided as to why fitness for the state or parties' interests could be neglected. When the state's interests are emphasized and preferred, it should also be examined how it would affect parties' interests, but so far there has been no proper mechanism to adjust the state's and parties' interests.

This article proposes to take both parties' and state's interests on equal footing without assuming that territoriality should be the principle. Since taking such an approach enables us to examine the pros and cons of various PIL rules without prejudice.

4.3 Party Autonomy[24]

Under certain circumstances, party autonomy could play absolutely desirable roles, i.e. if all stakeholders in a specific cross-border relationship could discuss and decide with full capacity, with sufficient information, without causing any transaction costs, effectiveness and fitness for the stakeholders would be ideal under such circumstances and there would be no need for improvement. If a condition that their decision on applicable law would not affect anyone else, including any state, would be fulfilled, party autonomy would be absolutely the optimal PIL rule. However such ideal conditions could be rarely satisfied. Therefore functions of party autonomy should be analyzed by modifying conditions.

(1) The first situation would be that the choice of law by parties' agreement would cause externality to third parties. In other words, there would be some entities who would be affected by the choice of law, but it would be too costly for them to participate in the negotiation and decision-making processes. The applicable law identified by parties' negotiations, which may be optimal for them, could then badly impact third parties' interests. Therefore it would become necessary for third parties to control the choice of law.
(2) The second situation is imperfect information, i.e. if information on the nature of goods or other stakeholders or their behaviors is limited, or to obtain such information would be costly, such information is called imperfect information. Under the situation with imperfect information, there would be no guarantee that the parties' negotiations would bring about the optimal solution. If for example parties do not have exact information on the value of IP or its contents, they could not negotiate applicable law properly. This means fitness for parties would be lowered. Alternatively, in such cases where it is too costly to observe a debtor's behavior (replacement of collateral, change of his/her domicile etc.), the applicable law chosen by the involved parties cannot materialize anticipated legal effects. In this instance the effectiveness for parties would be damaged. A situation with imperfect information could be adjusted by paying high transaction costs, but the significance of party autonomy would then be lost. In such cases, other types of PIL rules over party autonomy should be opted for.
(3) The third situation is intertemporal consistency, i.e. if optimal acts *ex ante* and *ex post* could be different, how should they be coordinated? For example, at the time of conclusion of a contract, to make sanctions strict in the case of default would make sense to encourage the debtor to pay debts, even despite high transaction costs. But at the stage at which default occurs, it would perhaps be desirable to impose sanctions which would not cause high costs. However if it is anticipated in advance that the strict sanctioning would not be applied to

---

[24]In this context, see Borchers (2008), pp. 1645–1661, Lehmann (2008), pp. 381–434, Rühl (2009), pp. 153–183, Kramer and Themeli (2016), pp. 27–49, and Maultzsch (2016), pp. 466–491, Bebchuk and Guzman (1999), pp. 775–808 identified that, applying economic analysis, party autonomy enhances global welfare much more than territoriality.

avoid transaction costs, payment could not be encouraged. If originally anticipated strict sanction should be applied in any case even where events unexpected at the time of contract conclusion caused default, such a strict stance could discourage or prevent the conclusion of contract. To adjust these inconsistent situations *ex ante* and *ex post* is usually difficult for parties. This is because they could decide the best possible option at each time and have no incentive to adjust them.

(4) In the above-stated cases, party autonomy may not be the best option. However if pursuing parties' interests is absolutely crucial despite externalities, party autonomy could be justified. Or despite imperfect information, if it would be even more difficult for third parties to obtain information or to analyze it due to the complex relationships between parties, party autonomy could be justified as less problematic option. Or even if intertemporal adjustment would be important, since several countries could often be involved in cross-border situations, it could be very complicated to look into various scenarios *ex ante* and *ex post* in several countries. Eventually party autonomy may make intertemporal adjustment more easily.

Thus although party autonomy cannot always be the optimal solution, it does not mean that party autonomy is always inadequate. Party autonomy should be placed, as an option, on the same level as other PIL rules and its pros and cons in its functions and effects should be equally compared with those of other PIL rules.

5 Functional Analysis of PIL Rules on Security Interest in IP[25]

5.1 Party Autonomy and Its Conditions

In order for party autonomy to be a useful tool to choose law applicable to security interest in IP, based on the considerations above, the following should be the conditions for party autonomy to function better than other types of PIL rules:

[1] Parties are highly rational,
[2] It is easy for parties to negotiate,
[3] Parties have enough information,
[4] No big externality or compatibility issue,
[5] Agreed contents can be accurately and certainly carried out with low costs.

[25] Harris (2007), Akseli (2011), Gullifer and Akseli (2016), Matulionyte (2011), Dornis (2017). Tosato (2011), pp. 93–104 discusses on security interest in IP. See Thomas (2016).

In addition, in the case of party autonomy *ex ante*, the following conditions should be fulfilled:

[A1] Parties' negotiation *ex ante* is easy,
[A2] Parties have sufficient information in advance; in other words they would not obtain important information *ex post*,
[A3] Parties' *ex ante* agreement would not affect their activities or results *ex post*,
[A4] Parties' *ex ante* agreement could surely be implemented with low costs.

In the case of party autonomy *ex post*, these conditions should be modified as follows:

[B1] Parties' negotiation *ex post* is easy,
[B2] Information obtained *ex post* is more important than information in advance,
[B3] Parties' *ex post* agreement would not affect their activities *ex ante*,
[B4] Parties' *ex post* agreement could accurately and certainly be implemented with low costs at the time of agreement.

In short, party autonomy is desirable, provided that an appropriate agreement is made at the time of the parties' negotiations, that the agreement is consistent throughout the process of contractual arrangement, and that the agreement can be implemented with low costs.

Some of these conditions, especially conditions [3], [4], [A1], [A2], [B1] and [B2], may be difficult to fulfill, if these conditions should be applied to security interest in IP.

Hence, other types of PIL rules will be analyzed in the following sections, focusing on each function of security interest which we identified in the previous chapter.

The methodology is as follows: first, we identify conditions which make each function of security interest work, then we single out the factors that would impact these conditions. Last, but not least, based on these factors, we clarify (the best) possible PIL rules, taking into consideration effectiveness and fitness for parties and the state.

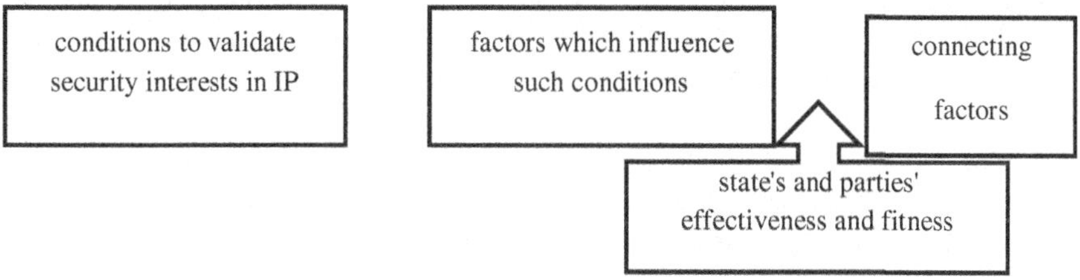

5.2 *Function 1: Debt Collection and PIL*

We identified five conditions which positively influence the debt collecting function in the previous chapter. If we could determine applicable law which could fulfill these conditions, the debt collecting function could work well.

5.2.1 Condition 1: High Possibility of Debtor's Default

If the risk of default is low, the involved parties would lose their interest in the effective function of security interest. To be noted here is that how to calculate the possibility of default is not crucial, but the involved parties' awareness on debtor's default is. Influential factors on debtor's default would be the debtor's business condition and environment, other creditors' intentions, and legal mechanisms to control these factors. If a PIL rule could raise participant parties' awareness on such factors with minimal costs, such a PIL rule would be a desirable one.

If party autonomy would be adopted and different laws would be chosen in the relationship between the debtor and each creditor, the transaction costs to obtain information on the debtor's business condition and business environment based on each applicable law would be enormous. The costs to integrate all creditors into one negotiation process would be prohibitive. Therefore an objective connecting factor is a realistic solution.

Such a connecting factor should be justified from the view point of effectiveness and fitness for parties. The law of the state of debtor's domicile seems the best option for the following reasons:

[1] The state of the debtor's domicile usually, compared to other states, has more means to directly intervene for disclosure and acquisition of information on the specific debtor. In addition, a debtor and other individuals and firms in the debtor's neighboring areas influence one another. Therefore we could assume that the law of the place of the debtor's domicile fits best the policy goal, the legal system and business customs of the state of his/her domicile.

[2] It is easy for parties to predict and specify the law of the place of the debtor's domicile in advance. Thus effectiveness for participant parties is enhanced. In addition, a debtor's business and transactions are often regulated by specific local rules or customs. This means that the place of a debtor's domicile is the place where the information about the debtor's business is more accurate and creditors' awareness could be raised further.

[3] As stated above, a parties' subjective awareness is at stake. Such awareness itself does not cause externality. Hence, there is no need to examine externality.

5.2.2 Condition 2: High Enforceability of Collateral

This condition depends upon not only the speed and certainty of the enforcement of collateral, but also of transfer of ownership of IP as well as deposition of IP. These elements are usually different in each contract to set up IP as collateral, so that situations are more complex and individual than the condition 1. Instead of the legislator or the court, parties are in better position to collect relevant information on enforceability of collateral and to analyze the circumstances. Party autonomy could be a choice, since it would be easier for parties to join an agreement which could enhance enforceability of IP collateral as a common goal of all creditors.

However, if consistency between *ex ante* and *ex post* stages or the absence of certain parties in the process to agree on applicable law could cause problems, the advantage of party autonomy would be lost. Hence the possibilities of objective connecting factors should be examined. Although there may be a number of possible options, we take only the law of the place of debtor's domicile and *lex loci protectionis* in order to make our analysis simple and clear.

The threshold here is also the effectiveness and fitness for the state and relevant parties. To be noted is that there is a specificity in that we should differentiate creditors who hold collateral and creditors without collateral. Because the former has a stronger position in terms of enforceability compared to the latter creditors. Also, states should be distinguished as those having interests in collateral agreement contract and those related to the protection of IP. These can be summarized as indicated in the chart below:

	Parties			States	
	Creditors		Debtor	IP protection	Debtor's domicile
	With collateral	No collateral			
Effectiveness					
Fitness					

[1] Debtor's domicile as objective connecting factor

1. Effectiveness and fitness for the debtor would be enhanced by applying the law of the place as the center of his/her activities.
2. For creditors, a certain degree of effectiveness is secured by the law of the place of the debtor's domicile, because it is easily identifiable. But this law is not necessarily familiar to creditors, so fitness for creditors would be low. There would be no different interests between creditors with collateral and those without collateral, since they would have obtained the debtor's information before they entered into transactions with the debtor. As for intertemporal consistency, a change of a debtor's domicile after validation of IP or conclusion of a collateral agreement might affect consistency between *ex ante* and *ex post*.

But information on the debtor's new address would be relatively easy to obtain, as long as the business relationship continues, so its negative influence would not be so big.
3. The law of the state where the debtor holds his/her domicile is designed to apply to its residents, so that its effectiveness and fitness for the state is high.
4. As long as the state with a debtor's domicile belonging to WTO, an internal minimum standard of IP protection is guaranteed. Thus a certain degree of effectiveness would be guaranteed. But to what extent the enforcement of IP protection is carried out could differ from state to state. Therefore the level of effectiveness of the law of the state of a debtor's domicile may not be high for the IP protecting state. In addition, the law of the state with a debtor's domicile would not fit IP granted by its protecting state well. If institutions in two countries are not compatible, it would be even worse and may result in losses.

This analysis is summarized as below:

	Parties			States	
	Creditors		Debtor	IP protection	Debtor's domicile
	With collateral	No collateral			
Effectiveness	○	○	◎	△	◎
Fitness	△	△	◎	×	◎

◎: almost optimal, ○: desirable, △: not desirable, ×: seriously problematic

[2] IP-Protecting State

1. Legal protection of a collateral agreement is affected by the security interest system under the IP-protecting state. Creditors with collateral could incorporate such a scheme into their collateral agreements, so that effectiveness and fitness of the law of the IP-protecting state is high for such creditors, while it is low for creditors with no collateral. Positions of creditors with no collateral could be even worse after new creditors have obtained collateral.
2. Effectiveness and fitness for a debtor is ensured, since the law of the IP-protecting state is predictable through the existence of IP or negotiations to conclude a collateral agreement. But these cost to the debtor, so that the law of an IP-protecting state is not optimal for the debtor.
3. The IP-protecting state can manage its legal system to enforce IP rights on its own initiative, so that the effectiveness and fitness of its own law is high. However, under such circumstances where issues of compatibility with other relevant systems would arise, effectiveness and fitness would be worsened.
4. For the state of a debtor's domicile, application of the law of the IP-protecting state could be a surprise and may threaten the certainty of transactions or assets in its territory, so that effectiveness and fitness for the state of a debtor's domicile would be low. However such a surprise would be smaller among member States of WTO.

5. Applying the law of an IP-protecting state means the application of multiple laws in a case, irrespective of setting up collateral. Hence costs to collect information on all applicable laws, negotiations as well as costs caused by incompatibility among relevant laws could become so high that effectiveness and fitness for all stakeholders, tates and parties, would be lowered.

	Parties			States	
	Creditors		Debtor	IP protection	Debtor's domicile
	With collateral	No collateral			
Effectiveness	○	△	○	○	×∼△
Fitness	○	△	○	○	×∼△

From the above-stated considerations, party autonomy is not a realistic solution for condition 2. Comparing the two charts above, the state of a debtor's domicile is a more appropriate connecting factor. But under exceptional circumstances, such as if a debtor's domicile is not identifiable or there is little compatibility between relevant systems (IP, collateral, contract etc.) , the law of IP-protecting state could be appropriate.

5.2.3 Condition 3: High Disposability and Usability

Even if a creditor obtains assets as collateral, these assets must be converted into a monetary value in order to achieve the function of debt collection. Hence, how effective such conversion could be made is at stake for security interest. In the case of security interest in IP, collateral is a right which depends upon the legal system in each state. This means that key business factors such as the stability of IP as a property right, possibilities to find business partners, business negotiations, or ensured enforcement heavily depend upon legal systems and business customs.

High disposability or usability of collateral depends upon a number of factors, including the situation of the market of properties. At the end of the day, whether collateral has high disposability or not relies on a creditor's judgment who should take such factors into consideration.

Since the final decision should be made based on a creditor's subjective judgment, it is not necessary to care about its externality to third parties. Also the debtor would not have direct interests concerning condition 3: When conversion in cash should be realized, it is only after the enforcement of collateral. At this stage, the debtor has already lost his/her power to dispose or use the assets. Therefore, for the debtor, condition 3 (high disposability or usability of collateral) would only apply as a tool to improve his/her position in contractual negotiations at the *ex ante* stage. For the creditor, on the other hand, fulfillment of condition 3 is desirable anyway. Hence there is no big conflict of interests between the creditor with collateral and the debtor. The most desirable option for the involved parties would therefore be for the creditor to choose *ex post* applicable law which enhances disposability and/or usability as much as possible.

This option would raise no issue from the viewpoint of intertemporal consistency. The creditor would not oppose the idea, since he/she could only strengthen his/her position by choosing *ex post* appropriate law to enhance disposability or/and usability of assets. The debtor on the other hand would not oppose at the *ex ante* stage, since he/she could enhance his/her position in negotiations, while at the *ex post* stage he/she would have already lost the assets.

5.2.4 Condition 4: High Value of Collateral

Also this condition comes into play only after IP as collateral has been transferred to creditor. So the situation is similar to condition 3. Both the debtor and creditor have also interests in raising values of collateral to improve each position. Therefore party autonomy is a valid option for them. Intertemporal consistency is not an issue under this situation, since the original collateral agreement has been terminated after the enforcement of collateral.

However there is a specificity of condition 4; if a state has a security interest system where collateral with excessive values compared to the size of debt should be restricted, it means that the system pays due attention to possible impacts caused by such a collateral arrangement for third parties. In this case, the state's effectiveness and fitness come into play, so that, different from condition 3, an objective connecting factor would be more desirable than party autonomy.

The threshold to identify a desirable objective connecting factor should be whether higher IP-values could be realized smoothly and promptly with low costs. The state of a debtor's domicile and the IP-protecting state should be compared from this viewpoint.

The law of the IP-protecting state has high effectiveness and fitness, since its law applicable to security interest in IP is compatible well with its other legal systems and mechanisms related to the IP-transactions. On the other hand, the law of the State of debtor's domicile also has high effectiveness and fitness, since the law is familiar to a debtor's business partners and competitors in neighboring areas, so that disposition of IP obtained from the debtor would become easy. For instance, when a firm in an industry cluster is insolvent, if other firms in the cluster take over IP, facilities, employees and customers, it could raise the values of IP with less costs.

Due to different reasons of effectiveness and fitness, it is difficult to determine *ex ante* which should be adopted, the State of a debtor's domicile or the IP-protecting state. A possible idea could be these two as alternative connecting factors, depending upon more important circumstances identified *ex post*.

Conditions		Connecting factors
High possibility of default	⇒	Debtor's domicile
High enforceability of collateral	⇒	Party autonomy or Debtor's domicile
High dispositionability or Usability	⇒	Creditors' choice *ex post*
High value of collateral	⇒	Debtor's domicile or IP-protection, as alternative connecting factor circumstances
Diverse transaction costs	⇒	No appropriate option

Summary conditions for function 1 (ensuring debt collection) and possible connecting factors

5.3 *Function 2: Insulation of Collateral*

5.3.1 Condition 1: Insulation of Assets as an Advantage

Assuming that each debtor's asset has its own risk, insulating prime assets from risky assets helps to save costs in obtaining information about a debtor's assets. Risks of asset depend upon factors which determine values of the asset. In the case of IP, the factors could be divided into the way of legal protection of a specific IP and the way to use the IP. If the outcomes of an IP protection scheme are unpredictable or if there are a number of difficulties to commercialize the IP (e.g. the lack of an IP-evaluation scheme), the risk becomes bigger.

Each creditor has a different capacity to evaluate and cope with such risks. If a debtor who owns different types of assets would offer his/her entire assets as collateral, the total transaction costs for the debtor would become higher. These costs increase because the creditor may not have sufficient capacity to properly evaluate certain types of assets. On the other hand, if the debtor would offer only specific types of assets as collateral to a specific creditor with better capacity to evaluate the assets and to cope with risks, the costs for the debtor would decrease. Insulating specific assets from other assets contributes to this function. Cost reduction for each debtor achieved in this manner would lead to a reduction of costs for the entire society and improve social welfare. Therefore insulation of prime assets is desirable not only for parties in a specific case, but also for the entire society.

In order to keep the insulation function beneficial, each party's value and risk judgments must be properly made. To be noted is that judgment on values and risks of assets is each party's subjective decision and that each party's capacity plays a crucial role for decision making. Therefore judgment on values and risks of assets has no externality to other parties. Thus effectiveness and fitness for the state are not related, and only the parties' effective and fitness are at stake. In such a case, party autonomy *ex ante* is usually an appropriate mechanism to choose applicable law. In cases where party autonomy does not adequately function, for example a party's risk judgment was misguided by other parties, the law which the respective parties would have chosen must be identified. For example, if the debtor uses IP for his/her business, the place where the business should be developed would be an appropriate connecting factor. If predictability under an IP protection scheme is at stake, the IP-protecting state would be relevant.

5.3.2 Condition 2: Small Costs to Obtain Information on Collateral, and Taking Collateral Brings About no Risk (Surprise) for Other Creditors

If the debtor would have consulted with all creditors and decided with which creditor and what type of collateral agreement should be concluded, no externality would occur, so that party autonomy would be desirable. However in real world settings it would be difficult to assume such a situation. In addition, the debtor has an incentive to negotiate with a specific creditor to conclude collateral agreement. Hence an objective connecting factor would be needed.

From the viewpoint of effectiveness and fitness for the involved parties, neither the IP-protecting state nor the state of the debtor's domicile would be adequate.

Because, without establishing a scheme to publicly notice collateral agreements concluded somewhere in the world, it would be impossible to control the debtor's incentive to make a special deal with a specific creditor. Appropriate applicable law should be such a law which controls the debtor's incentive and the creditor's behavior. From this viewpoint, the connecting factor that other creditors would determine *ex post* would be adequate. In this case, other creditors who suffered damages due to the debtor's surprise acts should be able to choose the most preferable law for them. Hence they should be able to recover the damages by applying such a law. If the debtor should know *ex ante* that the choice of law by other creditors could happen *ex post*, the debtor may be discouraged from making a special deal with a specific creditor.[26]

5.3.3 Condition 3: Assets Are Legally Isolable, Without Being Overwritten by Bigger Policy Goals

This condition's main point is to maintain independence of specific assets from other assets without being overwritten by an insolvency procedure. It would be

[26]Applicable law chosen *ex post* by other creditors may not satisfy effectiveness and fitness for state. If the debtor received benefits through a special deal with a specific creditor, and such benefits are much larger than damages caused to other creditors, the state of the debtor's domicile may accept the result and justify the outcome of the debtor's behaviour. This could be legitimate, since the world's welfare would be raised as a whole. As this example suggests, a decision based on weighing parties' interests and states' interests is crucial.

desirable that all parties could agree on where the insolvency procedure should be commenced, but such an agreement would be impossible to reach in the real world. Generally speaking, the place where the insolvency procedure commenced should be the connecting factor, which is usually the debtor's main office of business.

Maintaining the independence from the insolvency procedure has externality against third parties. Hence party autonomy is not relevant, instead an appropriate objective connecting factor should be identified.

The place of a debtor's domicile is often identical to the place of commencement of the insolvency procedure. Usually domestic security interest law and insolvency law are in harmony. But if the state has a rehabilitation-oriented insolvency procedure, such a procedure probably imposes some restriction on collateral. Security interest law is usually so designed as to accept such restriction. Hence, the law of debtor's domicile may not satisfy condition 3.

On the other hand, the IP-protecting state is not relevant to such an issue whether collateral should be restricted in the case of insolvency. Instead, parties' expectation on the independence of collateral would be ensured by the laws of the IP-protecting state.

Under this law, fitness for the involved parties would be achieved as well, i.e. for creditors with collateral, the law of the IP-protecting state ensures collateral, therefore effectiveness and fitness for the parties should be high. In addition, if the debtor knows in advance that the position of a creditor with collateral would be enhanced, it is a useful negotiation tool. Effectiveness and fitness would become high for the debtor as well.

5.3.4 Condition 4: Unintentional Information Delivery Does not Occur

If a debtor does something unusual in the business circle in a specific area, it may trigger doubts about the debtor's solvency. Like this example, deviation from a specific culture or custom may attract people's attention, although it should not happen when specific assets should be insulated. The situation detailed in this example would happen between the debtor and his/her still potential creditors or potential business partners. Therefore there would be no room for party autonomy.

On the other hand, such potential creditors and business partners usually exist in neighboring areas of the debtor's business. Whether a debtor's acts are "unusual" or not, would be judged based on local business customs. For example, if a security interest in IP is rare in a region, IP as collateral alone may send some negative signs on the debtor's financial situation.

From this viewpoint, the law of the place of the debtor's domicile would show high effectiveness and fitness for the state: the state of debtor's domicile would be impacted by such negative signs, but the state would be equipped with the best possible means to cope with it, understanding social and economic conditions of such a negative sign. In addition, other parties should be aware of the law of the state of the debtor's domicile, so that fitness with a specific transaction is also high. Hence, a negative sign on the debtor's solvency could be well controlled by using the debtor's domicile as a connecting factor. Other connecting factors would be less adequate from each viewpoint of effectiveness and of fitness.

5.3.5 Condition 5: No Overwriting by Alternative Schemes

If raising capital should take place in a place, alternative schemes other than collateral may be available, which have also an insulation function similar to collateral. Governing law applicable to security interest in IP should clarify such questions whether using such alternative schemes would be appropriate, and, in the case of "yes", how to coordinate it with the original law applicable to collateral agreement.

Even in the context of domestic law, new schemes with insulation function similar to security interest could be developed. These alternative schemes often emerge outside of the framework of the existing legal system and may not yet be established in such a sense that parties would negotiate *ex ante* in details about the legal protection of an alternative scheme. Thus the parties could not agree on the scheme nor make evidences to the level where even third parties could clearly understand *ex post* the details of the scheme. Such incompleteness of the alternative schemes would be improved with the development of legal rules and interpretations, but due to such incompleteness, it would be difficult to judge *ex ante* whether an alternative mechanism should be preferred to security interest.

This would be more complicated in the cross-border context. Classification in the sense of PIL of an alternative mechanism could be difficult due to the incompleteness. Identification of applicable law might not be possible. Such complexity could differ in each alternative scheme. Hence party autonomy could be an adequate solution, since it could deal with specificity in individual cases. If parties could agree on applicable law, choosing collateral or alternative schemes, and as long as their *ex ante* agreement on applicable law would remain valid, this condition "no overwriting by alternative scheme" would be fulfilled.

However, party autonomy may be less effective for parties, if to obtain information on alternative schemes would be costly. Also intertemporal consistency between *ex ante* and *ex post* stages might not be maintained due to the incompleteness of alternative schemes. Hence options for objective connecting factors should be examined.

Because of low effectiveness for participating parties, which stems from incompleteness of the scheme, results expected in the parties' agreement may not be materialized. On the other hand, the fact that parties agreed to take the alternative scheme despite such uncertainty implies that collateral has lower fitness for parties than the alternative scheme. This dilemma (collateral has lower fitness, while the alternative scheme is less effective) could be solved only by restricting the overwriting of the original collateral agreement.[27]

An example of a PIL rule, according to which overwriting would not occur after a collateral agreement was concluded, should be party autonomy in such a situation where applicable law, agreed *ex ante* by parties, has high fitness for involved parties. The implementation of the agreement should be ensured by evidencing the contents of the agreement to a certain degree. By this PIL rule, the agreement will be accurately and certainly carried out. As a result, effectiveness for parties would be added to the applicable law with high fitness.

How about a case where a law agreed *ex ante* by parties has fitness, but evidencing the agreed contents is difficult? Collateral agreement could make objective evidence available more easily than an alternative scheme, but in the case of movable property or IP as collateral, the contents of an agreement may be unclear.[28] But the court should be careful to accept parties' arguments based on alternative connecting factors and should stick to the originally chosen applicable law.

An additional advantage to restrict overwriting the original collateral agreement would be to lower unexpected surprise risk for other creditors. From these considerations, concerning condition 5, party autonomy *ex ante* under certain conditions would be desirable. Technically speaking, such a restriction may be imposed, using the framework of public policy.

Conditions		Connecting factor
Advantage for insulation • Risk differs in each asset • Save costs to obtain information	⇒	Party autonomy + Supplementary connecting factors
No restriction on insulation (1) • Small costs to obtain info on collateral • No risk for other creditors	⇒	Choice by other creditors *ex post*
No restriction on insulation (2) • Legally insolable • No overwritten by bigger purposes	⇒	IP-protecting state
No restriction on insulation (3) • Ignore signaling effects	⇒	Debtor's domicile
No restriction on insulation (4) • Not overwritten by alternative schemes	⇒	Party autonomy

[27]This applies at least to situations where the collateral agreement was concluded first, then parties may switch to an alternative scheme. This however needs more elaboration. For example, cases where parties chose an alternative scheme first, then they decided to switch to security interest, or cases where an alternative scheme becomes desirable ex post, should be examined.

[28]For example, a registration system for these kinds of collateral is not well developed.

5.4 *Function 3: Control Function of Security Interest and PIL*

The main function here is how to control a debtor's behavior, focusing on closed and specific agreement between parties.

5.4.1 Condition 1: Parties Are Aware of Conditions and Mechanisms to Make This Function Work

This condition concerns a party's specific agreement. Thus party autonomy is appropriate. Collateral agreement as the basis of this control function should contain a clause on applicable law, since applicable law and its legal effects influence the involved parties' decision making and its process. Involved parties should *ex ante* negotiate, collect/exchange information, and consult each other under this law. Although it may turn out *ex post* that pre-determined applicable law may become less desirable, instead of jumping to an objective connecting factor, the originally agreed applicable law should be respected. Not only because it would give parties stronger incentives to carefully choose applicable law, but also because respecting the originally agreed applicable law can be justified also from the viewpoint of effectiveness and fitness for the state. As long as there is no externality, enhancing the effectiveness and fitness for involved parties means satisfying the state's interests. When participating parties would choose the law and the law is effective to control the debtor, effectiveness for the state would be strengthened as well. Also parties would carefully choose applicable law with high fitness in order to cope with sensitive aspects of control function. This would lead to the enhancement of fitness for the state. In addition, respecting the originally agreed upon applicable law contributes to intertemporal consistency.

5.4.2 Condition 2: Proper Incentives

The control function aims at controlling debtor's behaviors in order to achieve specific goals set up by the parties. Therefore objectives of the control function should be decided upon by parties' agreement. This article takes three typical examples of controls over the debtor.

Example 1: The debtor should make his/her best management efforts

These kind of efforts enhance the possibilities of other creditors to collect their debts (positive externality), so that other creditors would not legally demand the debtor to make more efforts. Only very few disputes would occur, so the state would have little incentive to get involved. The important consideration is how to achieve effectiveness and fitness for the involved parties. Thus party autonomy seems appropriate.

Example 2: The debtor should make efforts to pay to specific creditors

If a debtor's efforts to pay to a specific creditor would negatively affect other creditors' possibilities to collect their debts, other creditors may request to make less efforts (negative externality). Due to such externality (which could be bigger, when it develops as a legal dispute), party autonomy is inappropriate and objective connecting points should be preferred.

Taking into consideration effectiveness and fitness for the creditor with collateral and other creditors as well as for the debtor, the debtor's domicile would be appropriate connecting factor. The law of the state of the debtor's domicile serves also effectiveness and fitness for the state, since externality usually occurs in areas neighboring the debtor's domicile.

Example 3: The debtor should make efforts to maintain values of IP as collateral

The debtor may not make sufficient efforts to maintain values of IP due to information asymmetry between the debtor and creditors. Hence, it is desirable to choose a law which could prevent the loss of value in IP. Party autonomy is a good basis to begin with from the viewpoint of effectiveness and fitness for parties. Other connecting factors are difficult to justify.

5.4.3 Condition 3: Outputs Exceeding Costs

It is desirable to choose applicable law which could increase outcomes brought about by control function and at the same time to reduce costs. Both outcomes and costs depend upon factors in the relationship between debtor and creditors. Therefore party autonomy is desirable from the viewpoint of parties' interests. Whether outcomes of the control function exceed costs or not, does not cause any externality, so that there is no need to pay attention to the state's interests.

5.4.4 Condition 4: Stability of the Control Function

Under this condition, it is expected to identify an applicable law which would not allow the state to intervene or modify or parties to deviate from the original collateral contract, must be identified. If intervention by the state or deviation from the original agreement by parties would easily occur, the control function would lose its basis. However in a number of states, rules for state's intervention are integrated in the legal system, such as rules to cancel collateral or rules to change the priorities among creditors. These rules for the state's intervention usually have a persuasive rationale. Hence, whatever law is chosen as applicable law, as long as the purpose of condition 4 is to exclude the state's intervention, condition 4 would be difficult to fulfill.

Another option would be, accepting that the state's intervention is inevitable, to identify an applicable law under which the state's intervention is less strong. In this case, parties may be in the best position to identify such law. However, this approach would have two shortcomings. First, laws with weaker state intervention might be "softer" law and it may have ambiguous requirements or legal effect of security interest. This would be a problem from the viewpoint of effectiveness for parties, since to obtain sufficient information on such ambiguous rules would be costly. Second, such "softer" law would not satisfy the state's interests, since intervention by the state should be an effective tool of the state to pursue its policy goal, irrespective of parties' agreement.

Control function relies on the involved parties' relationships, so that party autonomy should be the main PIL rule. However, conditions to identify applicable law for this function could be difficult to fulfill. Hence, an alternative would be to identify an objective connecting factor, which refers to the place which would be affected by collateral. The state's intervention would decrease fitness for parties, but effectiveness for parties may improve. Because the law becomes more predictable through the objective connecting factor and obtaining information on the law would be less costly. But if several states want to intervene, setting up connecting factors in advance might be difficult.

Conditions	Connecting factors
Parties know conditions and mechanism well	Party autonomy
Provide appropriate incentives	Party autonomy Debtor's domicile (if negative externality would occur)
Outcomes exceed costs	Party autonomy
Mechanism which makes control function work	IP-protecting country or Debtor's domicile, but anyway with limits

6 Comparative Analysis with the CLIP Principles

(1) The most detailed rule on the security interest in IP is proposed in the CLIP Principles (Art. 3:802).[29] This provision proposes two connecting factors, i.e. grantor's habitual residence at the time of the creation of the security right and the IP-protecting state (the State for which protection is sought), and allocates certain issues to each connecting factor.

[29]European Max-Planck Group on Conflict of Laws in Intellectual Property (CLIP) (2013), pp. 354–369, p. 507.

As a rationale for choosing the IP-protecting state, several advantages are pointed out:

[A1] this approach "avoids *dépeçage* between the property right and the security interest, which makes it easier to comply with registration requirements in the country of protection which may be a prerequisite for third-party effectiveness of the security right"[30];
[A2] "assignees or licensees in the country of protection may expect that any transaction affecting their position is governed by the same law which governs the intellectual property right itself"[31];
[A3] "the application of the law of the country of protection may be seen as the closest equivalent to the *situs* of corporeal property".[32]

On the other hand, its shortcomings are identified as follows:

[S1] *lex loci protectionis* leads to a fragmentation of the secured transaction;
[S2] whether the justification of *lex loci protectionis*, i.e. the protection of the economic, social and cultural policy of the country of protection applies equally to a mere security interest;
[S3] while there are some aspects of security rights which clearly concern the interests of third parties or of the registration authority, others seem to be relevant primarily or exclusively for the relationship between the parties of the transaction;
[S4] the application of several laws may lead to frictions in insolvency;
[S5] a study of substantive law reveals that only certain aspects of secured transactions in this field are governed by specific IP legislation, while others fall under the general rules of secured transactions law.[33]

As the result of these considerations, the CLIP Principles distinguish those matters which concern IP rights as such, to which the laws of the IP-protecting state are applicable and other matters on the general law of secured transactions, which are referred to the law of the grantor's habitual residence.

Issues connected to the grantor's habitual residence are (a) the security agreement that creates or transfers the security right, (b) any registration requirements in general security rights registers, (c) the security right's dependence on the existence of the secured obligation, (d) the transferability of the security right, (e) the enforcement of the security right[34] (Art. 3:802, para.1).

---

[30]CLIP (2013), p. 355.

[31]CLIP (2013), pp. 355–356.

[32]CLIP (2013), p. 356.

[33]CLIP (2013), p. 356.

[34]But if the enforcement involves the transfer of ownership in an IP right, the law of the state of protection applies to the question whether and under which conditions ownership in the IP right may be transferred. Art. 3:802 (1) (2) of CLIP. See CLIP (2013), p. 354.

Issues referred to the IP-protecting state are (a) the existence, validity, scope and all other issues concerning the IP rights, (b) the ownership of the IP right, (c) the bona fide acquisition of an IP right or security interests in such rights, (d) any registration requirement in IP registers of the State of protection and the effects of registration or non-registration in such registers, and (e) the property and the third-party effects (Art. 3:802, para.2).

And the CLIP Principles do not "address the law applicable to the obligation for which security is provided, the law applicable to insolvency proceedings or the effects of such proceedings" (Art. 3:803).

(2) As the CLIP Principles clarified in [S2], the function of security interest in IP should be clearly distinguished from general policy goals of IP rights on which the state of protection has much to say. The-*lex-loci-protectionis*-only-approach should be excluded, as the CLIP Principles rightly did. Also the CLIP Principles are right to acknowledge that only some aspects of the security interest concern third parties, but some others do not, and that IP legislation is applicable to only certain aspects of security interest.

The CLIP Principles selected certain matters related to third parties and referred them to the law of the IP protecting state (Art. 3:802 (2)), while other matters are made subject to the general rules of secured transactions (Art. 3:802 (1)). Assuming from such characterization of issues, the CLIP Principles seem to be led by the prototypical legal structure of security interest against the prototype of a contractual relationship, i.e. always-more-than-two-parties-relationship against two-parties-relationship. It further led to a focus only on states' interests. As its result, party autonomy was not analyzed at all. Consequently a control function for which parties play crucial roles was not analyzed either. As we argued above, as long as no externality occurs, party autonomy could bring about optimal results. The prototypical approach prevents analysis under what circumstances such externality would occur, where party autonomy would be inappropriate.

Second, as for the debt collection function, only one condition out of four in our analysis, i.e. enforcement of the security right is on the list in Art. 3:802 (1) (e), where the law of the grantor's habitual residence is applicable, with reservation of the applicability of the law of IP-protecting state to the transfer of ownership in IP. We are also of the view that the law of the place of the debtor's domicile should be applicable, so that we could support this provision. An aspect on which the CLIP Principles' position is unclear is the usability of IP as collateral. As we analyzed, the usability is generally based on a creditors' subjective decisions for security rights. The difference between real property and IP as collateral in this aspect for example is the quality and quantity of available information for decision-making. Due to the lack of widely accepted valuation methods and schemes for IP as collateral, such subjective nature is stronger for IP. As for value judgments, although party autonomy could be justified due to the subjective nature of the value judgment, we proposed the debtor's domicile and IP-protecting state as alternative connecting factors. The position of the CLIP Principles on these issues is not clear.

A possible reason might be that the parties' interests were not considered. Even objective connecting factors should have been examined from both parties' and state's perspectives.

Third, as for insulation function, we proposed to apply the law of IP-protecting state to lawful insulation of specific assets. Art. 3:802 (2) (a)[35] of the CLIP Principles may be similar to our view, but the language "all other issues concerning intellectual property right" in this provision makes its scope blur and needs more clarification. Other conditions we identified are not listed as the issues identified in the CLIP Principles. Or they may be covered by "all other issues concerning intellectual property right" in Art. 3:802 (2) (a). In the latter case, our conclusions are different, since we propose to apply the law of the place of the debtor's domicile or chosen by creditors, depending upon conditions. In the former case, as above said, the text needs clarification. For such a purpose, the CLIP Principles would need a behavioral analysis of the involved parties.

7 Conclusions

This article aims at contributing to academic debates on PIL rules on security interest in IP by functional analysis. For this purpose, this article clarified functions of the security interest and its conditions first. It places party autonomy and two objective connecting factors on the same level for detailed analysis; we identified what option as a PIL rule would be appropriate for each condition of individual function of security interest in IP. Outcome of this analysis provides tools to clarify what was discussed and what not, and to highlight not fully conceived parts of previous discussions. The CLIP Principles were compared with our proposals from this perspective. They seem to have applied the prototypical legal structure of the security interest to draft its text, so that some issues to be analyzed from the viewpoint of functions of the security interest do not appear on the list of issues identified in the CLIP Principles. Perspectives from both states' and parties' interests should be properly integrated in the analytical process.

References

Adler BE (1998) Secured credit contracts. In: Newman P (ed) The new palgrave dictionary of economics and the law, pp 405–410

Akseli NO (2011) International secured transactions law: facilitation of credit and international conventions and instruments. Routledge, Abington

[35]The law of the state for which protection is sought shall apply to (a) the existence, validity, scope and all other issues concerning the IP right as such which is used as security, including the question whether a particular IP right may be transferred or encumbered to create a security right.

Armour J (2008) The law and economics debate about secured lending: lessons for European lawmaking? Eur Co Financ Law Rev Spec 2:3–29
Baird DG (2004) Secured lending and its uncertain future. Cardozo Law Rev 25:1789–1800
Baird DG, Gertner RH, Picker RC (1994) Game theory and the law. Harvard University Press, Boston, p 314
Basedow J, Kono T, Rühl G (eds) (2006) An economic analysis of private international law. Mohr Siebeck, Tubingen
Bebchuck LA, Fried JM (1996) The uneasy case for the priority of secured claims in bankruptcy. Yale Law J 105:857–934
Bebchuk LA, Guzman AT (1999) An economic analysis of transitional bankruptcies. J Law Econ 42(2):775–808
Borchers PJ (2008) Categorical exceptions to party autonomy. Priv Int Law Tulane Law Rev 82(5):1645–1661
Bowers JW (2000) Security interests: creditors' priorities and bankruptcy. In: Bouckaert B, De Geest G (eds) Encyclopedia of Law and Economics, vol II. Edward Elgar, Cheltenham, pp 90–128
Bradley CA (1997) Territorial intellectual property rights in an age of globalism. Va J Int Law 37:505–586
Buxbaum HL (2009) Territory territoriality and the resolution of jurisdictional conflict. Am J Comp Law 57:631–676
Castellano GG (2015) Reforming non-possessory secured transactions laws: a new strategy? Mod Law Rev 78(4):611–640
Coco G (2000) On the use of collateral. J Econ Surv 14(2):191–214
Cook T (2014) Territoriality and jurisdiction in EU IP law. J Intellect Prop Rights 19:293–297
Dinwoodie GB (2009) Developing a private international intellectual property law: The Demise of Territoriality? William Mary Law Rev 51(2):711–800
Dornis TW (2017) Trademark and unfair competition conflicts. Cambridge University, Cambridge
European Max-Planck Group on Conflict of Laws in Intellectual Property (CLIP) (2013) Conflict of laws in intellectual property the clip principles and commentary. Oxford University, Oxford, pp 354–369
Feng M, Gramlich JD, Gupta GS (2009) Special purpose vehicles: empirical evidence on determinants and earnings management. Acc Rev 84(6):1833–1876
Flint GL Jr (1999) Secured transactions history: the fraudulent myth. New Mexico Law Rev 29:363–405
Gullifer L, Akseli NO (2016) Secured transactions law reform: principles policies and practice. Hart Publishing, Oxford
Guzman AT (2001) Choice of law: new foundations. Geo LJ 90:883–940
Harris SL, Mooney CW Jr (1994) A property-based theory of security interests: taking debtors' choices seriously. Va Law Rev 80:2021–2072
Jackson TH (1982) Bankruptcy, non-bankruptcy entitlement and the creditors' bargain. Yale Law Rev 91(5):857–907
Jackson TH, Kronman AT (1979) Secured financing and priorities among creditors. Yale Law J 88:1143–1182
Kagami K (2006) The systematic choice of legal rules for private international law: an economic approach. In: Basedow J, Kono T (eds) An economic analysis of private international Law. Mohr Siebeck, Tubingen
Kono T, Kagami K (2013) Is a uniform law always preferable to private international law? Jpn Yearb int Law 56:314–337
Kramer X, Themeli E (2016) The party autonomy paradigm: European and global developments on choice. In: Lazic V, Stuij S (eds) Brussels ibis regulation: changes and challenges of the renewed procedural scheme. T.M.C. Asser Press, Hague, pp 27–49
Lehmann M (2008) Liberating the individual from battles between states: justifying party autonomy in conflict of laws. Vanderbilt J Trans Law 4:381–434
Mann RJ (1997) Explaining the pattern of secured credit. Harv Law Rev 110(625):625–683

Maultzsch F (2016) Party autonomy in European private international law: uniform principle or context-dependent instrument? J priv int Law 12(3):466–491
Metzger A (2010) Applicable law under the clip principles: a pragmatic revaluation of territoriality. In: Basedow J, Kono T, Metzger A (eds) Intellectual property in the global arena–jurisdiction applicable law and the recognition of judgments in Europe Japan and the US. Mohr Siebeck, Tubingen
Michaels R (2008) The new European choice-of-law revolution. Tul L Rev 82:1607–1644
Matulionyte R (2011) Law applicable to copyright: a comparison of the ALI and CLIP proposals. Edward Elgar, Cheltenham
O'Hara E, Ribstein LE (2000) From politics to efficiency in the choice of law. Univ Chicago Law Rev 67:1151–1232
Ruhl G (2006) Methods and approaches in choice of law: an economic perspective. Berkeley J int Law 24(3):801–841
Rühl G (2009) Party autonomy in the private international law of contracts: transatlantic convergence and economic efficiency. In: Gottschalk E, Michaels R, Ruhl G, von Hein J (eds) Conflict of laws in a globalized world. Cambridge University, Cambridge, pp 153–183
Schwartz A (1981) Security interests and bankruptcy priorities: a review of current theories. J Leg Stud 10(1):1–37
Schwartz A (1984) The continuing puzzle of secured debt. Vanderbilt Law Rev 37(5):1051–1069
Scott RE (1997) Truth about secured financing. Cornell L Rev 82:1436–1465
Thomas S (2016) Security interests in intellectual property: proposals for reform. Legal Studies
Torremans Paul (2013) Holyoak and Torremans intellectual property law. Oxford University, Oxford
Tosato A (2011) Security interests over intellectual property. J Intellect Prop Law Pract 6(2): 93–104
Treppoz E (2014) International choice of law in trademark disputes from a territorial approach to a global approach. J Law Arts 37:557–571
UNCITRAL (2011) Legislative guide on secured transactions. https://www.uncitral.org/pdf/english/texts/security-lg/e/09-82670_Ebook-Guide_09-04-10English.pdf. Accessed 20 May 2017
Whincop MJ, Keyes M (2001) Policy and pragmatism in the conflict of laws. Ashgate, Aldershot

Index

T. Kono (ed.), *Security Interests in Intellectual Property*, Perspectives in Law, Business and Innovation, DOI 10.1007/978-981-10-5415-0